Lough Hyne
From Prehistory to the Present

Lough Hyne
From Prehistory to the Present

By Terri Kearney

With illustrations by Peter Murray

Chapter 6 by Dr Colin Little and Dr Cynthia Trowbridge

Foreword by Eoghan Harris

Macalla Publishing

First published in 2013 by:
Macalla Publishing,
Cunnamore,
Skibbereen, West Cork, Ireland.
macallapublishing@gmail.com

Macalla Publishing

This edition published in 2014 by Macalla Publishing.

© Macalla Publishing.
Images and text © Terri Kearney 2013 & 2014.
All rights reserved.

ISBN: 978-0-9926242

No part of this publication may be reproduced or transmitted in any form or by any means, electronic or mechanical, including photocopying, recording, or any information storage or retrieval system without permission in writing from the author and publisher.

Illustrations by Peter Murray:
Cover :   *Lough Hyne*
Page 1:   *Cross Slab at Glannafeen*
Page 16 :   *Wedge Tomb on Castleisland*
Page 37 :   *Viking Ships off the South-West Coast*
Page 43 :   *Cloghan Castle*
Page 49 :   *O'Driscoll Galleys in Baltimore Harbour*
Page 51 :   *The Inauguration of Fineen O'Driscoll*

Unless otherwise credited, all contemporary photographs in this publication were taken by the author with the following exceptions:
Aerial photo of Lough Hyne on page ii courtesy of R. McAllen, School of BEES, UCC.
Unless otherwise indicated, all images in Chapter 5 are from Skibbereen Heritage Centre archive.
Unless otherwise indicated, all photographs in Chapter 6 by Cynthia Trowbridge.
Unless otherwise indicated, all historic images in Chapter 7 are from Skibbereen Heritage Centre archive.
'The Rapids' on page 125 and 'UCC Pontoon' on page 161 by Mark Jessopp.
Aerial photo of Lough Hyne on page 183 courtesy of John Earley.
Painting on inside back cover by Sue Hawkins (marine scientist, see page 159), with thanks.

Design and layout: Star Creative, Skibbereen. www.starcreative.ie

Printed in Ireland.

> Please note that the majority of the places described in this book are on private property. Where possible, a similar site with public access is referred to in the text. Many of the archaeological sites, in particular, came to light because of the co-operation and goodwill of the landowners. The publication of this book allows such information to be shared but **does not** suggest or promote the idea that they be visited. Please **respect the privacy** of the landowners of Lough Hyne and do not attempt to visit sites on private property without permission to do so.

Contents

Foreword by Eoghan Harris .... *vii*

Thanks and Acknowledgements .... *viii*

Introduction .... *xi*

1 - From Prehistory to History *1*
Early Man in Ireland and Lough Hyne | The First Farmers in Ireland
First Farmers at Lough Hyne | From Stone to Metal
The Age of Iron | Early Medieval Lough Hyne | Early Christian Lough Hyne
Other Christian Sites at Lough Hyne | The Vikings at Lough Hyne

2 - The O'Driscolls *40*
The O'Driscolls in West Cork | The Arrival of the Normans | Trade, Piracy and Wealth
The Last Chieftain of Collymore Fineen O'Driscoll | Rebellion and Loss of Land | Cloghan Castle

3 - Pre-Famine Lough Hyne *72*
Land and Employment | Population | Agriculture | The Poor of Lough Hyne | The Poor Laws

4 - The Great Famine *94*
1845 – The Blight Arrives | 1845 – Famine Relief | 1846 – Famine Relief | 1846 – Public Works
Rapids Wall | 1846 – Soup in the Skibbereen Union | 1847 – Government-Run Soup Kitchens
New Poor Law System | Eviction – Disease – Emigration
The Effects of the Famine on Lough Hyne

5 - Marine Research *126*
Lough Hyne's Habitats and Hydrology | Marine Research in Ireland
Lough Hyne is 'Discovered' | Rowland Southern | Professor Louis Renouf
Professor Jack Kitching and Professor John Ebling et al. | The Research Work of Kitching et al.
UCC and Lough Hyne 1950s–1987 | Designation as Europe's First Marine Nature Reserve
Dr Colin Little et al. | Other Scientists at Lough Hyne | UCC and Lough Hyne – 1990s to Today

6 - The Ecology of Lough Hyne *162*
by Dr Colin Little & Dr Cynthia Trowbridge
The Rocky Intertidal Zone | Intertidal Gravel Beaches | The Rapids
Subtidal Cliffs and the Deeper Rocky Subtidal | Soft Bottoms | Saltmarshes and Shallow Mud
The Open Water

7 - Miscellany of Lough Hyne *182*
Formation of the Lough | Lough Hyne House | Set Dancing | Ellie O'Driscoll's Shop
Lough Hyne Schools | Creamery | Coffin Stone | Gate at Coomavarrodig
McCarthy's Cottage on Knockomagh | Sandboats and the Coosh Stone

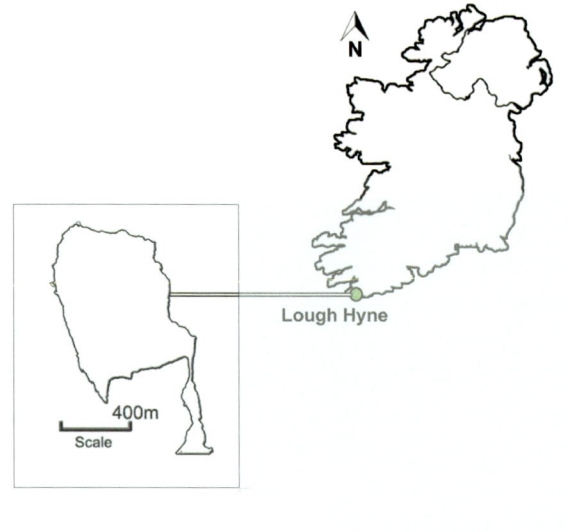

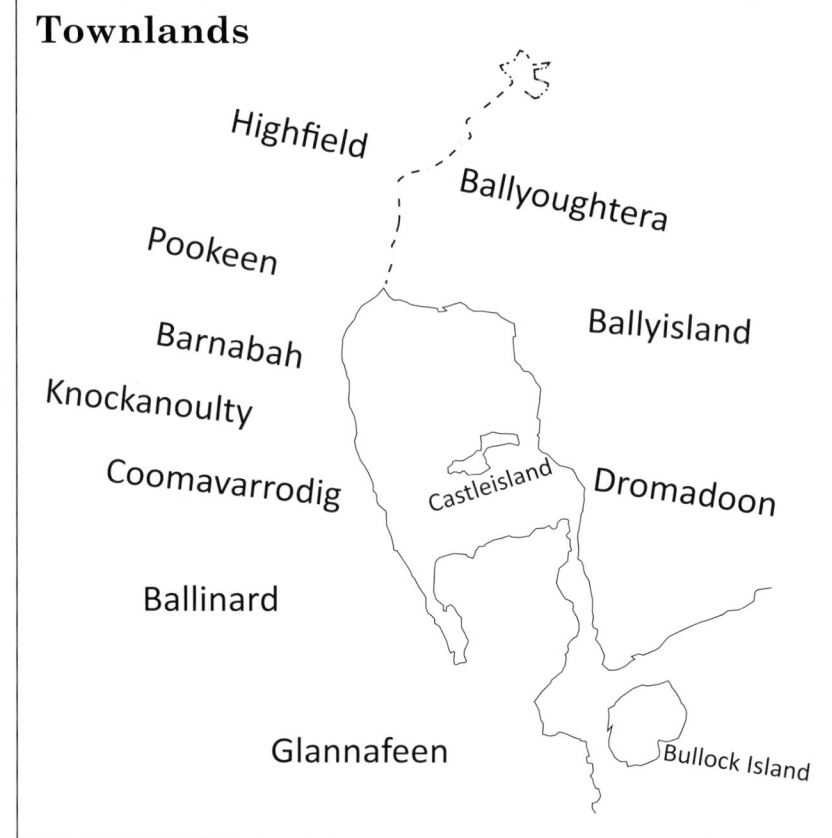

Townlands

Highfield, Ballyoughtera, Pookeen, Ballyisland, Barnabah, Knockanoulty, Coomavarrodig, Castleisland, Dromadoon, Ballinard, Glannafeen, Bullock Island

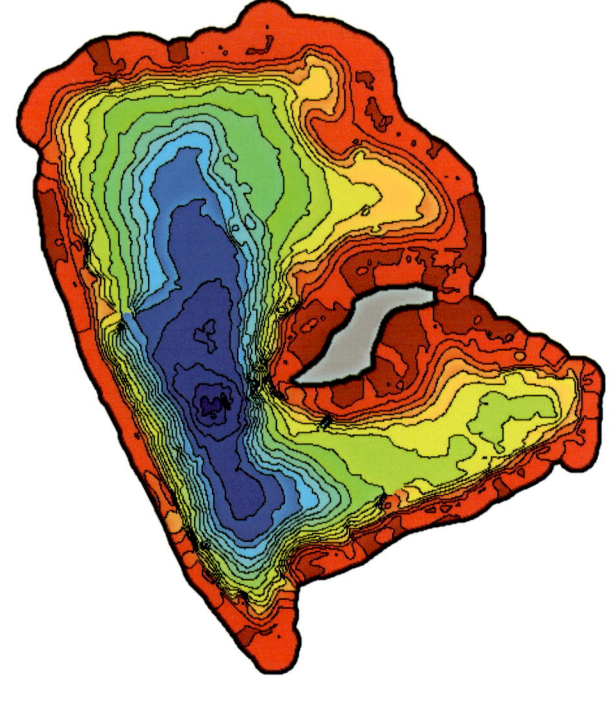

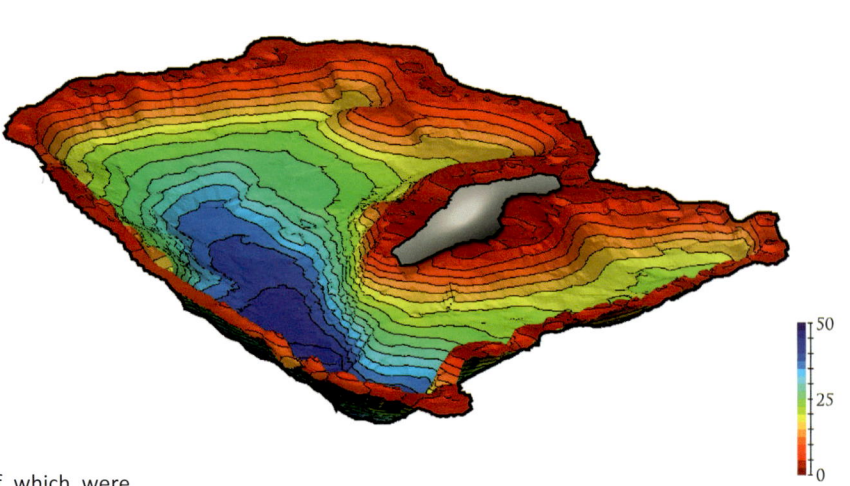

Images Courtesy of Jamie Mcwilliam and Tony Hawkins, some of which were produced from echo soundings within Lough Hyne using the Dr Depth program.

Depth (m)

Foreword

Down the years, swimming in Lough Hyne, I would glimpse the lithe figure of Terri Kearney, loping tirelessly around the lake, its woods and holy wells; or standing at its seawall, gazing at its glory, gravid with the labour of being the lake's first biographer. Her task triumphantly concluded, she wants me to say why I love Lough Hyne too.

Long ago, driving for the first time from Dublin to Baltimore, on a day when my life was tossed and torn, I saw a sign for Lough Hyne and took a twisty road less travelled that brought me beneath a brooding hill before suddenly lifting the veil on a vision that took my breath away and never gave it back.

Lough Hyne is a rock pool where serious scientists sport and play and local children learn to swim seriously; a sweet bower for lovers in full bloom, a sanctuary for the sore in mind or body, seeking the same consolation as Sir Fineen O Driscoll who came here, in a state of 'disabilitie and wante of means', to die in peace.

Lough Hyne is a sacred place, a natural amphitheatre with perfect acoustics, where we can guess our pre-Christian ancestors gathered to worship the lost gods of the Druids; came later as Christians to convert the pagan pools to holy wells; came later still as freezing Famine starvlings to build its stone walls, leaving their bones behind to sanctify it forever.

Lough Hyne is linked to the life-giving oceans from whence our species struggled to the shore, a birthing pool, a school of natural history, a training ground in the triathlon of life, a safe harbour when it is time to rest and return to our salty womb.

But the sacred is not solemn. All my memories of Lough Hyne are happy; my favourite being of a fine summer's morning, watching a line of burly County Council workers leaning on their shovels and cheering the Maids of the Isles as they splashed and screamed in its sparkling waves.

But much as I love Lough Hyne, I was not lucky enough to be born a local. We summertime visitors can sing its praises but we cannot recapture the locals 'first fine careless rapture' nor walk beside its waters through the four seasons.

That is why we are haunted – in the happy sense the word is used in Cork – to have this brilliant book, this long love-letter by a local woman, as our permanent, portable link to Lough Hyne. Thank you, Terri Kearney, the lady of the lake.

EOGHAN HARRIS

Thanks and Acknowledgements

This book is a collaborative effort involving people from a variety of backgrounds who have one thing in common – a deep love of Lough Hyne. First and foremost, a thank you to my co-conspirators, Peter Murray, Colin Little and Cynthia Trowbridge for their wonderful contributions and to Eoghan Harris for writing such a beautiful foreword. Peter's rich illustrations allow us to 'time-travel' to the Lough Hyne of the past via his imaginative portrayals of people, places and events. Colin and Cynthia's chapter on the ecology of Lough Hyne offers a clear and informative insight into the complex submarine world of the lough, featuring extraordinary underwater photographs. And Eoghan's foreword eloquently expresses why this small lough is so unique and worthy of conservation and protection.

A sincere thank you also to the landowners around Lough Hyne for sharing their stories and their properties with me. Their generous hospitality led to the discovery of many previously unrecorded archaeological sites through field names, personal knowledge and stories. Particular thanks to Annie and Neily Bohane, Paddy and Mary Burke and Michael and Denis (Denny) O'Donovan for the many hours they spent talking to me and for their hospitality while doing so. Sadly, Denny passed away before he got to see his contribution in print but I am honoured to record some of the vast amount of information that he had on the lough. Thanks also to Breeda Cahalane (née O'Sullivan) and her daughter Cathy Lynch; Karen McCarthy (née O'Sullivan) and John O'Sullivan; likewise to Margaret Kelleher, Philomena Bohane, Stan and Gráinne Rispin, Anne and Jens Mueller and the Kellys. Thanks also to the Beard family for granting access to the deeds of Lough Hyne House, the Holmes for letting me walk their land and Stephen and Kathleen Hegarty, Denis McSweeney and Jim and Brigit O'Donnell for their help. Sadly, another Lough Hyne resident, Billy Andy O'Driscoll, also passed away during the writing of this book but his contribution is not forgotten. Nor is that of Eileen Stafford, also recently deceased. With her extensive knowledge of the Irish language, Eileen was a great help as was Beatrice O'Higgins (née Hegarty).

I am hugely grateful to the many friends who have supported this research over the last number of years. In particular Margaret Murphy, both for the time she spent walking around the archaeological sites of the lough with me, and for her friendship, help and advice. Likewise, Philip O'Regan for sharing his extensive knowledge of the Famine in Skibbereen and for reading and critiquing this material. Philip has offered quiet support to this 'learner historian' for many years, for which I am very grateful. William Casey, too, has offered invaluable help and advice and has put me back on track with this research several times, while also being a great friend. My thanks to Patricia and Kevin Tomlinson who also offered feedback and support and, again, much-valued friendship. Another big thank you to John Earley for sharing his opinions, his scientific knowledge and some of his photographs, and to my niece Elaine O'Flynn and close friend Flor MacCarthy, for their long-distance encouragement.

A huge thank you to Connie Kelleher for her generous help and advice and for sharing the document featuring the signature of Fineen O'Driscoll. Also a special thanks to Maeve Sikora of the National Museum of Ireland for her critique on the archaeology chapter and to Mary Sleeman, Peter Woodman and Lee Snodgrass for their help and support. Paddy Leahy tramped around many archaeological sites with me and also helped in scanning and researching the early marine research material and was both fun and supportive while doing so – thank you Paddy. A sincere thanks is also due to Moyra Curran (née Macaura) for sharing her memories of Lough Hyne and to her daughter Patricia Curran, for facilitating this. I would also like to acknowledge the work done by Georg Dose on the archaeology of Lough Hyne and the many sites that he recorded before this project even started, as well as his continuing interest and help. Thanks also to the supervisor of my archaeology dissertation, John Sheehan, for his fantastic support and sense of humour and to the supervisor of my MA thesis on Lough Hyne, Malgorzata Krasnodebska-D'Aughton, who was so kind, patient and helpful. I also met some wonderful people, and gained new friends, among my fellow students on the UCC DLRS and MA courses.

There were many contributors to the chapter on marine research and I am extremely grateful for their willingness to help. Again, top of the bill must go to Colin Little and Penny Stirling who gave so much of their time and likewise Cynthia Trowbridge. To Trevor Norton for sharing his archival material and to Rob McAllen of UCC for making contacts, sharing material and giving fantastic support. Michael Sleigh, Tony and Sue Hawkins, Máire Mulcahy and Declan O'Donnell have given a huge amount of guidance on this chapter for which I am very grateful. Thanks also to Dan Minchin, John Davenport, Frank Hegarty, Alan Myers, Mark Jessopp, Mark Johnson, Adrian Smith and Conor Duggan for their help.

The superb photos by Cynthia Trowbridge, Redmond O'Regan, Sharron Franks and, of course, Peter's beautiful illustrations really bring this book to life. There were many others who contributed images and I would like to particularly thank Skibbereen Heritage Centre, the Crawford Art Gallery, Cork Public Museum, the National Library of Ireland, the Royal Irish Academy, Trinity College Dublin, the Irish Architectural Archive, the Royal Society of Antiquaries of Ireland, the *Green Dragon,* Newport County Archives, the *New Phytologist,* the Director of the National Archives of Ireland, the Cork Historical and Archaeological Society, the National Museum of Ireland, Mark Jessopp and Rob McAllen, UCC and the Chapter and Dean of St Fachtna's Cathedral Ross for images used in this publication; as well as Prof. Werner Sarges and his wife Elke for sharing their seventeenth century maps. Thanks also to Mark Benson and Stefanie Jaax and the Crockett family for granting permission to photograph each of their respective properties. Thanks also to all of those who helped to scan the Skibbereen Heritage Centre archival material, much of which is used here.

This publication could not have gone ahead without the support provided by the Gwendoline Harold Barry trust for which I am truly grateful. Also to the West Cork Development Partnership and the board of Skibbereen Heritage Centre for their help and support. A big thank you also to the staff of Skibbereen Heritage Centre for being so supportive and encouraging throughout this project. Thanks too to the wonderful library staff in various libraries: particularly all the staff in Skibbereen, Mary Lombard in the Boole Library and Kieran Wyse in Cork County Library. Thanks also to Gloria Greenwood for 'checking' it all and special thanks to Alan Tobin of the *Southern Star* for his wonderful design work and patience.

And finally, my thanks to the lough itself. Since my childhood, it's been there for me as a haven to go to and remember what's really important in this world. A place to enjoy nature and beauty, to find peace from daily anxieties and worries; where the past, present and future flow together to grant me a moment of pure joy on each and every visit there.

Some of the interviewees come from families who have lived on the same farms at Lough Hyne for many generations. Their knowledge of the area reflects this, and they have so kindly and freely shared information passed onto them by their ancestors. For example, the Bohanes of Dromadoon, the Burkes of Ballyoughtera, the O'Donovans of Glannafeen and the O'Sullivans of Coomavarrodig have all lived on the same farms for many hundreds of years. Some of these interviewees are pictured here.

Neily and Annie Bohane at their home in Dromadoon.

Michael and Denis (Denny) O'Donovan in their home at Glannafeen. Sadly, Denny is now deceased but his contribution to this publication is gratefully acknowledged.

Paddy and Mary Burke in their garden at Ballyoughtera.

Breeda Cahalane (née O'Sullivan), who was originally from Coomavarrodig.

Introduction

Lough Hyne is a small salt-water lake in West Cork where there has been human settlement for at least 4,000 years. This is the story of the people of Lough Hyne – or what we know of them – and the place where they lived, loved, worked, worshipped and died, through some of the major events in Irish history.

Some aspects of Lough Hyne's heritage are unique, including its long association with marine research. The first biological observations were made in the lough in 1886 and sustained scientific research has been ongoing there since the early 1920s. This small West Cork lake was designated as the first Marine Nature Reserve in Europe in 1981 and is now one of the most-studied marine sites of its size in the world. This came about due to the efforts of the many extraordinary people who have worked there over the years, many of whom came to care deeply about Lough Hyne and its conservation and protection. Two of these scientists, Dr Colin Little and Dr Cynthia Trowbridge, offer an insight into what the researchers have learnt over the years in their chapter on the ecology of Lough Hyne.

Like many areas in West Cork, Lough Hyne has a rich archaeological landscape. There is material evidence relating to this area from practically every era over the last 4,000 years or so, which offers information on how the area was used by man from prehistory. What is remarkable is the type of monument that predominates there. Many of the sites and monuments around the lough are of a ritual or religious nature and these tell us something about the past perceptions of the lough.

The Gaelic O'Driscoll clan ruled over this part of West Cork for centuries and are an integral part of the history of Lough Hyne. The ruins of an O'Driscoll stronghold, Cloghan Castle, can still be seen on the island in Lough Hyne today. It is in this small castle that 'Fineen the Rover', the last wealthy and powerful O'Driscoll clan chieftain, is said to have lived out his final years. The story of this family's loss of land and power in the seventeenth century is a microcosm of a huge transition in Ireland, which saw an ancient system of clan rule give way to English plantation and colonisation. The society and economy of Ireland was irrevocably changed and the shift in land ownership continued to have effects over the centuries that followed.

By the nineteenth century, Lough Hyne was densely populated with a high level of poverty and dependence on agriculture. The area was devastated by the Great Famine, with the townlands around the lough suffering a 45% drop in population between 1841 and 1851. Lough Hyne's experiences, in the loss of its people through death and emigration, reflect what happened in the area generally. The Famine years changed the physical and social landscape of West Cork and continued to have effects long afterwards. The area around the lough was utterly transformed and its population continued to decline into the twentieth century.

Much has been written about all of these events on a national and international level but – as the saying goes – 'all history is local'. Each one of us experiences our life history on an individual basis and, after that, as part of our local community. This is the story of how people have interacted with Lough Hyne over the millennia and it could, perhaps, be argued that such a small place is not important enough to warrant such a study. However, when 'the gates of perception are cleansed' we can see the importance of such local studies. When history is explored on such a personal level, it has a resonance that is felt at the level of the heart. As integral as the heart itself, past events help to shape and create us as human beings, both as individuals and as part of society. There is nowhere better to explore 'the history of the heart' than in Lough Hyne, a place with which so many people have fallen in love.

From Prehistory to History

There are numerous archaeological sites and monuments, from various eras, in the townlands surrounding Lough Hyne.[1] By viewing them as an archaeological landscape, rather than a series of individual, unconnected monuments, they give us an indication of how the lough was used and perceived by man from prehistory.

We can get a sense of when people lived at Lough Hyne, the types of society that might have existed there and how the landscape was utilised. There has been human settlement at Lough Hyne for at least four thousand years and the presence of man is evident there through practically every period since then. The kinds of monuments found there also give an indication of how Lough Hyne was perceived by the people of the past. A large proportion of the sites around the lough are of a ritualistic or religious nature. The fact that this type of monument predominates may tell us something about the way that man has interacted with the landscape of Lough Hyne over the millennia.

The Coming of Man

Because prehistory refers to the time before writing was adopted, the study of this era is based on material remains. Monuments, tools, weapons, bones, seeds and pollen are used to tell the story of early man. Prehistoric eras are roughly classified by the materials used for weapons and tools. This gives us the periods of the Stone Age, the Bronze Age and the Iron Age, but, in practice, the dates of these eras overlap and should be used as a guideline only. For example, some Stone Age tools were still widely used into the Bronze Age. However, we can use them to take a general overview of man's presence in the Lough Hyne area.

Mesolithic

8000–4000 BC. Humans start to adapt as foragers in the post-glacial environment. There is no evidence, as yet, of these early settlers in West Cork but objects found near the River Blackwater in north Cork suggest a human presence in that area from around 4500 BC.

Neolithic

4000–2500 BC. This is the era of the first farmers and there is clear evidence of settlement at Lough Hyne during this period.

Bronze Age

2500–600 BC. Numerous sites around the lake date to this period.

Iron Age

600 BC–400 AD. There is a paucity of evidence throughout Ireland relating to this era and Lough Hyne is no exception.

Early Christian/Medieval

400–1200 AD. Several sites at Lough Hyne date to this time.

St Bridget's Church in Glannafeen, Lough Hyne, as depicted by marine scientist Professor John Ebling (image use courtesy of the Ebling family).

Early Man in Ireland and Lough Hyne

Temperatures in Ireland started to rise from about 8000 BC and brought an end to the last great glaciation of the prolonged Ice Age. This warmer period meant that vegetation gradually began to develop and this provided a home for wildlife that was starting to make its way from Europe. Hare, stoat, pine marten and otter slowly started to colonise the landscape, alongside larger animals such as wolf, bear and wild pig.

About 8,000 years ago, the sea level outside Lough Hyne was around 15m lower than it is at present, so the shoreline would have looked completely different to how it appears today.[2] The land, too, was dissimilar, as the area around the lough would have been heavily forested. The make-up of these woodlands was changing as the predominant hazel was being slowly replaced by oak. Over time, pine, which was also part of the mixed woodland, became dominant.[3] The lough itself would have contained fresh-water, as it did not become a marine lake until much later.[4]

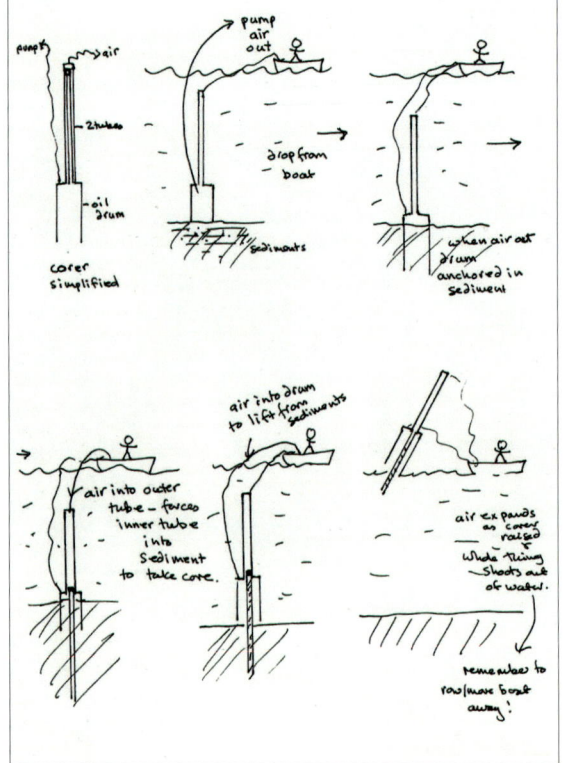

As organic matter falls on the ground, it is laid down in 'layers of time' in the soil, new over old each year, which, over time, gradually results in an increase in the level of the earth. Each plant has its own type of pollen which is encased in a shell. Every pollen shell has a unique shape which identifies it. These shells are practically indestructible so remain in the soil within each level of the 'layers of time'.

By extracting a vertical core of sediment from a lake, it is possible to get information about what grew in the surrounding area by analysing the content of each level. The base of the core would show what was there first, whereas the upper sediments would be the most recent. The proportion of different types of pollen at the various depths of the core are a guide to what species were present in the area at the time the sediment was laid down. A pollen core was taken from Lough Hyne in the 1970s by Dr Jenny Buzer and her sketch of the process, shown here, illustrates how this process worked.

This photograph shows the core coming to the surface of Lough Hyne. (Images courtesy of Dr Jenny Buzer.)

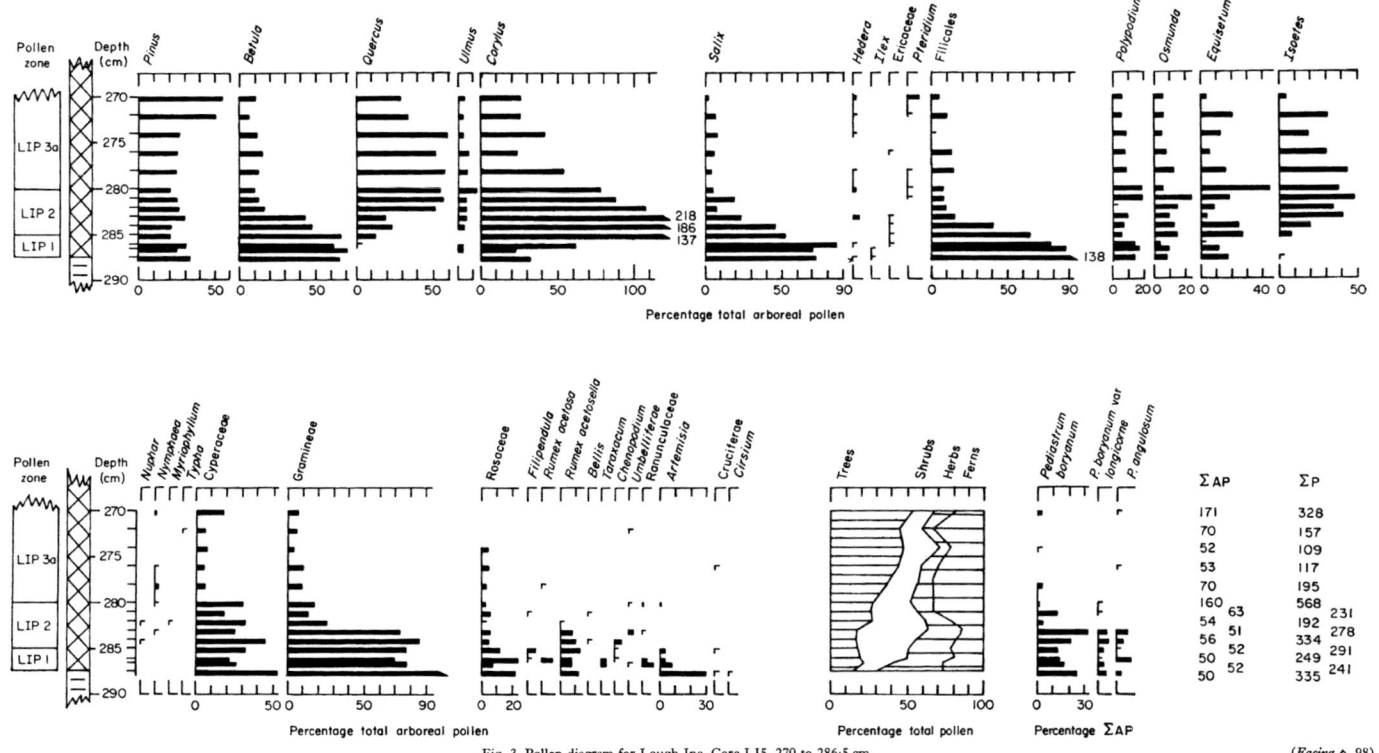

Fig. 3. Pollen diagram for Lough Ine. Core LI5, 270 to 286·5 cm.

Buzer's analysis of the core gives us information on what has been growing in the area around Lough Hyne for millennia. It shows that, about 4,000 years ago, there was a decrease in arboreal (or tree) pollen and an increase in the types of pollen associated with farming. This suggests that early farmers cleared some of the woodland at Lough Hyne in order to grow crops. (Image courtesy of Dr Jenny Buzer and *New Phytologist*.)

By analysing marine algae, called planktonic diatoms, Buzer was also able to establish an approximate date for when the lough transformed from a fresh-water to a salt-water lake. About 2000 BC, rising sea levels drove seawater through Barlogue Creek and the Rapids and into the lake itself, and thus it gradually became a marine lake. The cores extracted from Lough Hyne, shown here, have a darker section, which dates to the period when the lough contained fresh-water, and a section that is lighter in colour, which is from the salt-water era. The darker part of the core therefore pre-dates the part that is lighter in colour. (Image courtesy of Dr Jenny Buzer.)

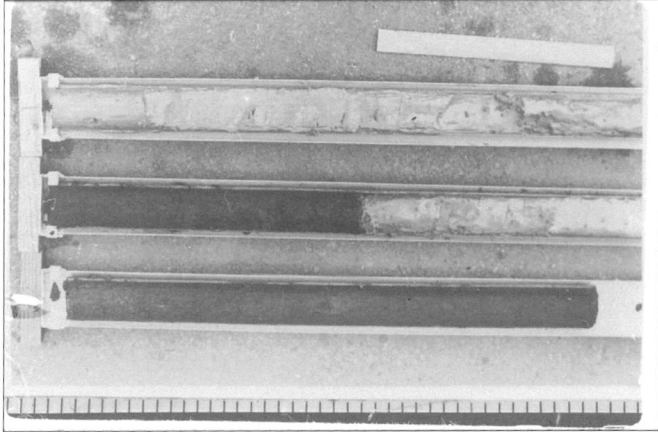

The earliest evidence of human settlement in Ireland that has been found to date is from around 7500 BC.[5] With the exception of Norway and Finland, this is much later than other parts of Europe. Unlike these Scandinavian countries, large parts of Ireland had been ice-free for thousands of years by this stage and so the land could have supported a human population long before this.[6] The reason for this delayed colonisation by man is unknown and evidence of an earlier settlement may yet be discovered.

The earliest Irish settlers lived by foraging and hunting at a time when the climate was warmer than it is now. Their tools were made of bone, stone and wood and their clothes of animal skins. They had to move location to follow food sources, as fish, hazelnuts and wild fruit were utilised on a seasonal basis. Evidence from this period is scant and mostly consists of flint flakes, which were used as tools and weapons.

There was certainly human occupation in the southern part of the country during the later Mesolithic period. Ferriter's Cove in County Kerry shows evidence of settlement from around 4600 BC.[7] By this stage, technology had developed and larger flakes of flint were being used as single-piece weapons or as composites in spears and other weapons. These flints are difficult to find and identify but a Mesolithic presence in Cork has been established by their discovery in the valley of the River Blackwater.[8]

There is no evidence, as yet, of human occupation in West Cork during this period. However, if we make an assumption that man could have reached this part of West Cork, Lough Hyne would have been an ideal location to settle. At the time, Lough Hyne was a fresh-water lake, adjacent to the sea and abundant with fish. There was no shortage of fish and shellfish, which would have been very important in the Mesolithic diet. It was surrounded by woodland, which could have provided materials for boat- and house-building, as well as animals to hunt and wild berries and nuts to eat. In addition, the sheltered position of the lake would have meant that it was accessible in all seasons.

The first tools developed by early man were made of stone and were used in hunting, fishing, food preparation and even in making clothes. When it was available, flint was used for producing sharp tools. Flint is a very hard stone but chips easily and breaks like glass, resulting in a razor-sharp edge. The creation of flint tools involved breaking, or 'knapping', small pieces of flint off a larger core piece. The resultant sharp flakes of flint were sometimes worked further by the knapper. In a process called 'retouching', the flint flake could be re-shaped, sharpened or smoothed to create a variety of tools including scrapers, arrowheads and blades.

Flint found at Ballinard, Lough Hyne, in 2012 by Jim O'Donnell. This piece of worked flint is difficult to date but is thought to be about 4,000 years old.

The flint found at Lough Hyne is the remains of a core which would have been worked on, or knapped, by a skilled stone-worker to create such tools. When its use was exhausted, the waste flint, known as debitage, may have been disposed of as it served no further purpose. This tells us that it is most likely that it was worked on in situ at Ballinard and suggests that there was human settlement there around 4,000 years ago.

The provenance of the Ballinard flint is unknown. The primary source of flint in Ireland is the Antrim area and it is not generally found in West Cork. However, flint nodules that are found on West Cork beaches and 'moonstones' that are regularly brought ashore by fishermen may offer a clue as to the source of the Ballinard flint. The 'moonstones', large and small lumps of flint, are caught in the trawling nets of fishermen about 15 miles south of the Galley Head. This off-shore source of flint can result in flint finds along the shoreline of West Cork. The Ballinard flint may have originated from a nodule washed up on the shore as pebble flint, but it could also have come here as a result of trade.

The First Farmers in Ireland

There was a radical change around 4000 BC as the hunting and foraging way of life began to be replaced by a society based on agriculture. These first farmers were not the Mesolithic inhabitants of Ireland but small groups of pioneers who came here by boat, each vessel carrying about a tonne of cargo.[9] They shipped animals, trussed in the base of the boat, and plants, alongside the tools required for early farming. They brought in cattle, sheep/goats, pigs, wheat and barley, but they still made use of Ireland's abundant wild resources, such as fish, deer, wildfowl, nuts and berries.[10] The indigenous Mesolithic people also adapted to the agricultural way of life over time.

This new lifestyle meant that crops had to be tended and harvested, so communities were more likely to remain in one place rather than move around seasonally, as they had done in the Mesolithic. They cleared woodland to make open spaces for cultivation, and established more permanent settlements as they tended and maintained these cleared areas. These early Irish farmers lived together as family units in village-type communities, in rectangular houses with walls of split-oak timbers.[11] They utilised small stone tools, such as blades, knives and scrapers, and used quernstones to grind wheat, which they grew in small fields close to the settlement.[12]

The decorated slab from the Cape Clear passage tomb, now held at Cork Public Museum, features decoration similar to that found in the passage tombs of Newgrange, Knowth and Dowth. Similar motifs are also found in passage tombs in Brittany. The art form on this slab suggests that this tomb dates to about 3000 BC.[15] (Image courtesy of Cork Public Museum.)

Cemeteries are a feature of settled communities and large stone tombs, or megaliths, began to be built within a few hundred years of the first arrival of farmers in Ireland. These megaliths were not only used for burials but also possibly for other ceremonies. While the houses of this era left few traces above ground, these substantial stone monuments were built to last into the future. The passage tombs in Cape Clear and Ringarogy islands show that there was human settlement in West Cork at this time.[13] The tomb at Ringarogy, first reported by Robert and Beibhinn Marten in 1993, is within walking distance of Lough Hyne, while Cape Clear is *c.* 13km off Baltimore.[14] Again, there is no evidence that Lough Hyne was settled during this period but it may have been used as a seasonal site, with its resources exploited at different times of the year.

First Farmers at Lough Hyne

Farming was generally adopted in the south-west area from around 2500 BC onwards.[16] A pollen analysis carried out at Lough Hyne shows evidence of forest clearances in the area, dated at *c.* 2000 BC, about the same time that the lake changed from a fresh-water to a salt-water lake.[17] By analysing the pollen core taken from Lough Hyne, Dr Buzer was able to establish a decline in arboreal pollen and a corresponding rise in grass pollen, which suggests that these early farmers cleared woodland for farming.[18] This is the first clear evidence of a human presence at Lough Hyne and the polished stone axe-head found at Ballinard may also date to this period. The 'new stone-age axe' was found in 1954 by Edward Sheehy in Ballinard, Lough Hyne, and is now on display in Cork Public Museum.[19] It may have been used to clear the woodland around Lough Hyne, as a clear correlation has been established between the widespread use of this type of axe in the Neolithic period and the felling of trees.[20]

Lough Hyne had everything that these Neolithic people needed. Their settlement sites were generally positioned in a sheltered area overlooking a lake. Access to water, arable and grazing land, as well as fuel and building materials, were their primary requirements, all of which were available at the lough.

We do not know how many people would have lived in the Lough Hyne area at this time but the introduction of farming did increase the population generally.[23] Hunter-gatherers would have had to keep their numbers down to what the environment could support, but farming meant a steady food supply, and required more people to carry out the work, so the population increased accordingly. In terms of scale, these Neolithic societies would have started at household level, with groups of perhaps a couple of hundred people who were linked by ancestry and common ownership of resources, and also, in turn, perhaps larger groupings with a shared cultural identity.[24] The construction of megaliths would have required the management of a large workforce, which suggests that some sort of organised society was in existence.

This stone axe-head was found in Ballinard in 1954 by Edward Sheehy and is now on display at Cork Public Museum. The ground-stone axe gained prominence during the Neolithic period as a tool for clearing woodland, both for grazing and cultivation, and for providing the raw material for house and boat-building. The polished axes were hafted by slotting their butts into a hole or mortice in a wooden haft, held in place by rawhide.[21]

We know that there were forest clearances in the Lough Hyne area around 4,000 years ago and this kind of tool would have been used in this process. The polished stone axe-head also acquired symbolism during this period and was bartered and used for gift exchanges over long distances. It also had religious and fertility significance.[22] (Photo courtesy of Cork Public Museum.)

From Stone to Metal

Around 2500 BC, stone-based tools gradually began to be replaced by those made of metal. A new technology can bring about a radical change in society and the introduction of metalworking was a significant event. The skills of metallurgy may have been brought to Ireland by new groups of people, but the knowledge may also have found its way here by way of cultural contact and the trade that existed with Britain and Continental Europe at that time.[25]

The Bronze Age is divided into distinct periods, each differentiated by the growing sophistication in the use of metal. The earliest items of this era were made of malleable copper and gold. Copper was replaced by the more durable bronze in the later periods. Bronze is an alloy of copper and tin, which required the importation of tin from Britain.[26] Besides the trade in tin, probably carried out with Cornwall, the metal users traded with Denmark. Later in the Bronze Age, Ireland was an exporter of fine metal objects.[27] The Bronze Age period had a great variety of burial customs, which possibly reflects the interaction with these external influences. The early metallurgists continued the pre-existing tradition of erecting stone tombs by building wedge tombs in this area, and the later period saw a new practice of individual burials.[28] These metal workers were highly organised, so it is most likely that there was a social hierarchy, but what that consisted of is unknown.

This bronze axe-head was found in 1940 by Jeremiah O'Sullivan, a native of Coomavarrodig townland in Lough Hyne. The socketed axe-head dates to the Later Bronze Age and was found in a bog in Rath (Rathmore) at a depth of *c.* 1.2m from the surface.[29] Rath is *c.* 3km from Lough Hyne. The socketed axe-head was a very versatile tool, used for both heavy and light wood-working.[30] (Image courtesy of the National Museum of Ireland.)

The Later Bronze age was a volatile period in Ireland and new types of weaponry began to appear here around the seventh century BC.[31] Many metal items that date to this era have been found in bogs in Cork but why they were placed in this particular environment is far from clear. Such watery locations would have made the retrieval of these objects easier, but they may also have been left in these environments for religious reasons.[32] Whatever the reason, the deposition of this bronze axe-head in a bog in Rath was significant, as this was an extremely valuable object. To put it in context, it has been calculated that it would take up to seven hundred working days to produce forty of the simplest bronze axe-heads, so this complex item would have been highly prized.[33] The fact that this valuable axe was found near Lough Hyne shows that there was considerable wealth in the area during the Later Bronze Age.

The demand for metal led to mining and there was extensive copper-mining in the West Cork area, as we know from the discovery of over thirty small mines at Mount Gabriel near Schull on the Mizen peninsula.[34] Some of these have been dated to as early as 1700 BC.[35] The copper mine at Lick Hill, situated about one kilometre from Lough Hyne, has not been dated but its layout is consistent with the type of fire-setting mining methods used during the Bronze Age.

The 'cave' at Lick Hill has been visited by the people of the locality for generations. There is a custom associated with the site of inscribing one's name into the rock on its interior. The majority of the inscriptions date to the nineteenth and twentieth centuries but there are also some that date to the eighteenth century including these 1790 and 1797 inscriptions.

The 'cave' is not a naturally occurring phenomenon but a man-made copper mine that was first identified as such by Brian Marten. Copper minerals become oxidised when they come into contact with the air, causing them to be stained green. This characteristic green colour of the copper carbonate, called malachite, is clearly visible at Lick and the two mine entrances follow the ore via this blue/green staining.

The two main mining periods in West Cork were the Bronze Age and the nineteenth century, with no other reports of mining in this area in between.[36] The absence of any historical reference to this site in the latter period, alongside the eighteenth-century inscriptions, suggests that it pre-dates the nineteenth century. Nor is it shown as a mine on the 1842 Ordnance Survey of Ireland map. The layout of the mine and the concave appearance of its roof alongside the presence of a spoil heap suggest that the 'fire-setting' mining method of the Bronze Age was used here.[37] This involved setting bonfires against the rock face for hours, causing it to fracture, after which the loose rock was pounded with stone cobble hammers.[38] The rock was processed outside the mine to separate the valuable copper deposits from the unwanted waste. This resulted in a 'spoil heap', a large mound of rock usually located outside the mine entrance, which can be seen here at the Lick mine.

Another type of megalith, the wedge tomb, is quite often found in areas where such copper outcrops and primitive mines are located.[39] There is a wedge tomb at Ardagilla, about one kilometre south of the Lick mine, with another possible tomb on the island in Lough Hyne. The latter monument is partially submerged by the tide and has been eroded over the millennia, so there is very little left of it now. There is a belief that the settlers who built these tombs may have had a strong interest in the copper deposits of this area.[40] The siting and distribution of these tombs suggests that copper was of economic importance to them, as was agriculture and fishing.[41]

Wedge tombs are the most numerous type of megalithic tomb in Ireland and they broadly date to *c.* 2500 – 1800 BC.[42] Their size and appearance can vary greatly between sites but they generally have a west-facing wedge-shaped opening, which gives them their name. Wedge tombs are found in the same general areas as stone circles, which are found throughout West Cork.[43] The exact purpose of wedge tombs is unknown but they are thought to represent a claim to a territory and, perhaps, a similar belief system.[44] Their consistent alignment suggests a religious imperative connected to the core beliefs of the people who built them.[45]

Wedge tombs vary considerably in size and form but have a consistent alignment, with the entrance always located on the west or south-west side.[49] The entrance generally decreases in height and width from the opening to the rear. Because of the extensive erosion of this site on Castleisland, it is not possible to see if this would have been the case here; however, what remains suggests that the characteristic wedge-shaped opening featured here. The other end of this monument is U-shaped, which, again, adheres to the wedge tomb convention.[50] Very little remains of this megalith but it was excavated by the antiquarian C.J.F. McCarthy, who said it was a 'very old grave' after he had excavated and replaced its contents of 'bones and shells'.[51] It has suffered considerable erosion over the millennia but its orientation, size and shape is consistent with that of the wedge tomb tradition.

For the community ... its megalithic sanctuary served not only as an ancestral shrine and ritual centre but also as a visible translation into stone of their fundamental conceptions of the cosmos. For that community, it was the centre of the world, the point at which heaven and earth met ... they were sanctuaries that made the entire territory of the community sacred and so served as the most appropriate place where the social unit could commune with itself and with the gods, goddesses and ancestors.[46]

Most wedge tomb communities probably engaged in agriculture and forest clearances for farming purposes are a feature of this period.[47] The Bronze Age diet was primarily based on agricultural output, but fishing, hunting and natural resources were also used.

Altar Wedge Tomb on the Mizen peninsula is an excellent example of this type of tomb and it is fully accessible to the public.

> Only a society with great material and intellectual reserves could have envisaged [such] monuments in the first place, and perhaps spiritual reserves were needed as well. These large edifices are surely the concrete embodiment of a belief in the hereafter.[48]

'Rock art' is the name given to markings and engravings on rock made by humans in prehistoric times. These carvings are found all over Cork county but their highest concentration is along the coastal area from Rosscarbery to the Mizen peninsula.[52] They come in a variety of abstract forms but the most common is the 'cupmark'. This is a shallow depression picked out of the natural rock or boulder with a hammer and a sharp implement. There are nine cupmarked stones around the perimeter of Lough Hyne, many of them discovered by Georg Dose.[53]

The significance of these engravings is not fully understood, however there is a lot of effort required to create such art so it must have had some strong meaning for its creators. Cupmarked stones are most commonly found close to, or in view of, substantial bodies of water, or river sources, giving credence to the concept that the engravings had a ritual or religious function.[54] The concentrations of rock art in this south-west copper mining area has also prompted the suggestion of a link with copper mining but this remains in the realm of conjecture.[55] The precise date associated with these monuments is uncertain but they are believed to date to 3000 – 2000 BC.[56]

This cupmarked stone at Barnabah, discovered by Georg Dose, is one of nine such monuments found in the townlands around Lough Hyne. (Photo: R. O'Regan.)

The next group of monuments that were built at Lough Hyne are the standing stones in the townlands of Ballyoughtera, Ballyisland and Barnabah. There are about three hundred individual standing stones found in West Cork and the majority of these are thought to date to the second millennium BC.[57] Again, their meaning has been lost in antiquity but interpretations have been made:

> Standing stones may have been seen as playing a number of roles and standing as metaphors for different things ... a general link with the idea of ancestral figures seems likely ... the conventional Bronze Age date given to standing stones ... on the basis of burials at the base of them may have involved ... placing a burial at a location that was considered ancient and sacred.[58]

The precise meaning of standing stones and cupmarked stones has been lost in antiquity but a lot of effort was expended in their creation so they must have been of considerable importance to the people who made them. This standing stone at Barnabah has numerous cupmarks, both deep and shallow, on its surface.

The houses of the Bronze Age were predominantly built of wood and therefore left few traces above ground.[59] However, settlement traces can be found around Lough Hyne in the form of a *fulacht fiadh* in Ballyoughtera. This type of monument consists of a horseshoe-shaped mound of burnt stones with an opening oriented towards a stream or water source. Excavations have shown that a hearth lies in the hollow of the mound, usually built of flat stones. Outside this hearth, between it and the water source, is a trough, either lined with wood or stone. Stones were heated in the fire and then put into the water of the trough to bring it to the boil. These inauspicious sites are the most numerous prehistoric monuments in Ireland, with over 2,000 recorded in Cork county alone.

The most common interpretation of these sites is that they were used for cooking but alternative uses have also been proposed. It has been argued that they could have been covered by light structures and used as sweat-houses, or for bathing, or for some semi-industrial use such as dying cloth or in the preparation of animal hides.[60] Whether *fulachtaí fiadh* were an example of permanent settlement or nomadic use, they would have to have been used repeatedly in order to build up the surrounding mound.

> the large numbers [of *fulachtaí fiadh*] so far identified and the clustering and large size of some of the excavated examples suggests that they were an integrated part of a wider settlement pattern, one in which they served some particular but periodic function.[61]

Unfortunately, the *fulacht fiadh* recorded at Ballyoughtera, Lough Hyne, is no longer visible but the one near Drombeg Stone Circle (about 14km east of Lough Hyne), shown here, is an excellent example of such a site. Heated stones were put in the water to bring it to the boil and the discarded remains of these stones can still be seen in a horseshoe shape around the trough. A cooking experiment was carried out by a team led by Professor O'Kelly in a *fulacht fiadh* in Ballyvourney in the 1950s. Hot stones from an adjacent hearth were immersed in 454 litres of cold water, bringing it to the boil in 35 minutes. A leg of mutton was cooked in this water for 3.5 hours and was eaten as part of the experiment.[62] Drombeg Stone Circle, on opposite page, is fully accessible to the public.

Tombs and graves in Neolithic times were frequently covered in mounds of stone, which were known as cairns. This practice extended into the Bronze Age, when they were often used to cover important burials.[63] Many of them were placed in locations with commanding views over the countryside and they are found in areas where there are a variety of Bronze Age sites.[64] There are the remains of a cairn high up in the townland of Knockeencon, Lough Hyne, which, it has been suggested, dates to the Bronze Age.[65] Another three cairns are located in a single field in Dromadoon townland at Lough Hyne, known as the '*cill* field'. Both sites command spectacular views over the sea and surrounding countryside.

This cairn in Dromadoon is one of three to be found in a single *cill* field. It has a wonderful view of the surrounding area, as does another cairn at Knockeencon.

With the existence of a *fulacht fiadh*, alongside the relatively high number of standing stones and cupmarked stones around Lough Hyne, we can assume that there was a healthy Bronze Age population in the area. This was a prosperous time in Ireland, with some form of structured hierarchical society and strong ruling dynasties. The emergence of strong regional powers and the production of large amounts of bronze weaponry and gold suggest that this was a period of great wealth but also of political instability and warfare.[66] The increasing population, alongside a change in the weather, began to put pressure on land resources. The Later Bronze Age in Ireland was a period of volatility, with extensive metal production using vast resources. Strife, environmental change and new ritual practices were features of this turbulent time. By the end of the Bronze Age, weapons such as rapiers, spears, swords and shields began to appear and in such numbers as to suggest that personal protection may have been necessary. There have been discoveries of hoards of valuables, which date to this era, deposited in various locations including bogs. Some of them are of a votive nature, but others were put there for safe-keeping, suggesting that these were unsettled times.[67] The bronze axe-head found in a bog in Rathmore (*c.* 3km west of the lough) shows that this was also the case in the Lough Hyne area.

The striking appearance of boulder burials in the landscape strongly suggests that they served as monumental markers above burials.[68]

The Age of Iron

The complex, wealthy society of the Later Bronze Age led into the so-called 'Dark Age' of the Iron Age, about which we know very little compared to other periods. The first contacts between Ireland and the iron-using world of the Continental Celts began in the centuries after 700 BC. The arrival of iron-working in Ireland comes about the same time as the appearance of a new art style known as La Tène. This was once linked to the belief that there had been a major movement of Celtic people into Ireland, but this theory is no longer accepted. There is no evidence that Iron Age groups living in Cork county were intrusive populations or 'invaders'. Instead, the archaeological evidence points to a gradual acculturation of the indigenous population over several centuries of contact with the Celtic peoples.[69] This suggests that there was a slow transformation of the Late Bronze Age society in this area, as it developed culturally to gain new skills and technologies. However, there is really very little known about the Cork/Kerry area during this era. What is certain is that the smelting of iron is a difficult technological process and was unlikely to have been discovered by accident.[70]

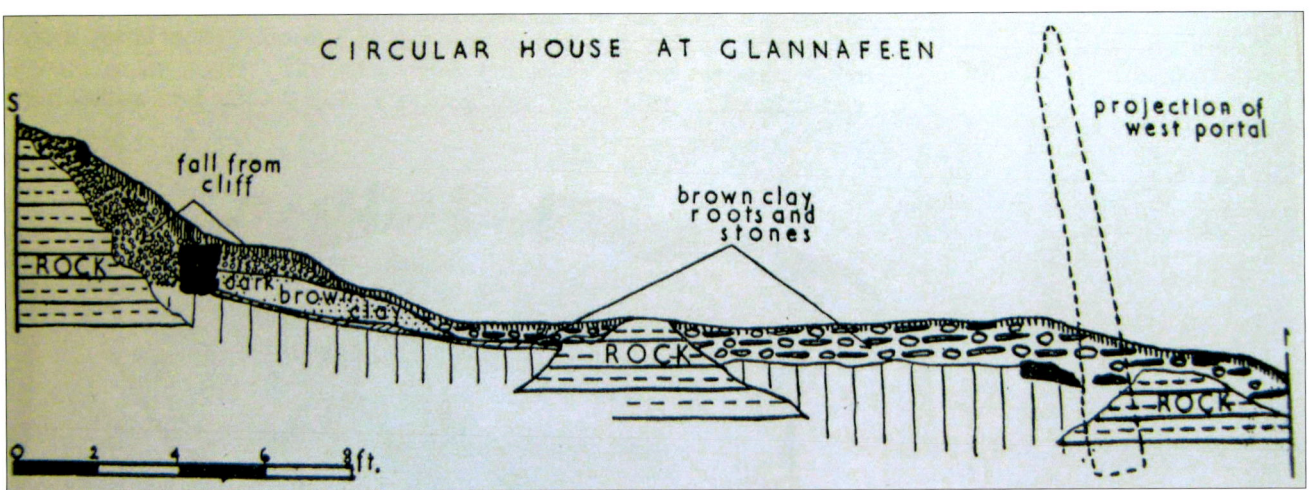

The absence of evidence of domestic occupation at the metal-working site in Glannafeen, excavated by Ó Cuilleanáin in 1953, may indicate that this was a commercial site. The nearby hut site may have been a habitation site. However, without further excavation and radiocarbon testing being carried out, neither can be confidently dated so it is not known if they were contemporaneous sites. (Image Courtesy of the *Royal Society of Antiquities of Ireland*.)

There is remaining evidence of a metal-working site in Glannafeen townland at Lough Hyne. Known locally as 'Druids' Altar', it was believed to be a stone circle prior to its excavation in August 1953 by Conchubhar Ó Cuilleanáin.[71] Unfortunately, material from the site was not radiocarbon dated so it cannot definitely be classified as belonging to the Iron Age. However, it was dated by Ó Cuilleanáin as not earlier than the Iron Age and the presence of furnace bottoms, fragments of tuyère and a flue are consistent with Iron Age smelting methodology.[72] There is a hut site approximately 100m from this site which was not included in the excavation.

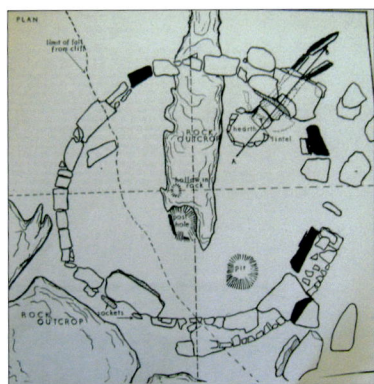

Ó Cuilleanáin's sketch of the same site. (Image Courtesy of the *Royal Society of Antiquities of Ireland*.)

The metal-working site as it appears today.

The hut site, *c.* 100m from the metal-working site, as it appears today. The presence of a stone lintel on its eastern side gives an indication that the entrance was on this side.

In Iron Age Ireland, lakes and waterways were very important for votive offerings. Lakes were sacred to the Celtic peoples of Europe and many deliberately-placed fine metalwork examples have been found in lakes in Ireland. The explanation offered for this practice is that these people deliberately deposited such high-quality weapons and other martial equipment in deference to some religious ritual.[73] A discovery of human skulls in another Irish lake, Loughnashade in County Armagh, where four superbly made bronze trumpets were also found, adds weight to this argument.[74] Lough Hyne, as such a magnificent example of a lake site, would surely have been considered a place of significance during this period.

Early Medieval Lough Hyne

The next group of monuments to be found at Lough Hyne are small circular enclosures, called ringforts, which date to the Early Medieval. An enclosure is a familiar monument in the Irish countryside and is also known as a *rath, lios, dún, caher* and *cashel*.[75] The term 'ringfort' is a misnomer, as it is not a fort in the military sense. A ringfort was a farmstead which would have enclosed a single farming family and its workers. Some of the internal structures were houses and others were farm buildings, named in ancient law tracts as a byre, pigsty, sheepfold and calf-fold.[76]

The majority of these sites were constructed and occupied between *c.* 600–900.[77] Because the remains of four ringforts are still evident in the townlands surrounding Lough Hyne, we know that there was settlement there during that period. The written evidence suggests that this was a time of relative prosperity. Despite a series of plagues and famines in the second half of the seventh century and the first half of the eighth century, the population of Ireland increased considerably between AD 600 and 800.[78]

Some booley huts were associated with old field walls, as may be the case with the site shown here in Glannafeen. Such sites were used to safely enclose cattle at night.[82] There were wolves in West Cork in the Early Medieval Period (and much later, up to 1710), which would have been seen as a major threat to animals.[83]

These ringfort dwellers were strongly attached to the land, with cattle-rearing as their primary economic pursuit. This period also saw the development of an advanced mixed-farming economy. As well as cattle, the medieval law tracts mention nine different cereals, with a predominance of oats, and there is an entire law tract devoted to bees and bee-keeping.[79]

Land was divided into different categories, one of which was commonage. This category included woodland, mountain upland, bog and wasteland.[80] Access to mountain land permitted extensive summer grazing, known as 'boolying', a practice well documented in early Irish sources.[81] The stone hut at Glannafeen, a possible 'booley hut', could date to this period or later.

There is evidence remaining of four ringforts in the Lough Hyne area but there were probably many more. There is a popular belief which says that each ringfort had a view of five neighbouring enclosures, which would have meant a much higher density.[84] However true that is, it is thought that up to 42% of ringforts were destroyed between 1773 and 1843–45 alone.[85] The current townland boundaries may once have corresponded to those of an independent farmstead, each of which would have held a ringfort.[86] The area around the lough would have been highly valued in view of its access to seaweed and fish, and for the woodland in the area, all of which were greatly prized at this time.

Early medieval Irish society was hierarchical and the sites themselves reflect this hierarchical nature. Below the king, or *rí*, were four divisions of lords, or *aire*. Below these were the freemen: the independent landholder farmer, or *bóaire,* and the small independent farmer who held no land, the *ócaire*.[87] Slavery was extensive in Ireland and the most commonly used names were *mug,* for a male, and *cumal,* for a female.[88] The smaller ringforts were occupied by the lower grades, who were compelled to provide a fixed amount of manual labour to their superiors. This included time constructing the lord's ringfort, so it followed that those higher in the hierarchy had larger enclosures.[89] The ringfort at Ballinard, the only such structure still intact, is considerably bigger than what remains of the other ringforts at Lough Hyne, reflecting these social differences.

The ringfort at Ballinard is considerably larger than what remains of other such sites at Lough Hyne, which suggests that its owners had a higher ranking in the social hierarchy of the time.

Early Christian Lough Hyne

Christianity was introduced into Ireland during the late fourth and early fifth centuries and, by the sixth century, it had become the dominant, if not exclusive, religion in Ireland. During the second half of the sixth century, monasticism spread across Ireland and some of the monastic sites functioned as small, isolated hermitages, while many served local families as proprietary churches.[90]

In the south-west, the predominant name associated with early church sites is *cill* or *kill*.[91] This term was commonly used in the naming of ecclesiastical sites in the period *c.* 550–1050 and there are many *cill* field names around Lough Hyne.[92] The earliest church sites were small enclosures sometimes containing inscribed pillar stones with simple crosses and a small church.[93] Other features of these sites are bullaun stones, souterrains and a cemetery, usually located on the site.[94]

Bullaun stones are stones with hollows ground into their surface and their exact function is unclear. They may have been used as communal altars but they could, too, have had a more utilitarian purpose.[114] While their use cannot be definitely established, they were certainly associated with early church sites. This is an example of a bullaun stone in Ballyoughtera townland.

The early ecclesiastical site at Glannafeen, with its souterrain and hut sites located in a *cill* field, may be an example of one of these early sites. Souterrains are frequently associated with church sites. A souterrain is an underground passageway which sometimes, but not always, ends in a chamber. The one at Glannafeen had a chamber which has now collapsed. The purpose of these underground 'caves' (as they were sometimes called) has been debated by scholars but it is thought that they were used either as places of refuge in times of attack, as storage places, or as a combination of both.[95] Some suggest that the early ecclesiastical centres used them as secure places for church valuables and personnel and that they also housed property deposited by lay neighbours who wished to avail of church protection.[96] The major period of their construction and use in Ireland was *c.* 500–1200.[97]

Souterrains in Cork are usually simply tunnelled from the earth and not stone-lined, as is the case with the one shown here in Glannafeen.[98] The purpose of these underground passageways is unclear but their construction took some effort, especially the 'dry-stone' variety. This type of souterrain had the advantages of stability and strength but its construction would have required the knowledge of a highly skilled souterrain-engineer.[99] This would suggest that this site was significant enough to warrant such 'outside involvement'. There are two types of underground passage and this one would fall into the 'restricted' category of *c.* 60–90cm in width and in height.[100] Such passages usually ended in an underground chamber, as is the case with the one in Glannafeen.[101]

Many of the early church sites would subsequently be known as *cills* or *cillíns*, some of which were also referred to as 'children's burial grounds'. This was the name given to the designated resting places for unbaptised infants and other members of Irish society who were considered unsuitable for burial in consecrated ground. These sites were used for this purpose from the seventeenth century onwards, because of changes in church law regarding burials in the wake of the Counter-Reformation.[102] In addition to unbaptised babies, oral history suggests that others buried there included the mentally ill, strangers, the shipwrecked, criminals, famine victims and people who committed suicide.[103] When the early ecclesiastical church sites were abandoned because of changes to church law, the sites were still regarded as consecrated ground. When later church law prohibited the burial of unbaptised children in graveyards, some of these *cill* sites began to be used as a burial place.[104] There were at least two *cillíní* at Lough Hyne: the remains of one in Dromadoon, in addition to a site that once existed at Ballyoughtera.[105]

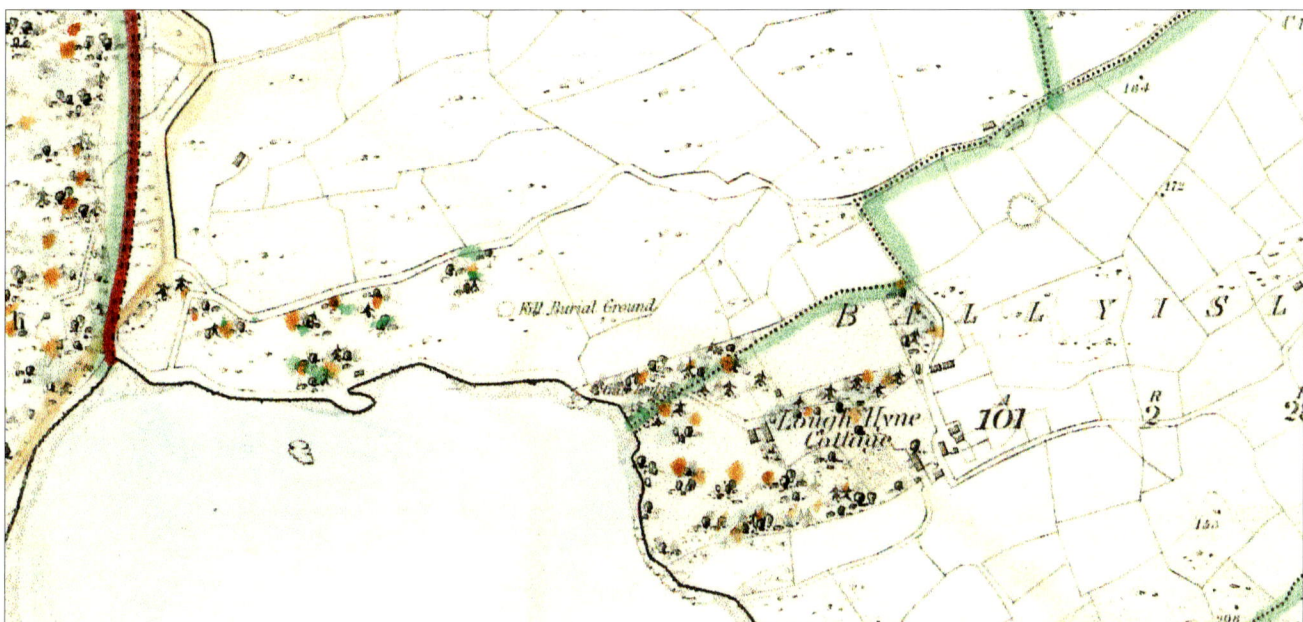

Many of the early church sites would later be known as 'children's burial grounds' as they were used for burials of unbaptised infants and others when later church law prohibited their burial in graveyards. In addition to deserted church sites and graveyards, archaeological sites such as ringforts and megaliths were also utilised for these burials. The site at Ballyoughtera was once used for this purpose, as it is shown here as '*Kill* Burial Ground (Children)' on the 1842 Ordnance Survey of Ireland map. This site is depicted as circular, which may indicate that it was once a ringfort, but little evidence remains of it today. By using ringforts and other archaeological sites as *cillíní*, these burial grounds were clearly identifiable in the landscape, which afforded them some protection against destruction. *Pishógs* and superstitions also protected them from harm in many cases. (OSI Map permissions: © Ordnance Survey Ireland/Government of Ireland Copyright Permit No. MP 000714.)

Some studies carried out on settlement patterns in Ireland have shown that ringforts and ecclesiastical sites had a common distribution pattern.[106] The relationship between them was symbiotic. The ringfort provided cattle, patronage/population and surplus wealth, while the ecclesiastical centre provided grain, served the population's spiritual needs and also offered treasury services.[107] The fact that both these contemporaneous sites are found at Lough Hyne may be an indication that such an inter-relationship existed in the society there.

Members of the clergy were included in a special classification of high-ranking people in Ireland at this time. The *áes dána*, or 'men of art', were a learned class that was accorded a high status.[108] The fact that the personnel of these early church sites were included in such a high-ranking group gives an indication of their importance in the society of the time.

| These circular hutsite foundations are near the site of the souterrain in Glannafeen.

Templebreedy Church in Glannafeen at Lough Hyne is, according to Webster, 'the most primitive church in the Diocese of Ross'.[109] Also known as St Bridget's Church, it is thought to date to before the twelfth century.[110] However, it may well have been built on the site of an even earlier wooden church. With its simple, small structure and associated cross-slab and holy well, it is another example of an early church site at Lough Hyne.

Templebreedy has a lintelled doorway on its northern side as its original entrance. An arched doorway on its western gable is a later addition. During the twelfth century, lintelled church doorways were replaced by highly elaborate round-arched doorways, influenced by the English Romanesque architectural tradition.[111]

Close to Templebreedy Church is St Bridget's Holy Well, also known as Tobarbreedy. This well was visited by local people each year on the festival of St Bridget, the first day of February.[112] There are indentations in the rock on either side of the well which are said to have been made by the knees of the saint as she knelt there.[113] The well could also be regarded as a possible bullaun stone, as the catchment basin could be man-made.

Tobarbreedy Holy Well at Glannafeen. There has been a custom of placing coins in this well and the coins that still remain in the well today date to the pre-decimal era.

The broken cross-slab at Glannafeen, near Templebreedy Church, as it appears today. The Halls' sketch of the same site, from c. 1840, shows the cross-slab with the titulus, its engraving, intact.[115] By 1876, the slab is described as being broken.[116] There is a piece of folklore associated with the slab that says it was taken by a coastguard and thrown into the Rapids, only to constantly reappear in its original position.[117] Finally, the frustrated coastguard ordered the slab to be broken but, try as he might, he could not break the portion of the stone which was inscribed.[118] There was a coastguard station at Lough Hyne in the intervening period and such tales often owe their origins to an actual event, but over time become embellished and exaggerated in the retelling.[119] '[Nothing is certain other than] the holiness of the Heart's affections and the truth of the imagination'.[120]

Mr and Mrs Hall's sketch with their commentary: 'Not far from Skibbereen is a singular salt-water lake … in the centre is a long island, upon which are the ruins of one of the castles of the O'Driscolls. It is surrounded by picturesque hills … [there is] a churchyard, particular to Ireland, devoted exclusively to the interment of children and where there was formerly a chapel dedicated to St. Bridget. In the foreground is one of the singular ring-stones, or pillar-stones, engraven with inscrutable characters.'[121] Halls' comment on the 'interment of children' may mean that this was also used locally as a children's burial ground.

Other Christian Sites at Lough Hyne

There are two other holy wells at Lough Hyne, *Tobarín na Súl* and Skour Holy Well, both located on the small road that skirts the north-eastern side of Knockomagh Hill. They are within easy walking distance of the lake, with public access to both of them.

Skour got its name from Skour Church, which was situated on the hill overlooking the present well.[122] This church was in use up to *c.* 1795 and the name Skour, or 'Skeowr', comes from the Irish *Seipeal-an-sceabhrach*, which means 'church of the sloping hill'.[123] *Tobarín na Súl*, which can be translated as 'little holy well of the eyes', is about 100m from Skour Well.

Skour Holy Well is dedicated to St Ina and an annual mass is held there every May Eve.[126] The holding of mass there is a relatively new occurrence (within the last fifty years), but it was preceded by an annual pilgrimage there, held also on May Eve.[127] The holding of 'patterns' or pilgrimages on May Eve, the Celtic festival of Bealtaine, was common.[128] Folklore has it that the water from Skour Well will not boil.[129] There is also a piece of folklore relating to Skour Church which tells the story of a man hanging his coat on a sunbeam in the church.[130]

Tobarín na Súl has no known association with a saint and is known primarily as a 'cure for the eyes'. People with eye ailments would bathe their eyes in its water in the hopes of a cure.[131]

There was a mass rock at Barnabah, Lough Hyne, where, it is said, mass was celebrated in secret during Penal times.[124] There is also a 'monastery field' and 'monastery well' in Dromadoon townland, about which very little is known.[125]

The Vikings at Lough Hyne

An archaeological find at Lough Hyne places a Viking presence there somewhere between the eleventh and thirteenth centuries. By this stage, the Vikings were well established in West Cork.

The first Viking raid in Ireland took place in AD 795 and attacks continued sporadically over the following forty years.[132] The raiding intensified in the 840s with the use of larger fleets but gradually the Irish began to fight back in a more organised way and mounted a stronger resistance to the attacks.

From about the mid-ninth century, the Vikings began to engage in politics and to form alliances with Irish kings.[133] They started to assimilate with the native Irish, intermarrying and borrowing personal names.[134] Some towns had Viking enclaves, which became an integral part of a society in Ireland that consisted of numerous tribal kingdoms.

Cork city experienced the first raid in 820, when the great monastery of St Fin Barre was attacked.[135] The first Viking settlement in the city was established by at least 846 and probably even earlier.[136] By the early twelfth century, the Ostman Viking town of Cork was the largest urban settlement in south Munster.[137] The MacCarthy kings of Desmond established their 'capital' at Cork and became overlords of this Ostman settlement, utilising its ships in times of war.[138] By then, the Viking community had become fully integrated into the Gaelic world. They were Christian, and Gaelicised to some degree, and lived harmoniously with their native Irish neighbours.[139]

The Viking trading network reached Britain and possibly extended to France. Within Munster, there was trading between Cork city and the Viking trading posts at Youghal and Kinsale, as well as Gaelic harbours such as Dunboy in Beara.[140] Viking ships would have worked their way along the coast from Cork to the westerly harbours, with overnight stops along the way at navigable inlets. There is evidence to indicate that there were such Scandinavian way-stops scattered along this coast. It is possible that they existed in places like Crookhaven, Schull, Cape Clear, Fastnet (an old Norse name), Glandore and Clonakilty Bay.[141]

Viking ships regularly travelled along the south-west coast, following a trading route which took them past Lough Hyne.

A Viking hoard of silver was found in Rathbarry, *c.* 16km east of Lough Hyne, in 1799. It was found in a souterrain and is thought to have a concealment date of *c.* 945.[142] Sheehan proposes that the fact that this was found in a native Irish site means that it was under Gaelic ownership when it was buried. He suggests that it was likely that such wealth would have come into Irish hands as a result of trade, tribute or gift exchange with the Scandinavians. This could have come about in one of the way-stations of West Cork. If such exchange was being carried out along this coast, we could assume that the O'Driscolls, as overlords of this part of West Cork, would also have engaged with the Vikings.

As they had a presence along the coast of West Cork, the Viking stick-pin found by Colin Barnes at Lough Hyne is not an unexpected find. The sheltered site, positioned alongside a coast that their boats would have frequently travelled, could have offered a place or shelter in rough weather or perhaps more. Such a prime location could not have gone unnoticed by these experienced seamen and the sheltered anchorage of Barlogue, adjacent to a lough that was abundant with fish, would surely have been considered a prime site. That the artefact was found on the island in the middle of the lough suggests that the Vikings may have utilised the lough itself in some way.

A Viking stick-pin, which was used as a cloak fastener, was found by Colin Barnes at Lough Hyne in 2002 and is now held in Cork Public Museum. This places a possible Viking presence in the area somewhere between the eleventh and the thirteenth centuries.[143] (Image courtesy of Cork Public Museum.)

A Sacred Place?

The archaeological monuments that have been found to date in the Lough Hyne area span a period of *c.* 4,000 years. They are the only remaining evidence of the people who lived, loved, worked and worshipped there through the millennia.

The number of sites of a ritual or religious nature in the area is particularly high. These include the cupmarked stones and cairns of the Bronze Age, the Early Christian ecclesiastical centre and *cill* sites, Templebreedy and the cross-slab, the holy wells and mass rock and the Later Medieval Skour Church. It could be said that these sites are physical representations of how Lough Hyne was perceived by the people of the past. It is possible that there were once even more monuments of this nature there, as the remains of the megalith and other *cill* sites and cairns indicate. When compared with two other West Cork lakes located near the sea, Lough Hyne has a significantly higher proportion of sites of a ritualistic or religious nature.[144] Such a comparison suggests that Lough Hyne has been regarded as a 'special place' since prehistoric times.

> Ritual action is repetitive and formal, often carried out in defined, special places ... The encounters with the other world take place in special places which are luminal ... Natural places that would fulfill such a role might include mountain tops, caves, rivers and lakes.[145]

Early man viewed the landscape as a living thing and would have considered himself to be part of it to a far greater extent than we do nowadays. However, even today, the landscape of Lough Hyne has an effect. It is a much-loved place that is visited regularly by many people for different reasons. A variety of modern rituals, from ash-scatterings to wedding proposals, have taken place there in recent years. There are often flowers floating on its waters, perhaps placed there in memory of a loved one. People still visit the holy wells, as the numerous 'gifts' of rags, stones and beads around them show, and the annual mass at Skour Well is always well attended. Numerous poems have been written about the area and, even in this modern age, many people consider Lough Hyne to be 'sacred ground'. With the remaining monuments as testament to how the lough was perceived in the past, it would appear that this is not a recent phenomenon. It appears to be a place where man has experienced 'the magic worlds of another law' throughout the millennia.[146]

The O'Driscolls

Introduction

The ivy-covered ruins of a medieval castle still stand on the island in the middle of Lough Hyne. This is Cloghan Castle, one of the many tower houses built by the O'Driscolls, a Gaelic clan that once ruled over this coastal area of West Cork. Despite being one of the smallest of their castles, Cloghan is significant as the place where Sir Fineen O'Driscoll, the last Chieftain of Collymore, is believed to have spent his final years.[1]

The O'Driscolls were one of the chief families of the region from at least the sixth century.[2] By the fifteenth century, when most Irish tower houses were built, the family was well established as a powerful maritime force.[3] At the beginning of the sixteenth century, they were the premier maritime lords of the south-west and one of the most powerful clans in Munster.[4] However, by the early seventeenth century, the head of the clan, Sir Fineen, was financially ruined and was living in the small castle at Lough Hyne in 'great and decrepide age' and in a state of 'disabilitie and wante of means'.[5] Like many Gaelic clans, the O'Driscolls lost most of their lands and wealth in the course of that turbulent century. This once wealthy and powerful family sank 'into the ranks of the hewers of wood and drawers of water'.[6]

As rulers of the area, the O'Driscolls played an integral role in the history of Lough Hyne. While there are few direct references to Lough Hyne during these centuries, the experiences of the O'Driscoll clan give an overview of the fundamental changes that happened in the area. This family's lordship spanned a period that saw an ancient Gaelic system of land ownership and rule change to one of colonisation and plantation.

Cloghan Castle today.

The O'Driscolls

Before the arrival of the Normans in Ireland in 1169, society in Ireland was generally rural, consisting of a series of small, scattered settlements.[7] The land was under tribal ownership in that it was not owned by individual people but communally by family groups.[8] Each family, or clan, functioned as a political unit and elected its own chief, who ruled the tribe and its territory, the *tuath*.[9] The chieftain, or *taoiseach,* was known simply by the family surname, for example O'Driscoll, or O'Driscoll Mór. He was selected from a small group within the family, known as the *derbfine*.[10]

Genealogies were therefore very important in establishing family position and property rights and they were recorded in poems and local books of pedigree.[11] In this way, the O'Driscoll family can trace its lineage into the mists of mythology as one of the ancient Gaelic tribes.[12] It was the chief family of the Corcu Lóegde, which once ruled over a region that extended from Kinsale to Kenmare Bay.[13]

The family's territory was gradually eroded by intertribal conflict. Conflicts between clans were common, as were incursions and seizures of land.[14] In the eighth century, the O'Mahonys seized the Fonn-Iartharach, or West Land, comprising the parishes of 'Kilmoe, Scoole, Kilcrohane, Durris, Kilmaconoge and Caheragh'.[15] With the arrival of the Normans in the twelfth century, there were even more territorial encroachments as Gaelic clans were forced to leave their traditional lands. The O'Driscolls were pressed south and westwards by the O'Sullivans and O'Donovans, who were, in turn, being pushed out by the MacCarthy overlords.[16]

Cloghan Castle in ruins, shown here in the Lawrence Collection photo of the late nineteenth century. The remains of its ground-floor vaulted ceiling are still visible in this photo. This is a common feature in such castles and its purpose was to protect the inhabitants of the castle from being burnt out from below. (Image courtesy of the National Library of Ireland.)

The Arrival of the Normans

The Norman invasion changed the status quo for the Gaelic families and, by the early part of the thirteenth century, the newcomers had reached even remote areas like West Cork. A war within the MacCarthy family proved to be an opportunity for the Normans, as they acquired large areas of land in the south, where they settled and started to build castles of stone.[17] One of these castles was built in Baltimore in 1215 by Robert de Carew, who was also known as Sleynie.[18]

Over time, the Gaelic clans started to revolt against this Norman presence. There are few references to the O'Driscolls during this period, but, as Connie Kelleher puts it, 'it can be presumed that [they] took part in the general unrest'.[19] The resistance culminated in the Battle of Callan in 1261, where the Anglo-Normans were defeated by a branch of the MacCarthys, and the region started to come back under Gaelic control.[20] By 1300, the area was outside the scope of royal criminal justice.[21] Crown resources were drained by a series of wars with the French and royal authority was eroded in Ireland generally during this period.[22]

In the early years of the fourteenth century the climate deteriorated, with the 'Little Ice Age' bringing extremely cold conditions.[23] There was severe famine as a result and this was compounded by the arrival of the plague, known as the Black Death, in 1348–49.[24] This turbulent period, in which royal authority was waning, saw the Normans begin to rule almost autonomously in Ireland.[25] Known as 'the Old English in Ireland', they were by now intermarrying and dealing with the Gaelic families.[26] In Munster, the powerful earls of Desmond were trading with the native clans and also formed political alliances with them.[27]

In West Cork, where there was no strong Anglo-Norman presence, the MacCarthys became the dominant force through the fourteenth and fifteenth centuries.[28] A branch of the family, the MacCarthy Reagh, had begun establishing itself in West Cork from around 1232 and gradually acquired domination of the territory, becoming overlords to the O'Driscolls.[29] There are few accounts of the O'Driscolls during these two centuries, but they emerge in the fifteenth century as 'powerful maritime lords'.[30]

While the fourteenth century was a period of famine, plague and economic slump, the fifteenth century was a time of prosperity, during which most of the tower houses in Ireland were built.[31] This was a period of high economic growth, especially in port towns like Baltimore, where fishing was a lucrative industry.[32] At this time the O'Driscoll territory encompassed the areas of Collymore and Collybeg, which included the parishes of 'Myross, Glanbarahane (now Castlehaven), Tullagh, Creagh, Kilcoe, Aughadowne and Cleere'.[33] While they held tower houses all along the coast of this territory, their primary castles were located around Baltimore, where the seat of the O'Driscolls, Dún na Séad Castle, dominated the harbour.[34] The castle originally built by Sleynie in 1215 was later rebuilt by the O'Driscolls.[35] Tower houses were potent indicators of wealth and status, as well as symbols of power and control over a region, and the O'Driscolls were clearly a prosperous and powerful clan at the time.

Cloghan Castle

Trade, Piracy and Wealth

In the early sixteenth century, the Norman earls of Desmond were ruling over a considerable part of Cork county. They traded with and received dues from the native MacCarthy Reagh, who were, in turn, overlords to the O'Driscolls.[36] While the O'Driscolls had to pay the MacCarthy Reagh their dues, customs and royalties, in effect the O'Driscolls enjoyed considerable autonomy.

In areas where the authority of the government was weak, such as West Cork, English prohibitions against the use of Gaelic customs effectively meant nothing. Without royal judges the English common law could not function, and judges ceased to be appointed for Munster soon after 1400.[37] The Irish judges and lawyers, the Brehon, made legal judgements based on the Irish system and were appointed by the lord.[38] The O'Driscolls ruled under Gaelic custom, appointing judges and officials within their territory and levying taxation almost at will.[39] Sixteenth-century Ireland was divided politically into a multitude of these small, autonomous lordships.[40]

By the sixteenth century, the O'Driscoll territory covered an area between Castlehaven and Aughadown, with the centre of power around Baltimore and the islands. The overlords of Carbery, the powerful MacCarthy Reaghs, were paid dues by the O'Driscolls and other clans. Each of these local lords, including O'Driscoll, exercised a sovereign authority in his own area, levying taxation and appointing judges and officials within his territory.[41] (Image from *An Archaeology of Southwest Ireland: 1570–1670* by Colin Breen. Image used courtesy of the author and Four Courts Press.)

Although the area ruled by the O'Driscolls was small, with rough and hilly land, it included extremely rich fishing grounds.[42] Climatic changes of the late fourteenth century resulted in migrations of herring shoals to the south of Ireland, drawing Irish and foreign fishing fleets to the area.[43] Baltimore became a trading post, with Spanish and French fishing boats landing there, and the O'Driscolls, as the controllers of the port, exacted dues and grew very wealthy.[44] Because the herring had to be salted within twenty-four hours to retain its flavour, the catch had to be processed locally and the fishermen would pay dues to the local lord for doing so.[45] The sea around Baltimore was noted as being one of the richest fishing grounds in Europe in the fifteenth century.[46] The following century also saw extensive fishing activities, with a report of six hundred Spanish vessels fishing off the south-west coast in 1572.[47] The O'Driscolls received revenues from fishing up to 1601, at which time O'Driscoll Mór (Sir Fineen) was entitled to six shillings and eight pence for every barrel of herring or pilchard sold.[48] This was a significant amount, as, to put it in context, a good milch cow was valued at 30 shillings at the time.[49]

In the seventeenth century, pilchards, *Sardinia pilchardis,* were the primary catch in this area and these required even more on-site local processing.[50] Two of the so-called 'fish palaces', the name given to the buildings where oil was extracted from the fish, were situated at Ballyalla and Tralispean, east of Lough Hyne.[51] The labour-intensive fish processing provided employment to the local people and 'where the pilchards came great fortunes were made'.[52] However, by the time the pilchard trade reached its height in 1630, the chief Munster fisheries were run by Englishmen.[53] The Tralispean site is shown on Petty's parish map of the 1650s as a 'fishing pallice', so it was in existence at that date. This land at Tralispean was under Gaelic ownership in 1641 but was later granted to Colonel Richard Townsend, an officer of Cromwell.[54]

Petty's parish map, which dates to the 1650s, shows the 'fishing pallice' at Tralispean, *c*. 1km to the east of Lough Hyne. The ruins of this extensive structure still remain today. A second 'pallice' was situated on the eastern side of Ballyalla inlet, *c*. 500m east of Lough Hyne.[55] A 'fish palace' was the name given to the building in which pilchards were processed. Pilchards, which are larger versions of sardines, came to this south-west coast in great numbers during the seventeenth century. The fishing and curing (smoking, picking and pressing) of pilchards was an important industry in West Cork in the early seventeenth century, both for export and for home consumption.[56] (Image courtesy of the National Library of Ireland, MSS714.)

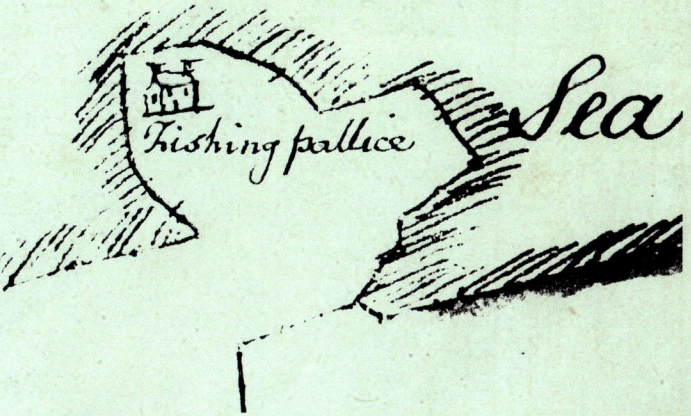

By the seventeenth century, pilchard came to dominate the fishing industry in Ireland and in huge volumes, with exports valued at £29,000 recorded in 1626.[57] Practically all these exports came from the south-west, with Baltimore, Crookhaven, Bantry and Kenmare ports accounting for 82% of the trade in 1617, 78% in 1622 and 75% in 1626.[58]

Two boats were used to catch these small fish. The 'seine boat', a large boat pulled by a dozen or more oars, carried the net, which was often 300–400 yards long, and this was accompanied by a smaller boat, the 'follower', with a crew of five or six.[59] From high land an experienced fisherman, called a 'hewer', directed the seine boat to the location of a shoal. The net was shot around the shoal by the seine boat, while the free end of the net was picked up by the follower, encircling the shoal. The weighted foot-ropes of the seine net were gradually drawn up until the fish were enclosed in the purse of net. They were loaded into the boat using baskets. This process would be repeated until the boats were full.[60]

As well as providing employment directly via fishing, the curing and preservation of pilchards also gave work to coopers, carpenters, clerks, etc.[61]

Pococke said of Sherkin Island in 1758:

> They are all fishermen, both on this island and Cape Clear; & they have on the coast, places for curing fish, commonly call'd fish palaces, & [fishermen] come to these parts from Cork and Kingsale … & make little huts in which they live during the summer; most in time of peace the French come here to fish: where the pilchards came great fortunes were made by them.[62]

These 'small huts' may well have been what was seen by a Spanish officer in Castlehaven in 1601 when he described the land as 'mountainous and without trees … all I can see are straw huts and these are small'.[63] This type of house was called a 'creat' and was a small, rounded or oval one-roomed house of post-and-wattle construction covered with sods and coarse grass.[64] As the sites at Tralispean and Ballyalla were isolated, we can only suppose that such huts could have been used there too, in support of the work at the fish palaces.

There were fish palaces all along this south-west coast, with very little trace remaining of them now. However, place names offer a clue, and a village on the western portion of Heir Island called 'Paris' is thought to have derived its name from a fish palace.[65] A field near Ballydehob is known locally as the 'Palleshes' and was known as a curing station for pilchards operated by the 'Spaniards'.[66] Others include a house known as the 'Palace House' on the north side of Schull harbour, with a 'Palace Strand' nearby, while there is a 'Palace Field' in Dunmanus.[67] Other fish palaces in this area were located at the Cove in Baltimore, Long Island off Schull, Cape Clear, Courtmacsherry, Crookhaven, and many were further west, at Bantry Bay, Dursey Island and Kenmare Bay.[68]

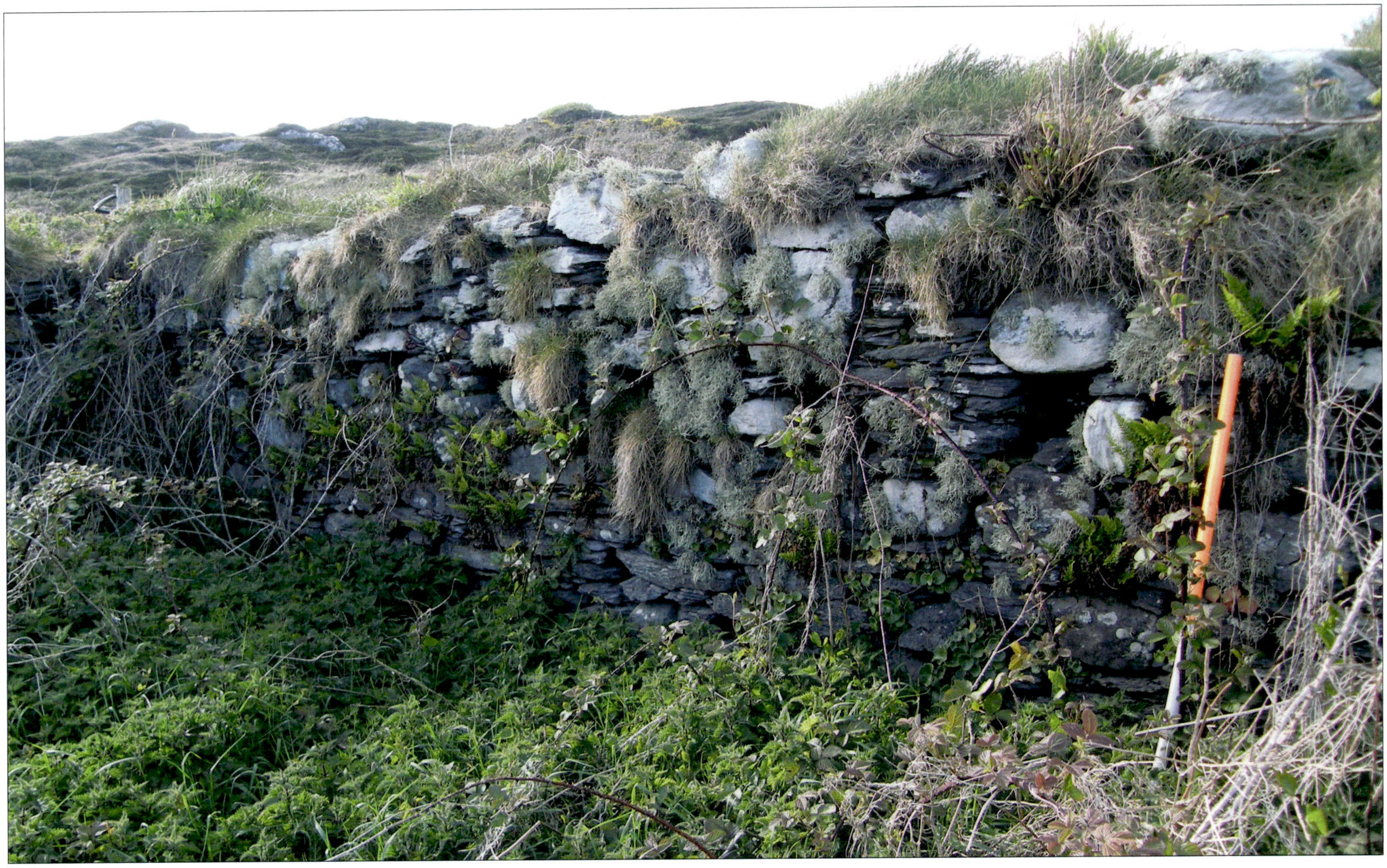

The fish processing methods in the fish palaces varied, with some smoked, some cured and some pickled. The cured fish were first laid out and covered in salt and left for up to three weeks before they were washed and pressed. The extracted oil from the pressing process was called 'train oil' and was a valuable by-product, used in preparing leather and as a luminant.[69] This was pressed from the pilchard by means of press beams and collected in barrels.[70] 'The fish being thus pressed, the barrels are headed and sent to market'.[71] Pickling was the method favoured for home consumption, while the pressed was more for export.[72] We do not know what processing method was used at the Ballyalla site, as nothing remains as evidence. The site at Tralispean still has visible beam niches or holes (shown here), so this was most likely to have been a processing site for fish to be exported.

Fig. 8.

A.—Elevation of pilchard press. Barrel and support for press beam shown in section. Contents of barrel omitted.

B.—Plan of pilchard press.

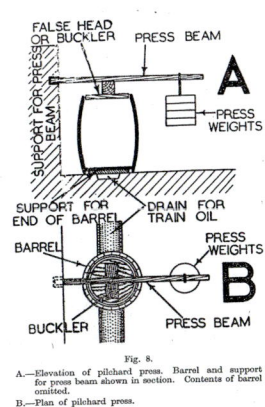

This diagram from Went shows the mechanism for pressing the fish using the press beams, which would have been used at the Tralispean site. (Image use courtesy of the Cork Historical and Archaeological Society.)

As well as charging fees for fishing and processing the fish, the head of the O'Driscoll clan, O'Driscoll Mór, was entitled to dues from all merchandise tendered for sale in his territory, including the lucrative wine trade.[73] He also controlled activities within the ports. Pilots, who guided ships in the harbours and on the river Ilen, had to hold a licence granted by him. He was also deemed to be the owner of all wrecks and material washed ashore.[74]

The O'Driscolls had a long history of controlling the use of the sea but also of attacking ships.[75] They were known for their habit of plundering ships and 'made themselves obnoxious to the people of Waterford, in particular by the piracy of their vessels on the high seas'.[76] The long-running feud between the O'Driscolls and the citizens of Waterford spanned several centuries, with the first record of an attack being in 1072.[77] The dispute continued until 1537, when a force of four hundred men, on a number of ships including the great galley of Waterford, sacked Sherkin, Cape Clear and Baltimore.[78] This ferocious attack fulfilled its purpose, as, after this dramatic event, the O'Driscolls did not take part in any more raids outside of their own territory.

Such was the O'Driscoll renown for piracy that, when William Syngyn and John Galvy were appointed as admirals for the ports of Cork in 1382, part of their duties was defined as 'to fight with God's aid the lineage of the Hinderscoles [O'Driscolls], Irish enemies, who constantly remain upon the western ocean'.[79] A law was enacted in 1450 'that no person ... shall fish at Korky [Cork], Baltimore nor go within the country of said O'Hedriscol ... and the town that receives said O'Hedriscol or any of his men shall pay £40 to the King'.[80]

However, as the ruling Gaelic family of the area, it could be said that the O'Driscolls were simply continuing to do what they had always done, long before the arrival of Anglo-Norman law. As Kelleher put it, 'such clandestine behaviour formed part of the tradition of seafaring in Ireland among the Gaelic maritime lords'.[81] Whether they should be regarded as pirates or lords of the sea, they were not alone in engaging in such activities along this coast. This remote region, where English authority was practically non-existent, drew pirates from England, who came here in great numbers from 1607 onwards and were provisioned by the new English town of Baltimore.[82] By 1610, 'the town and harbour of Baltimore were such notorious places of resort for pirates that even foreign governments complained to King James the First'.[83] The scale of these English pirate activities was far greater than anything that the O'Driscolls had ever engaged in.

During one of the many feuding raids that took place over the centuries between the O'Driscolls and the city of Waterford, three of the O'Driscolls' galleys were captured:

> On the third of June, 1461, the Mayor and citizens of Waterford [knowing that O'Driscoll was in Tramore] prepared themselves in warlike manner, and set forwards towards Ballymacdane, where they met the O'Hedriscols and Powers, gave them battle and gained compleat victory, 160 of the enemy being slain, and some taken prisoners, among whom were O'Hedriscol Oge and six of his sons, who with three of their Gallies were brought to Waterford.[84]

These 'gallies' were boats that were a combination of sail and oar. The three captured O'Driscoll galleys feature on the city Seal of Waterford in celebration of this victory.[85] The O'Driscoll galleys shown here heading out of Baltimore harbour are similar to those that feature on the 1556 Waterford Charter of Philip and Mary, which are said to represent the three captured in 1461.[86] The O'Driscolls also had a 'great galley of thirty oars', which was seized in the 1537 raid along with 'three or four score pinaces'.[87]

The Last Chieftain of Collymore, Fineen O'Driscoll

Fineen O'Driscoll was inaugurated as chieftain of the O'Driscoll clan in 1573 by the overlord, MacCarthy Reagh.[88] Under Gaelic custom, a chieftain was elected from within the *derbfine,* a group of the family that consisted of males whose great-grandfather had once been chieftain.[89] In some regions, including Carbery, the new chieftain would have been chosen not only by his own clan but by the overlord and the assembly of the country as a whole.[90] In practice, however, it was often the son of the former chieftain who was selected.[91]

The date of Fineen's inauguration in 1573 was a tumultuous period in Munster, as it was just after the outbreak of the First Desmond Rebellion, in 1569.[92] In the preceding years, the Crown had made attempts to regain its control over the region and tried to order the province along English lines, imposing English laws of land tenure and custom. The Norman earls of Desmond had been effectively ruling the area independently for centuries and the new regime brought about a series of revolts.[93]

This uprising caused savage reprisals and the Lord Deputy, Sir Henry Sidney, carried out a subsequent campaign of slaughter across Munster using brutal methods such as the erection of a grisly corridor of severed heads to induce abject surrenders. The destruction was so bad that the fields lay fallow for years afterwards, causing a terrible famine.[94] The Earl of Desmond finally submitted to the Crown in 1574. It is not clear what position the O'Driscolls took in the rebellion but they must have provided some help to the rebels, as Fineen received a pardon for his role in the events.[95] When Sidney made his vice-regal tour of Cork in 1575, after the rebellion had been quashed, the newly inaugurated chieftain Fineen went to meet him.[96] This tour, during the winter of 1575–76, was met with general compliance by the Gaelic chieftains of the province as a whole.[97]

Fineen was the last O'Driscoll chieftain to receive his Irish title in the traditional way, as he extinguished his Irish right under what was known as the 'surrender and regrant' system. This involved Gaelic chieftains 'surrendering' their Irish title and land to the Crown to have the land 'regranted' to them by letters patent to hold them in accordance with English law, along with an English title. Fineen was not the first West Cork chieftain to do so. MacCarthy Mór and O'Sullivan Beare had taken English titles in 1565.[98]

Fineen's inauguration ceremony would have been carried out in the customary way at some traditional, sacred site. The placing of a white rod in the hands of the newly appointed chieftain was one of the most characteristic features of the inauguration.[99] The white rod was the symbol of sovereignty and was thought to represent the righteousness of the receiver.[100] Fineen's genealogy would have been recited by a poet and his praises sung as part of the ceremony.[101] Fineen was the last O'Driscoll chieftain to be inaugurated in the traditional way as he surrendered his Irish title under 'surrender and regrant'.

The 'surrender and regrant' system was not new to Ireland, but it was reintroduced in 1540 in an attempt to incorporate Gaelic lordships into an anglicised kingdom of Ireland after the failed Leinster Geraldine Rebellion.[102] At the time, Henry VIII did not capitalise on the Crown victory, as he was otherwise occupied in his dispute with the Pope. Reluctant to engage in an expensive campaign in Ireland, he sent instead an envoy, who, under the generous terms of these early surrender and regrants, offered a concession to lordly authority.[103] However, by the time that Fineen had accepted his English title of Sir Fineen, the policy had changed to one of coercion and colonisation and the forced imposition of English norms.[104]

This was a turbulent period in Ireland and, even prior to the First Desmond Rebellion, the perception was rife that the English government meant to overturn the rights of the Gaelic clans and institute a widespread plantation.[105] Fineen may have entered his 'suit to surrender all his possessions to the Queen, and to hold them by such tenure as shall seem good to her', because he feared confiscation of his lands after the failed rebellion.[106] Whatever his reasons, by so doing Fineen secured the legal title of the property, which would, in turn, pass to his descendants. Irish law was not based on primogeniture, on passing property from father to son. The chieftain was elected by his clan, while the land remained the property of the entire clan, and the landholdings of the various members of the group were liable to redistribution from time to time.[107] By adopting the English system, Fineen was, in effect, claiming inheritance of clan property solely for his own heirs. This resulted in a subsequent protracted legal struggle with one of his cousins.[108]

During the Second Desmond Rebellion of 1579, it seems that Fineen sided with the government, as Baltimore was one of the few ports of the south available to Crown forces during that time.[109] The war dragged on until 1583 and resulted in another devastating famine. Even after it had ended, the famine raged on, with the population estimated as falling by as much as 30% as a result.[110] Fineen was reported to have 'loyally behaved in this dangerous time'.[111]

In the 1580s, when relations between England and Spain steadily worsened, Sir Fineen was seen to be a loyal subject to the Crown. A report in 1586 by a government official who was sent to appraise the ports of Munster as potential sites of attack from Spain says that:

> The castle [at Baltimore] belongeth to one of the O'Driscols … follower to Sir Finnin O'Driscol, by whom I learnt it would not be hard for Her Majesty to have that castle, if it should be required for any necessity of service.[112]

Fineen was High Sheriff of the County of Cork in *c.* 1592.[113] In this position, he acted as the local agent of the Crown, with responsibility for collecting revenues for the county.[114] He also held judicial powers, as well as performing military functions in this role.[115] In 1598, he is described as 'one of the principal men of the County of Cork'.[116] He was seen as a loyal subject, with the *Pacata Hibernia* stating that he 'never in the course of his whole life had been tainted with the least spot of disloyaltie'.[117]

'Loaghine' is shown clearly here on this 1612 Dutch map of the area, which features the 'O' Drifcall' family name. (The letter 'f' was frequently used to represent a double 's' at this time.)[118]

The arrival of Spanish forces in Kinsale and Castlehaven in 1601 altered the political situation, and the O'Driscoll alliances changed dramatically when Sir Fineen joined with other local chieftains to rebel against the English.[119] After the initial Spanish landing in Kinsale in early October, he had sworn allegiance to the Crown.[120] A letter from the Lord Deputy to Captains Harvey and Taaffe tells of Sir Fineen capturing rebels and handing them over to the English forces.[121] However, a month later, possibly inspired by Donal O'Sullivan Beare's offer to the Spanish of 2,000 of his men, Fineen and his son also offered their support to them.[122] As part of this alliance, he handed over his castles at Baltimore and Sherkin to the Spanish, who prepared them for defence against the English.[123]

The Spanish and Irish forces were totally defeated at the Battle of Kinsale.[124] After this victory, the English moved south, leaving 'neither corn, nor horn, nor house, unburnt'.[125] They quelled a subsequent stand by the O'Driscolls at Castlehaven in which Sir Fineen's son, Conchobhar, took part.[126] The English continued on to Baltimore, where the occupying Spanish force handed over Dún na Séad castle and also Dún na Long at Sherkin. The castle on Cape Clear, Dún an Óir, was pounded by heavy guns until it, too, surrendered.[127]

A detail, from 1612 Dutch map, shown off the coast of West Cork.

Fearfeasa O'Cainte sang this...

Not to rise up in warlike alliance,

After all the evils which they have sustained,

The tribe of the land of round-nutted woods;

'Tis wonderful how long their forbearance.

It is hard if victory they gain not,

For it is not excessive ambition, it is not injustice,

That drove this noble tribe of sharp spears

To take to steps of wars.

There is not one of them by the justice of God,

One to whom the heirship is more fitting,

To free her mountains, protect her cattle,

Than the best heir which is of them.

The son of O h-Eidirsceoil, of smooth breast,

For him it is the most becoming of all the men of Eire,

To fight for its sake in the battles,

The land famed for battling and wars.

Conchobar, heart of a lion,

Will fight, as for him it is right,

For the fertile, warm, music-loving land,

With the old English at the bank of Boinn.

Excerpts from a poem composed for Conchobhar O'Driscoll (son of Fineen) and his wife Eibhilin by Fearfeasa O'Cainte after the Battle of Castlehaven.[128]

By July 1602, English forces had taken control of '[various] castles strongly seated by the sea, where ships may safely ride, and fit places for an enemy to hold … except Kilcoe and Cloghan'.[129] 'Cloghan' is a common castle name, as it means 'heap of stones', and this may refer to the MacCarthy castle of the same name.[130] However, the MacCarthy castle is inland and the use of the term 'strongly seated by the sea' suggests that it refers to the castle at Lough Hyne.[131] The taking of the castle reflects the brutal methods used at the time:

> Captain Flower having the charge of Baltimore understanding that the castle of Cloghan was guarded by the rebels … had in his hands, a traitor, brother to the Constable [person in charge of a castle] … Then he told the ward that if the Constable did not presently surrender the Castle to him he would hang his brother in their sight, they persevered obstinately not to yield: whereupon Captain Flower in their sight hanged the Constable's brother.[132]

Four days later, this castle was surrendered to the English and Kilcoe Castle, the final 'castle in the Carbery that held out in rebellion', fell in 1603.[133]

Why Sir Fineen, up to then a royal subject, decided to side with the Spanish will never be definitively known. Prior to this, he was highly astute in his political dealings, which had enabled him to hold on to his position through volatile periods. He did this by changing alliances when necessary, a custom commonly used by Gaelic chieftains. His political acumen once more came into effect after the disastrous defeat, however, when he re-established his allegiance to the Crown forces and distanced himself from the rebellion. He was described as having 'growne very odious to the Rebels of these parts' as a result.[134]

Fineen was not alone in reasserting his allegiance to the Crown: 'the best of them, namely Sir Fynin O'Driscoll, O'Donovan and Sir Owen McCartie's sons … ask to be received to mercy'.[135] However, even though Fineen's lands were restored to him, he paid dearly for his involvement in the rebellion as he was financially ruined.[136]

A section of Speed's 1611 map of Munster, shown here, shows 'Loghyne' and a mixture of Gaelic and English names.

Though plantations of English settlers had taken place in the sixteenth century in other parts of Munster, it was post-Kinsale when English settlements began to be set up in this area of West Cork, and Baltimore was one of the largest settled towns. Thomas Crooke, an Englishman, obtained a Crown grant of Collymore, formerly O'Driscoll territory.[137] Sir Fineen, broke and no longer able to charge for fishing rights off Baltimore, entered into a lease agreement with Crooke for the town and surrounding areas.[138] This included the areas of Ballinard and Glanyfoyne (Glannafeen) in Lough Hyne.[139] The 'surrender and regrant' system allowed for land to be remortgaged and so enabled the transaction. Crooke established an extensive English settlement in Baltimore and, by 1608, the whole area was occupied by newcomers. He secured rights to hold a weekly market and two annual fairs in Baltimore town.[140] Government approval of this new English town was shown by its incorporation as a parliamentary borough in 1612.[141]

Fineen's signature, shown here on a 1583 document, shows that he was confident in his writing ability and its flamboyant style may offer an insight into his character. (With thanks to Connie Kelleher for this image. CSP., Vol. CIV. 106, 1583, 'Fynyn O'Dryscoyll to Lord. Courtesy of the Boole Library, UCC, Cork.)

Sir Fineen borrowed money from Walter Coppinger, a descendant of an Old English family from Cork city, and re-leased the land he had already given to Crooke.[142] A series of complicated land deals, also involving Thomas Bennett of Bandon, continued over several years, culminating in a court case in 1629 when Sir Fineen, with his son Donagh acting as his agent, made an attempt to regain his lands.[143] By this date, sixty new houses had been built by the English in Baltimore and the settlement was well established.[144] Sir Fineen is recorded as living in the castle at Ballyisland (Lough Hyne) in 'great and decrepide age' and in a state of 'disabilitie and wante of means'.[145] The case did not restore his property to him, so he presumably remained living in the small castle on the island at Lough Hyne. The date of his death has never been definitively established, but it is believed that he ended his days at Lough Hyne.[146]

In the course of his turbulent lifetime, Fineen had negotiated his way through rebellions, famines and land redistribution. As the last O'Driscoll Mór, chieftain of Collymore, he had ruled over one of the wealthiest clans in Munster. Yet he ended his days as an old man, poor in health and wealth, in this minor tower house at Lough Hyne, an area with which he will always be associated.

(Tadhg, son of Diarmaid Óg O'Dalaigh, sang this)

The powerful tongue, which I used to hear,

Is now bereft of its eloquence,

No feeble word it ever uttered,

It was forcible in time of difficulties.

The ear which is no longer watching

The beautiful borders of Corca-Laidhe,

The smooth lands of ancient ships,

Of oppression on them it would not hear.

The declension of his mental powers,

Has ruined that land of Finghin,

That smooth plain of hospitable mansions;

Their powers of thought are now overclouded.

The warning of the death of his noble hand

Shall lower the prosperity of the land,

It has poured out lamentations from its heart

For the shortening of the knight's life.[147]

Excerpt of a poem sung by an Ó Dalaigh on the death of Fineen.
[The O'Dalys (Ó Dalaigh) were a sept especially privileged because of their poetic gifts and chieftains would grant them land in recognition of their importance. They had a number of bardic schools, including one on Sheep's Head.]

Rebellion and Loss of Land

After the defeat at Kinsale and the end of the Nine Years War, the English forces engaged in fierce and heavy-handed military tactics. The effects of this, combined with continuing Catholic resentment at the loss of lands, political exclusion and sporadic religious persecution, created an explosive atmosphere in Ireland.[148] Land reforms, religious tensions and the increasing power of the English government undermined political stability.[149] A widening division between the English planters and Gaelic Irish eventually resulted in an uprising against the new settlers.

A rebellion started in Ireland in 1641 which brought about a series of events that ultimately led to Oliver Cromwell's invasion of Ireland in 1649.[150] The rebellion started in Ulster in October 1641 and broke out in Munster in the early months of 1642.[151] The O'Driscolls took part in the uprising, with seven of them declared as outlaws in 1643, including Donagh O'Driscoll of 'Glounyfeen' (Glannafeen, Lough Hyne).[152]

The 1641 depositions are witness testimonies, mainly by Protestants but also by some Catholics, about their experiences during the rebellion.[153] The official purpose of the depositions was to award compensation and return property to the deponents.[154] In reality, however, they were a means for the Protestant officials in Ireland to identify and take revenge upon those Catholics who were involved in the insurgence.[155] Irish Protestant leaders recognised the propaganda value of these testimonies and they were skilfully exploited to construct a seemingly irrefutable case for the reconquest of Ireland by an English army.[156]

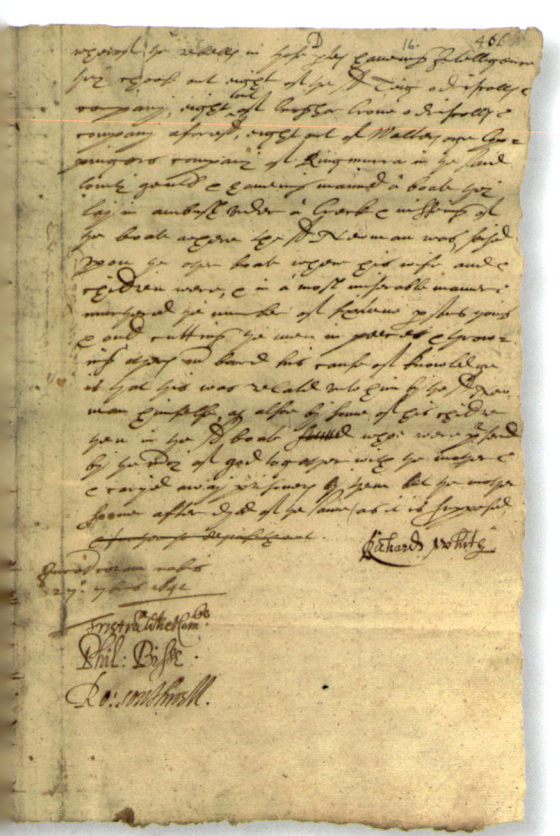

In one of the 1641 depositions, Donogh mc Cnoghor of Glannafoin (Glannafeen, Lough Hyne) was named by Robert White of Inishbegneclery (Innisbeg) as having:

> Tooke away this deponents said Cattle from of the lands of Inishbegneclery [Innisbeg] aforesaid & tooke possession of this deponents house & Caused his Corne to be threshed wherewith he sowed parte of his owne land & parte of this deponents land & that with his owne horses. Likewise he saith that aboute the same time his horses Cattle & Corne were taken away from of the lands of Ballylincheram [Ballylinch].[157]

(Image courtesy of the Board of Trinity College Dublin.)

After the uprising, the reprisals were fierce and St Ledger, the Lord President of Munster, launched an offensive whereby he executed large number of Catholics, regardless of whether or not they supported the rebellion. This resulted in the killing of at least two hundred people 'for a greater terror to all such as should adventure afterwards to follow their example'.[160]

The conflict effectively created a pretext for confiscating lucrative estates held by Catholics.[161] The Adventurers' Act of March 1642, passed to raise money for the campaign against the Irish, was based on the unconditional surrender of the rebels and offered 2,500,000 acres of forfeited Irish land as collateral. As a result of the subsequent English victory, this Act condemned Irish Catholic landowners to economic, political and social ruin.[162] The Quarter Sessions of Youghal held on 2 August 1642 'marked the death-sentence on the ancient civilisation … the decay of the ancient native families and gives us the arrival of the Planter Race'.[163] Most of the O'Driscoll lands were subsequently mortgaged, lost or confiscated.[164]

English settlers in the area became very nervous and many of them tried to escape from the area. Robert White also testified that a Thomas Newman of Baltimore made an arrangement to leave on a 'shipp out of Bristoll' which was at anchor at Castlehaven. Newman arranged for:

> The said masters mate to carry him & his family a boord the said shipp & thence into England with his goods & haueing agreed for the fraight & all the said Newman & he went in one boat & his wife & nyne children with some of his goods in another boate.

However, word got out of this arrangement and White stated that O'Driscoll and Coppinger forces:

> Lay in ambush vnder a Crecke & misseing of the boate where the said Newman was, seised vpon the other boate where his wife and children were, & in a most miserable maner murthered the number of sixteene persons young & ould cutting the men in peeces & throwing others ouer boord. [158]

(Image courtesy of the Board of Trinity College Dublin. [159])

Oliver Cromwell's fierce campaign in Ireland put an end to the war. Approximately 616,000 people, mostly Catholic, were killed, with the remaining population calculated (and probably significantly underestimated) at 850,000.[165] His short but brutal campaign, from his arrival in July 1649 to his departure in May 1650, broke the main enemy resistance and the final surrender of the war was in April 1653.[166] The last Munster surrender was in the summer of 1652.[167] Although some skirmishes continued, to all intents and purposes Ireland was conquered and destroyed.

After the war, Lough Hyne and the rest of the area would have been devastated. An outbreak of bubonic plague in southern Munster between 1649 and 1653 reached epidemic proportions, and much of the heavy death toll in the area could have been as a result of this.[168]

> A traveller might journey thirty miles along the public roads and not see a human face. When Cromwell's troopers were on the line of march, they used to wonder when they saw smoke arise from a chimney, or saw a light at night. Wolves roamed about unmolested ... Silence was everywhere, and it remained unbroken – save when the raven croaked as it soared into the sky; but the lively twitter of the birds, the buzzing hum of the bee, and the low of cattle, were absent. The latter were nearly all destroyed.[169]

The end of the war opened up a new phase of plantation and the reign of the O'Driscolls as lords of the area finally came to an end. All land automatically became the property of the government and was used to repay those who had funded the war or had fought without pay on its behalf.[170] These settlements fundamentally changed the nature of landholding in Ireland.

Because the new planters were to be paid their dues by way of land grants, the land had to be measured and mapped so that it could be divided up proportionally. Following two other unsuccessful survey attempts, William Petty started his 'Down Survey' in 1655, which he completed by 1659.[171] Petty measured the forfeited properties, as well as mapping the boundaries and classifying each parcel of land according to its value. This information would later act as the basis for its redistribution.[172] He created maps which divided each parish into different plots. Each plot was given a number that was cross-referenced to a list of 1641 landowners. From this, we can see that the O'Driscoll name clearly dominates the general area around Lough Hyne.

The settlement of Ireland and the imposition of English governance absolutely depended on the creation of a rational system of landed property based on a detailed survey. The 'Gross Survey' and 'Civil Survey' both proved inadequate and another, more ambitious, survey was subsequently carried out by William Petty between 1655 and 1659. His Down Survey parish maps show important topographical features alongside an accompanying description. They also show built structures; for example, the 'fishing pallice' and castle are shown at Lough Hyne. Each parcel of land has a narrative associated with it that cross-references the plot number on the map to a description of that area. This lists the landowners in 1641, gives the overall size of each plot and categorises it as profitable or non-profitable land. We can see from the Down Survey maps (so-called because they were written 'down') that Glannafeen was plot 370, Ballinard 371, Ballyisland 358 and Highfield (Gortard) 357. (Images courtesy of the National Library of Ireland. Ref. MSS 714.)

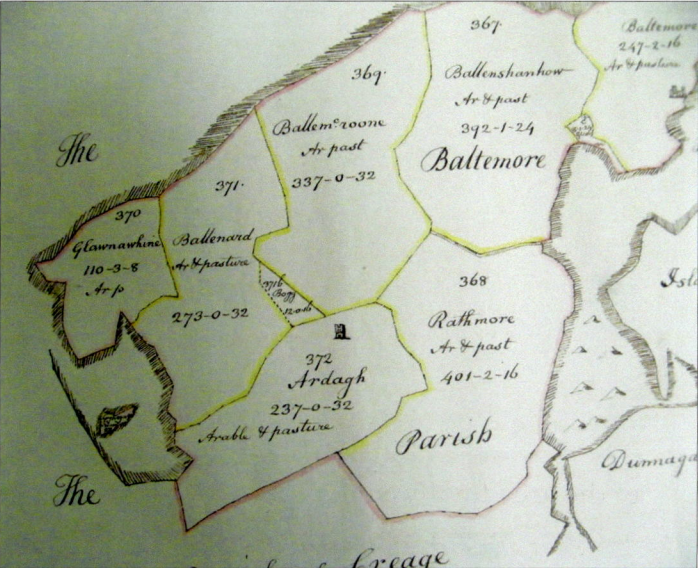

The accompanying narrative to Petty's parish maps shows that the O'Driscoll name repeatedly appears in the 1641 'proprietors' names' column.[173] The term 'Ir. Pa.' is frequently used, which means 'Irish Papist'. This classification, in itself, justified the transfer of lands into Protestant ownership. (Image courtesy of the National Library of Ireland. Ref. MSS 714.)

The *Books of Survey and Distribution* were compiled between the 1650s and 1680s and record the expropriation of each individual parcel of land that was listed in Petty's parish maps.[174] They show a seismic shift in land ownership. While Catholics owned 60% of the land in Ireland before the 1641 Rebellion, by 1660 their share had fallen to a mere 9%.[175] Power in Ireland shifted from Catholics of Gaelic and Anglo-Norman descent primarily to English and Scottish Protestants. It has been described as 'the most catastrophic land-confiscation and social upheaval in Irish History'.[176]

The *Books of Survey and Distribution* record the transfer of the land of Ireland from Gaelic ownership to the new planter class. Because they were based on Petty's Down Survey, the plot numbers refer to the numbers shown on the maps on the previous page. Ownership of the plots at Glannafeen and Ballinard was granted to the Bishop of Dublin and others, with just 3 gneeves (plot 371b) retained by 'Donogh McKnoghor' (O'Driscoll). Plot numbers 357 and 358 at Highfield and Ballyisland show the same amount of land on the left and right columns, showing that they were transferred in their entirety to James Coppinger. The Coppinger land subsequently passed to Edmund Galwey, who was outlawed in 1690, and it eventually came under the ownership of Sir Percy Freke in 1703.[177] Plot number 361, on which the Tralispean fish palace was located, was granted to Colonel Richard Townsend, an officer of Cromwell.[178] (Image courtesy of the National Archives of Ireland. Ref. NAI, Book of Survey and Distribution, County Cork, Barony of Carbery West, parish of Tullagh & Creagh.)

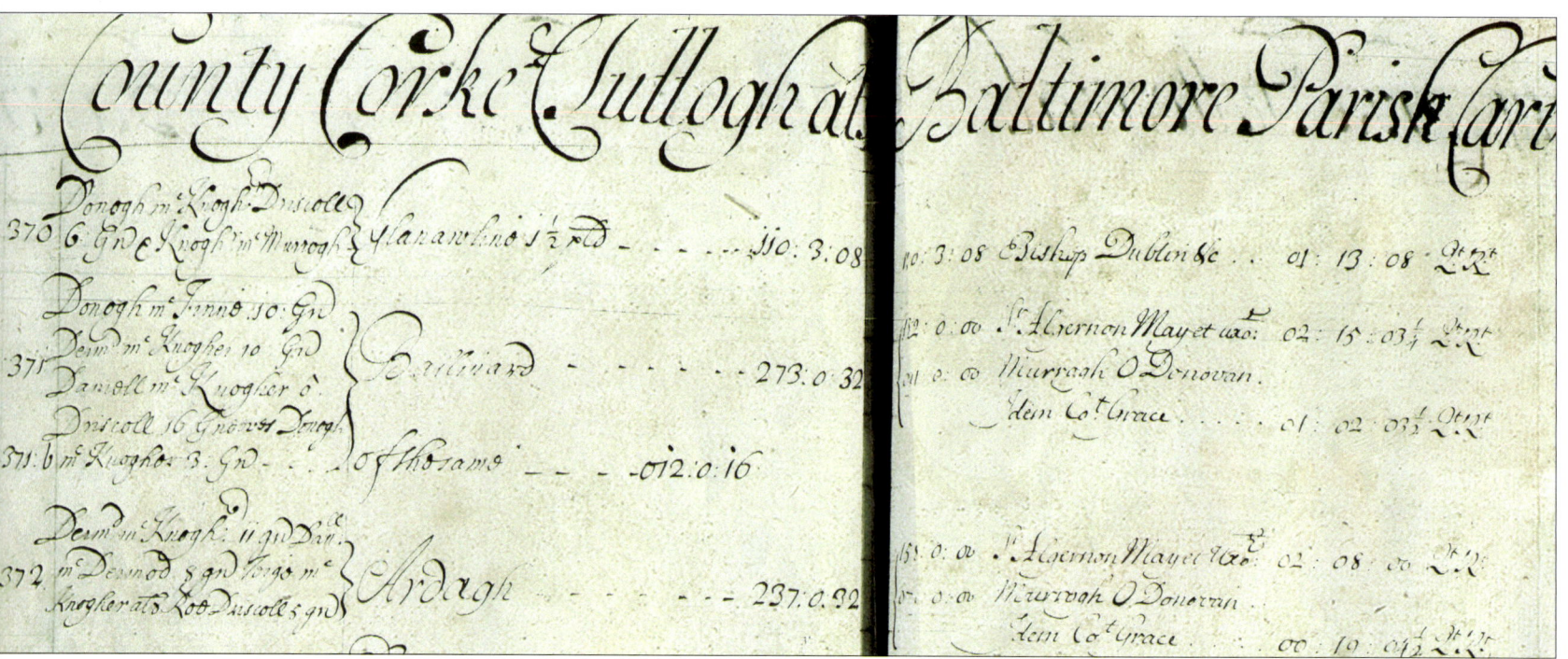

The 1659 census records thirty-five people living in Ballyisland, two of whom were English, while nearby Glannafeen had a total of nineteen people, four of whom were English.[179] The English settlement had reached even remote areas like Lough Hyne. The O'Driscolls were no longer the lords of Lough Hyne. Sir Fineen's great-grandson and heir, Donagh, was 'expulsed' from his inheritance in 1654 when it was redistributed to planters.[180] 'The O Driscoll family base at Ballinard was finally sold in 1670.'[181]

The O'Driscolls ruled over a vast area of West Cork for centuries but left little physical evidence in their wake. Other than the churches and ruins of Sherkin Friary, the remains of the O'Driscoll tower houses are the only testament to the lordship of this important Gaelic family. The castle at Lough Hyne, though one of the smallest of their properties, is particularly significant as the place where the last of the family's great Gaelic chieftains, O'Driscoll Mór, Chieftain of Collymore, lived out his final years.

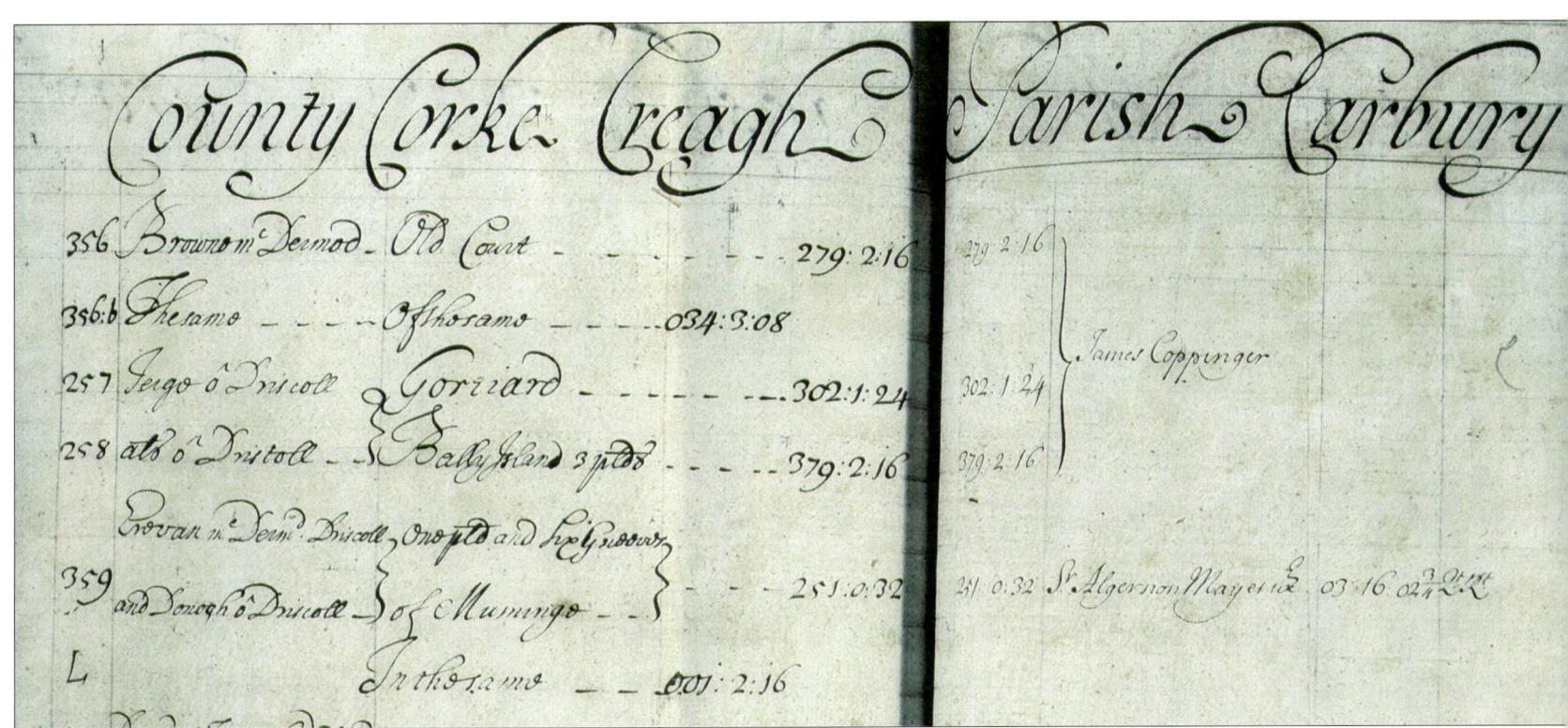

Cloghan Castle

Tower houses were an indicator of wealth and power and the O'Driscolls, as the principal Gaelic family of the area, held eleven tower houses built in the fifteenth and sixteenth centuries, with an additional four fortifications dating to the pre-Norman period or before.[182] Cloghan Castle at Lough Hyne was therefore just one of many belonging to this wealthy family.

Most of these castles were built by individuals who belonged to the *derbfine,* the senior family of a clan.[183] As we have seen, under the Gaelic system of land ownership property remained in the ownership of the family and individual family members held parcels of land for short periods only, as they were redistributed periodically among co-heirs.[184]

Castles were built in areas of significance and, even though Cloghan is small in size, its presence at Lough Hyne is an indication that the area was important to the O'Driscolls. Connie Kelleher has extensively researched the O'Driscoll sites and she suggests that Cloghan was built for purely recreational purposes, as it did not serve any defensive or strategic purpose. On the contrary, it was extremely vulnerable to attack.

> The O'Driscoll fortification at Cloghan on Lough Hyne may represent a site purely built with a private residential function in mind. Cloghan is located in an idyllic setting. From a defensive point of view, it would have been extremely vulnerable to attack, particularly given the potential of cannon bombardment … [As] access from the sea by boat was improbable … such a residence would have necessitated a permanent boat presence on the lake … Its obvious vulnerability, but also its seclusion, is suggestive of one that was used primarily as a family residence. It was a place where the O'Driscolls and their families could enjoy the peace and quiet of the lake, a place to swim, relax and enjoy themselves away from the demands of lordship … These native lordships displayed a sense of personal space and privacy in the location of some elite residences.[185]

| Trough on Castleisland, close to Cloghan Castle.

The tower house was the 'ordinary residence' of the Gaelic and Anglo-Irish gentry. Rincolisky tower house, shown here, is a recently restored O'Driscoll castle, situated in Whitehall, Lisheen. This property marked the westernmost limit of the family's territory.[186] Because so little remains of Cloghan Castle, we can only make suppositions as to its design. As only a minor tower house of the O'Driscolls, there are very few historical references to it. However, building methodologies of the time and the arrangements in other tower houses offer some information about its probable layout.

Like Rincolisky, Cloghan Castle was probably four storeys in height. The top-floor 'hall', which would have been the lord's main residential space, would have taken up between a third and a half of the entire internal volume of the tower house.[187] Windows were bigger on the upper floors, so the larger well-windowed rooms were at the top while the poorly lit chambers were further down.[188]

The main defence of a tower house was conducted from above, with battlemented parapets and machicolations.[189] These machicolations permitted downwards fire on the enemy without risk to the defenders. The roof was generally of oak and finished with slates or thatch.[190] Other features of tower houses included latrines – called garderobes – and some had secret chambers and fireplaces. We do not know what the interior of Cloghan was like but it did, most likely, have a garderobe and possibly a fireplace. (Photo: S. Franks. With thanks to the current owner Stefanie Jaax.)

There are several pieces of folklore associated with this castle, the best-known being the tale of King Labhra Loingseagh. There are several different versions of the fable, but the basic story is about a king who had the ears of an ass that once lived in the castle. He hid his disfigurement by growing his hair in such a way as to hide the ears and he had a barber fashion it so every year. However, as the barber would learn of his deformity by so doing, he would be sentenced to death. One year, as he lay dying, the barber whispered the secret to a tree (or a reed; there are two different versions – one says a tree, the other a reed).[195] This reed/tree was cut down subsequently by a bard to make a flute (or a harp in the case of the tree) and, at a big assembly in the castle, the bard began to play it in praise of the king. The instrument would play nothing but 'King Labhra Loinseagh has asses' ears, the king has asses' ears' and so Labhra was forced to abandon his kingdom as a result.

A much longer fable, told in the form of a poem, tells of a king who is deceived into marrying a hag. She puts a curse on him and gives him the ears of a horse (see page 71 for a transcription of this fable).[196] Daniel Donovan, in his 1876 *Sketches in Carbery,* gives yet another version of the fable and compares it to King Midas's tale in Greek mythology.[197]

Another piece of folklore tells of a crock of gold hidden under a flag near the castle which is guarded by a black dog. This was told to Daniel Donovan by Bill Barrett, the hero of the tale, in 1876.[198]

Petty's 1650s parish map shows Cloghan Castle and it is listed as a 'castle'.[191] However, by c. 1750 it is no longer in use, as it is described as 'the ruins of an old castle'.[192] (Image courtesy of the National Library of Ireland.)

The Carbery Estate maps show it as a 'castle in ruins' in 1788.[193] (Image courtesy of the Dean and Chapter of St Fachtna's Cathedral, Rosscarbery, Co. Cork.) In Hall's sketch of *c.* 1840, (see previous chapter) the walls are still standing, but we know that they fell around 1870.[194]

These two maps date to 1650 and 1651 and show two different spellings for Lough Hyne.[199] Both Lough Hyne and Lough Ine are still used today.

An alternative to the fable of King Labhra of Lough Hyne is given in this poem, as recited by Neily Bohane.

Long ago when our forefathers worshipped the sun
And kindled their Bael fires when darkness began,
'Ere the glorious Saint Patrick, that servant of Rome,
Set sail with his mission across the broad foam
And landed in Erin, that western Queen,
With its mountains of gold and valleys of green,
With the faith and cross that were destined to be
From henceforth the pride of the brave and the free,

There lived a great hero as bold as a lion
In a tall massive keep near the waves of Loughine.
Ah you should have gazed on that beautiful lake
When the morning sun beams on the neighbouring brake
And the zephyr steals down from the mountains above
To ripple the lake with its whispers of love
And the trees standing by in silent array
Like sentinels warning the storms away,
But oh what a bliss it must be to reside
In that spot where the glories of nature abide,
Where such heavenly peace in shower and shine
Forever live on by the waves of Loughine.

T'was King Labhra O'Loinnseagh as he was then known,
Had this huge castle raised built of mortar and stone,
For he was Lord of the Carberies then
And he had attendants five score of men.
T'was on tall Cnoc Cauma he hunted the deer
With his kinsmen and classmen twice in the year,
And when the day it was o'er with the chase and the sport
He invited his friends to be guests at his court
And it couldn't be said that there was lacking in wine,
There were cellars to hold it in the halls of Loughine.

Now Labhra was anxious to marry a wife,
Like most men are too at some time in their life,
In the freshness of youth or in manhood's full bloom,
Where the skies are still free from all shadows and gloom,
But as it so happened, it is a difficult thing
To win a young lady for even a king.
With his regal attraction, his horses, his hounds,
His personal charms, his castle, his grounds,
Cannot always be found their affection to gain
And Labhra to find one still laboured in vain.

Then one day as he journeyed to visit Con Mór,
His kinsman who lived by the town of Glandore,
He saw a young maiden as fair as the day
Walking slowly towards him along by the bay.
As he viewed her quite close, her eyes were as bright
As the stars that peep down from the heavens at night
And her cheeks were as red as the roses in June
When the sun shines upon them, all glorious at noon.

So he stopped, he saluted her and he loved her so fine
That he asked her to be the young queen of Loughine.
She told him her name and she promised him too
To wed him next spring and ere she bade him adieu
As she passed like a dream around the end of the bay,
To Labhra it seemed she just vanished away.
That the joys of the world were fruitless and vain
Would his eyes ever rest on this vision again.
For her beauty would ever excel like the flowers
When the cool breezes woo them in sunshine and showers.
His great heart of rapture filled his soul with delight
And made everything around him seem blissful and bright.

Six months rolled away and the springtime drew nigh
And Labra went forward to visit Cure Eye,
The father of her whom he met in Glandore
When he journeyed to visit his kinsman Con Mór.
He rode all alone with his heart quite at ease,
Dressed up in his best just as grand as you please,
Til at last he arrive at the gate of the keep

That drew up like a mountain quite close to the deep.
He was hailed by a maiden, young, handsome and fair,
Who glided towards him as if floating on air.
'Is it Labhra, great Labhra, the Lord of Loughine
That I now see before me so radiant and fine?'
Said he to this fair maid 'How is my Queen Maeve?'
'Alas, she is sleeping six months in her grave.'

Now then Labhra was struck with amazement and grief
And soft tears rolled down but they brought no relief,
His whole soul was moved with the tidings he heard
And for over an hour he spoke not a word.
Then he entered the castle a stranger to joy
And remained there a week as a guest of Cure Eye.
But that week put an end to his mourning for Maeve,
For it's useless to weep for a being in the grave,
So he married her sister, that maiden so fair
That he met on the morning he first entered there.
Now so a feast was prepared and a table was spread
And who should walk in but Queen Maeve that was dead,
She gazed on King Labhra now beaming with joy
and then, with fierce scorn at his wife and Cure Eye.

Her eyes seemed to blaze as she took in the scene
And she spoke with the loud haughty tones of a queen.
'Father, sister and brother all leagued against me,
They bound me and sent me far over the sea,
As for Labhra, he loved me with warmth and truth
And I loved him with all the fervour of youth,
But to part us you laboured by night and by day,
'Til at length you succeeded and drove me away,
And now I return to seek vengeance on those
Once I worshipped as friends but now hate as foes.

I tell thee, King Labhra, go home to Loughine,
For that old withered hag is no helpmate of thine.
She has used all the charms of the false one below,
For to freshen her cheeks and to make them aglow,'
As she uttered those words, the newly-wed wife
Looked just like a hag at the end of her life.
'Come, come with me,' sweetly murmured Queen Maeve,
'Away over the billowing white-crested wave.'
But his wife flew at Labhra before he could speak.
Although strong as a warhorse, in her grasp he was weak,
She clutched both his ears 'til they hung to the ground
And she swung him five times in a circle around.
She cried seven times, and each time was a curse,
Saying 'King Labhra, I give thee the ears of a horse.'
Then she turned on Queen Maeve and she killed her outright
And Labhra was forced to take refuge by flight.
So he jumped on his steed and rode like the wind
'Til he left that dread place a long distance behind.
The secret he told to his favourite oak,
But never a word to his kinsmen he spoke,
And day after day he was seen to decline
And his friends began to weep for the King of Loughine.

Death seized him at last and they laid him to rest
In that lone little island his heart loved the best.
Strange sounds were heard in the castle each night
And the servants withdrew from its precincts in fright,
'Til at length a great bard to that island came,
Who was longing for glory and panting for fame,
And he cut off a branch from King Labhra's oak tree
And he polished and pared it a nice harp to be,
But the only tune ever that this instrument played,
'T'was with horse's ears, King Labhra was laid.'
Tá scéal agam is deacair é innsint
Go bhfuil dá cluais capall ar Labhra Ó Laoinse.

Anon. Learnt by Neily Bohane from his father.
(Bael was the Pagan God of fire)

Pre-Famine Lough Hyne

The defining period of the nineteenth century in Ireland was undoubtedly the Great Famine of the 1840s. This pivotal event was 'a great abyss, a great chasm, between pre-Famine and post-Famine Ireland'.[1] As was the case in many other parts of West Cork, the Lough Hyne area was devastated during this tragic period, losing almost half of its population between 1841 and 1851. The years of the Great Famine fundamentally changed both the physical and social landscapes of Lough Hyne.

The potato blight struck in all the counties of Ireland but its adverse effects were felt to a far greater extent in some areas of the country. The circumstances in place in the lead-up to this catastrophic event – the system of land ownership, the rising population, the lack of employment, alongside the poverty of the people – were significant factors in the subsequent outcome of the Famine. How the people of Lough Hyne lived and worked in the pre-Famine era directly impacted not only on the years of the crisis itself, but also had long-term effects.

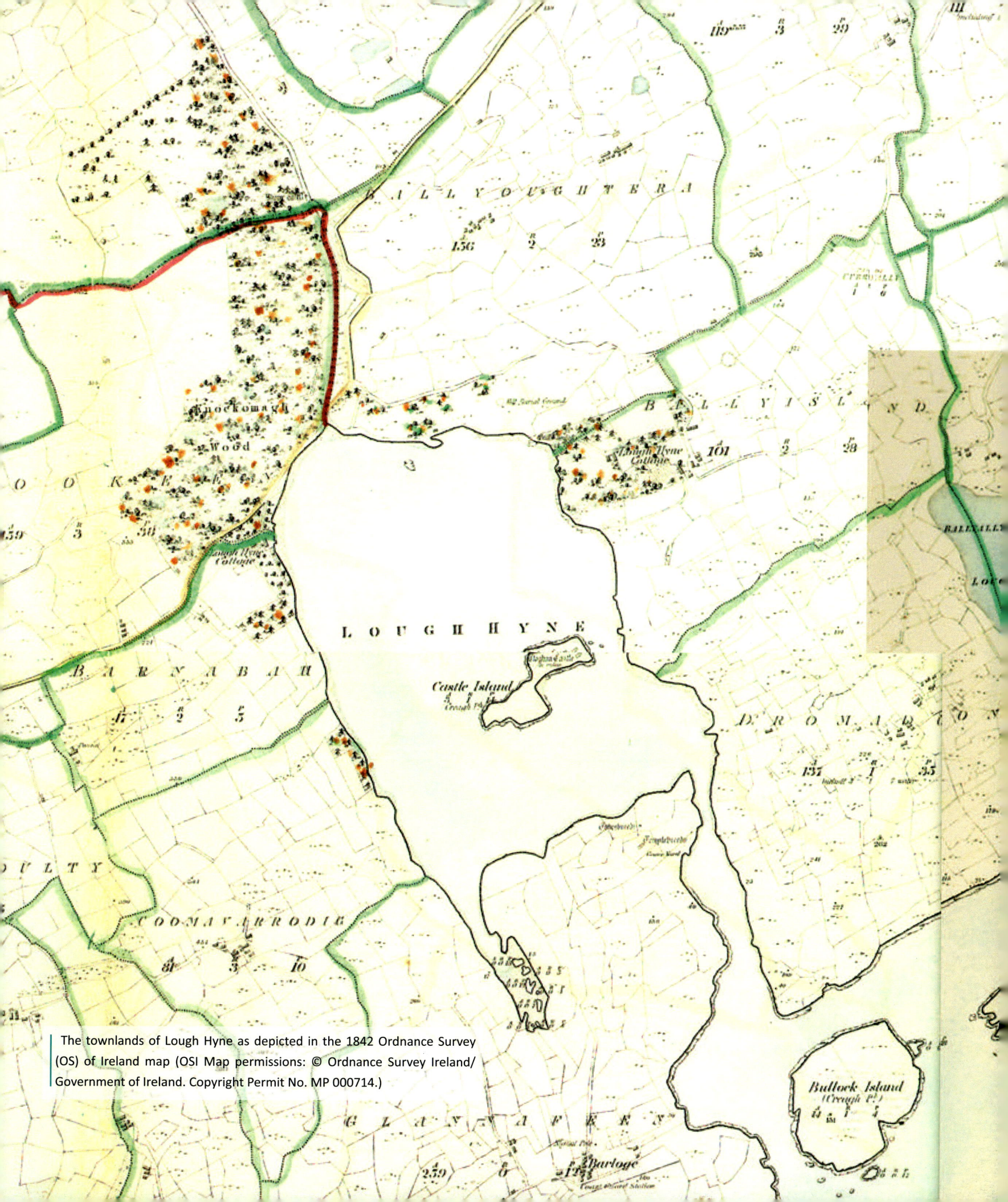

The townlands of Lough Hyne as depicted in the 1842 Ordnance Survey (OS) of Ireland map (OSI Map permissions: © Ordnance Survey Ireland/Government of Ireland. Copyright Permit No. MP 000714.)

Land and Employment

Land ownership in Ireland had changed dramatically in the 1600s, when practically all of the land in the country was granted to English settlers. Very few of the native Irish held on to their properties and, over time, ownership of the area around Lough Hyne transferred from the O'Driscolls to Anglo-Irish landlords.

After its colonisation, Ireland's social and economic conditions were slowly reconfigured over time to serve its ruler's needs. By the early nineteenth century, its primary role had developed into supplying food and labour to Britain's urban economy, which meant that, as a result, Ireland had not really developed industrially. The role of Ireland was to be a provisioner to Britain, not a potential competitor in the industrial revolution.[2]

Because there were few other employment opportunities, access to land as a means of earning a living was vitally important. Unless a labourer could get a piece of land to grow potatoes, he and his family were destitute. By the early nineteenth century, agriculture was by far the most important sector of the Irish economy. Two-thirds of the population of Ireland was living off the land in 1841 and this figure was even higher in some rural areas.[3] There was a high dependency in West Cork, with, for example, over 88% of the population of Tullagh parish in 1841 (which included part of Lough Hyne) relying on agriculture.[4]

This demand for land led to properties being divided and subdivided into smaller plots as part of a hierarchical rental system under which the land had to support several 'layers' of tenants. Many landlords rented their estates to a middleman, who, in turn, sublet it to tenant farmers and labourers. By the mid-nineteenth century, the land at Lough Hyne was fragmented into a multitude of smallholdings, sublet from two Anglo-Irish landlords, Lord Carbery and Sir William Wrixon-Becher.[5] The property at Lough Hyne was just a small portion of the overall estates of these two wealthy individuals. Carbery's estate brought in an annual revenue of £15,000, while Wrixon-Becher's realised £10,000, the two highest annual incomes in the greater Skibbereen area.[6] This system of ownership and access to land were fundamental factors in the outcome of the Great Famine.

The Carbery and Wrixon-Becher lands at Lough Hyne in the nineteenth century (with part of the townland of Glannafeen sublet to the middleman Atkins and part of Highfield also sublet to Dalcour Beamish). (OSI Map permissions: © Ordnance Survey Ireland/Government of Ireland. Copyright Permit No. MP 0006113.)

The Rental Pyramid:

The dependence on agriculture, alongside the rising population in Ireland, resulted in properties being divided and subdivided into smaller plots. Many landlords rented their land to a middleman, who, in turn, sublet it to tenant farmers and labourers. Everyone in this system paid rent, but the tenants of smallholdings paid a much higher rent proportionally than the middleman – or middlemen, as sometimes there were more than one in the rental pyramid. This graph is based on evidence given to the Devon Commission (1843–45) on examples of rents paid in the Skibbereen area.

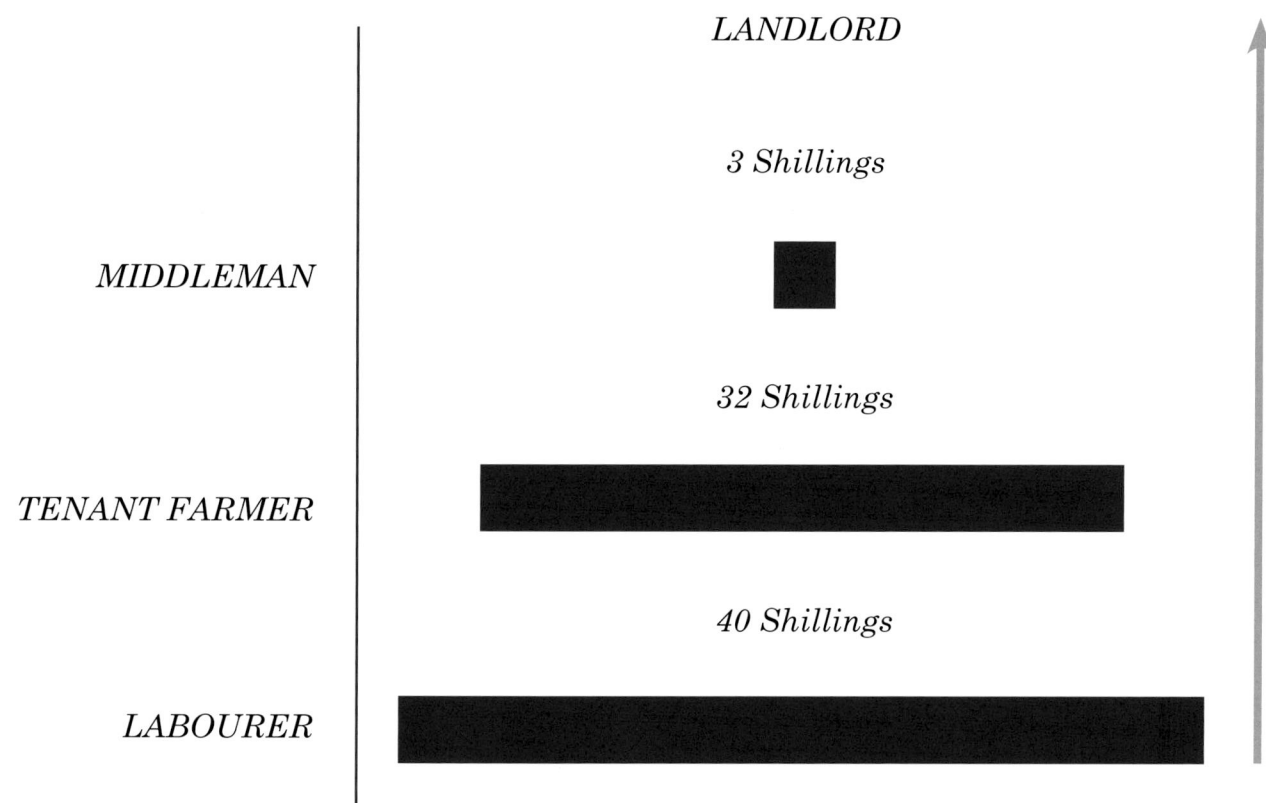

Agriculture was the main means of earning a living in the Lough Hyne area, despite the fact that the land there was of very poor quality. Because of its inferior nature, the townlands around the lough were given a very low valuation in the Griffith's Valuation of 1853 (see Table One). This was a survey of property ownership which rated the land of Ireland for taxation purposes. In the 1840s, the land and buildings of Skibbereen Poor Law Union, one of 130 such unions in Ireland, had a rateable valuation of under £1 per head of population, the second lowest in the country.[7] Based on the Griffith's Valuation, the valuation of the townlands of Lough Hyne was more than a third less again, indicating the extremely poor quality of the housing and land. It would have been even lower, but access to seaweed and sea sand for use as a fertiliser was regarded as an economic advantage to farmers, and such land was valued higher as a result. For this reason, some areas of Lough Hyne had their valuations increased. The townland of Glannafeen was raised by 10 shillings per pound for 'having the best situation for weed', while Knockanoulty and Pookeen were raised by 3 shillings and 4 pence per pound.[8]

Table One: Valuations per capita and acre based on Griffith's Valuation

Townland	1841 Population	Acres	Valuation
Ballinard	110	230	63
Ballyisland	64	101	73
Ballyoughtera	94	156	49
Barnabah	59	47	30
Coomavarrodig	49	81	28
Dromadoon	82	137	44
Glannafeen	164	259	101
Highfield	266	576	185
Knockanoulty	30	64	34
Knockeencon	65	108	31
Pookeen	66	159	29
	1049	1918	667

Outside of agricultural work, there were few other opportunities for employment around Lough Hyne at that time. The remains of the two seventeenth-century fish 'palaces' at Ballyalla and Tralispean, near Lough Hyne (see pages 46-47), are testament to a once-robust fishing industry in the area. However, by the nineteenth century, the situation had changed dramatically and Ireland was importing the kind of fish that it had once exported. Herring to the value of £58,197 was imported in 1818 and the export trade had fallen to just 5% of its former volume.[9] Various national incentives to encourage fisheries, including those supported by Glandore's James Redmond Barry, were unsuccessful in the long run. The fishing industry nationally was depressed and the West Cork area was no different. An 1835 inquiry into the industry found that the fishermen had no access to capital to purchase the necessary equipment.[10] Though fish were plentiful, 'want of apparatus' meant that they could not be caught, so almost all fishermen had a little land which they relied on to provide an additional income.[11]

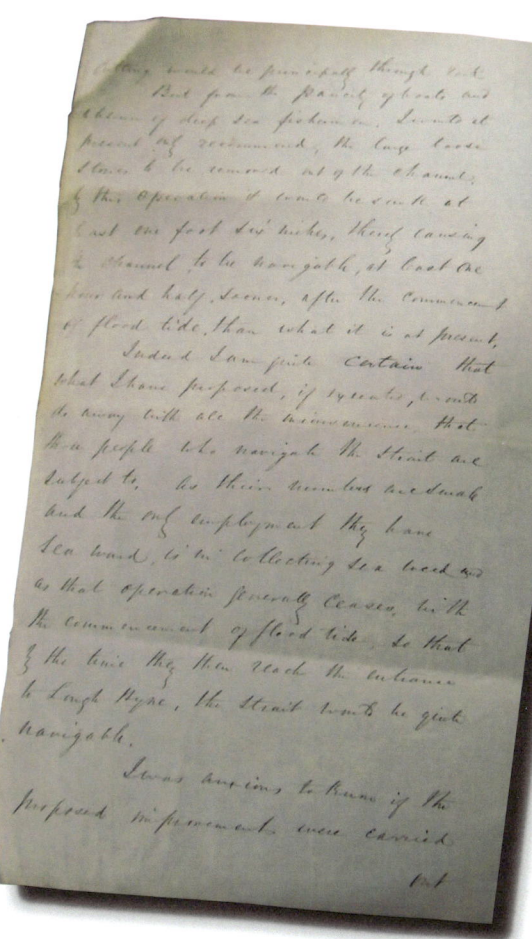

The written accounts of those who visited Lough Hyne in the century before the Great Famine all mention its abundance of fish, which would have helped to sustain its population.[12] However, there were very few boats on the lough. A letter written in 1848 describing the conditions at Lough Hyne mentions 'the paucity of boats and absence of deep sea fishermen'.[13] In the same letter, in response to an enquiry into whether completion of the Rapids retaining walls at Lough Hyne would 'be likely to induce any of the unemployed people to commence deep-sea fishing', a 'most intelligent coast guard at that place [said] that he feared that they would not'. The letter also mentions that 'the only employment they have is sea ward … collecting seaweed'. While fishing and seaweed collection supported the people of this area prior to the Great Famine, the sea did not give them a much better living than that of the poorest agricultural workers and their living conditions were described as 'miserable'.[14]

Excerpt from an 1848 letter which recommends finishing the work at the Rapids wall, which had been started under the 'Relief Act' during the Great Famine. The letter says that 'on the west side of the strait, a warping wall consisting of dry rubble masonry had been in course of construction, under the "Relief Acts" by Mr Treacey, county supervisor, but owing to stopping of the work, it was not completed.' (Courtesy of the National Archives of Ireland, Ref: OPW/8/ITEM381/1848.)

There was another industry which had thrived in eighteenth century Ireland, including this area of West Cork. The linen-manufacturing trade accounted for 80% of Irish exports to Britain in 1758 and provided substantial employment opportunities for rural areas at the time.[15] The industry grew in West Cork from around the mid-eighteenth century and Skibbereen developed into an important market centre for the linen trade. At that stage, the production of linen was a domestic industry, with spinners (female) and weavers (male) working in their own homes and selling their produce at market. However, the demand for linen decreased in the early part of the nineteenth century when cotton goods became cheaper, and the market collapsed as a result. With the drop in the demand for linen, former weavers in the parishes that included Lough Hyne were described in 1836 as 'now starving almost'.[16]

| *Committee of Inspection* by James Brenan. (Image courtesy of the Crawford Art Gallery.)

The landlord Wrixon-Becher generated local employment in the early part of the century when he carried out some improvements to his estate at Lough Hyne. This would have been part of the general trend of post-1815 reforms by landlords aimed at increasing efficiency on their properties during this major economic recession. His estate records show that he financed 'the road to Lough Hyne' in 1826 and 1827 and he also planted 'the wood' at Lough Hyne between 1826 and 1828.[17] Other cash payments for wages were made to 'McCarthy of the wood', the wood-ranger at Lough Hyne.

Daniel McCarthy, the owner of a substantial brewery in Skibbereen town, also provided employment at Lough Hyne. McCarthy leased Lough Ine Cottage in 1834 from Lord Carbery.[18] He is credited with building the original 'graceful-looking villa', which is now known as Lough Hyne House, and carried out many improvements to the property.[19] The refurbishment, upkeep and staffing of this sizeable house would also have provided work for local people.

The landlord, Wrixon-Becher, planted the wood at Lough Hyne and paid for road improvements in the early 1800s. The Creagh estate records show that Michael McCarthy, the wood-ranger, was paid wages of 18 shillings and 6 pence a month in 1827. They also show a payment to C. Minihane of £3 and 14 shillings for the 'Loughine road'. The improvements carried out by Wrixon-Becher reflect the general post-1815 trend where landlords sought to increase efficiencies on their estates in response to the prevailing deflationary economic conditions.[20] (Creagh estate records, with kind permission of the owners, the Donnelly family.)

A coastguard station was built at Barlogue, Lough Hyne, in 1822.[21] It was a small station in comparison to others nearby. In 1834, it employed one chief officer and four men, while Baltimore and Castletownshend employed ten and nine men respectively.[22] These were mostly English workers, as there were very few Irishmen in the coastguard service at that time.[23]

The coastguards were generally unpopular, as their role was to control illegal activities, many of which were regarded as traditional sources of income by local people. They sought to restrict the widespread smuggling activities of the time as well as the plundering of wrecks and cargo washed ashore. They were also responsible for investigating the making of whiskey (or poitín) in illicit stills, which would have been a common practice in West Cork at the time.[24] Such stations provided very little local employment, as they were generally self-sufficient. Instead, they probably restricted some of the illegal means of earning additional income for the people of Lough Hyne.

| The plan of the Barlogue coastguard station, *c.* 1841. (Courtesy of the National Archives of Ireland. Ref: NAI/OS58B/638.)[25]

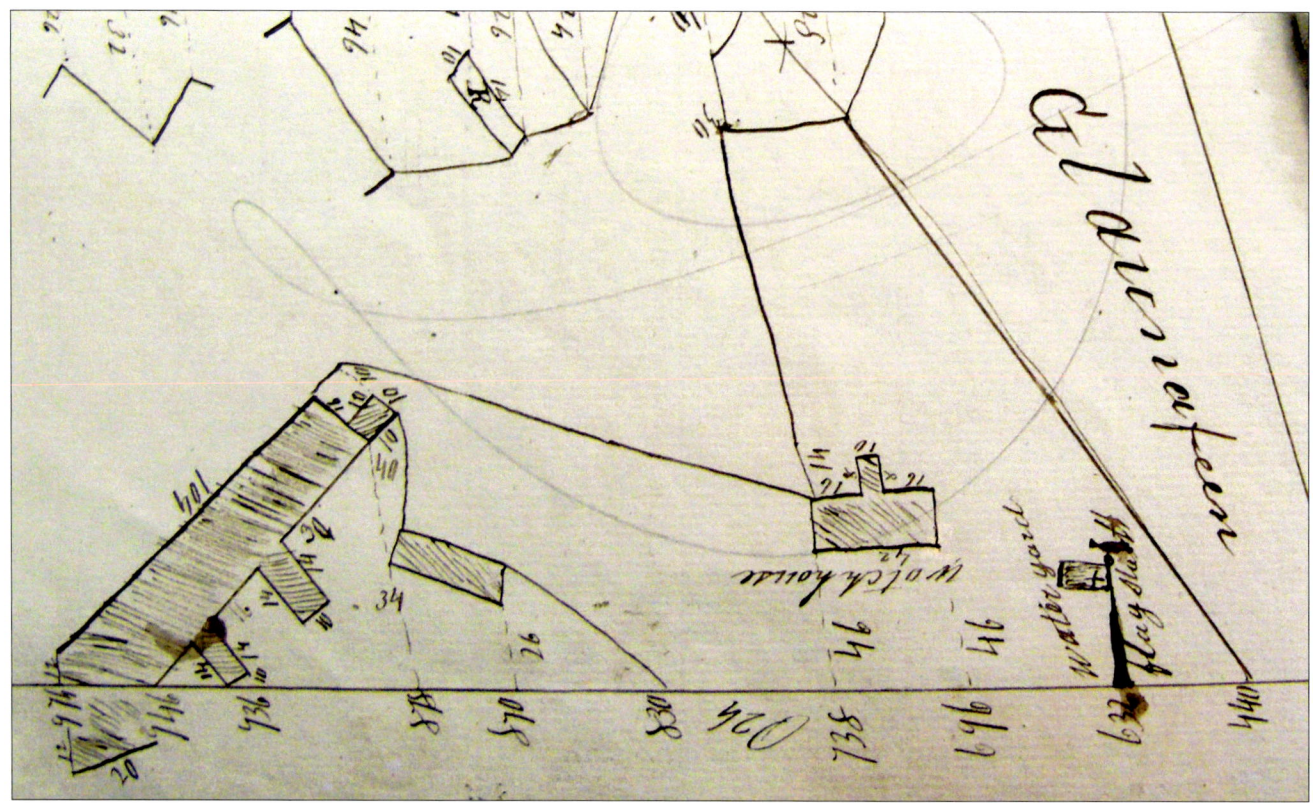

Population

The population of Ireland grew at an extraordinarily rapid rate, especially when the lack of industrialisation is taken into account. Between 1600 and 1845, Ireland's population went from around one million people to an estimated 8.5 million.[26] However, it was in the century preceding the Great Famine that the largest expansion occurred. A staggering 225% growth between 1750 and 1845 meant that the population increased from *c.* 2.6 million to *c.* 8.5 million, the fastest of 'any society in Europe in the century before the famine'.[27] This enormous increase was built on agricultural output, with dependence on the potato increasing accordingly. Because potatoes could be grown in poor-quality marginal land, an increase in their consumption meant a larger volume of land came under cultivation. Reclamation of previously untilled land, made possible by the robust nature of this crop, meant that bogs and uplands now started to be utilised for growing potatoes.

The population increase was highest in areas where there was marginal, unenclosed land that could be newly colonised, primarily by young people.[28] A large part of the area surrounding Skibbereen consisted of this kind of land, as indicated by its low valuation rate. By the mid-1800s, Skibbereen Union was densely populated, with over 400 people to the square mile, in contrast to the average for Cork county of 200 to 300 per square mile.[29] The area around Lough Hyne had a population density of about 350 per square mile, which is extremely high when the poor quality of the land there is taken into account.[30]

Despite the adverse conditions, the population of the parish of Skibbereen and Rath, which included the Lough Hyne area, continued to rise up to 1844, as can be seen in Chart One.

Chart One: Baptisms in the Catholic parish of Skibbereen and Rath, 1817–1901.

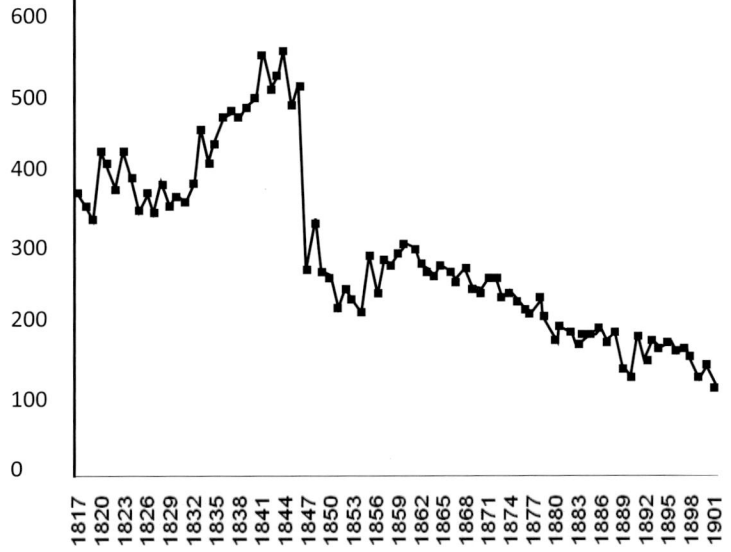

| Source: Roman Catholic Church Records for the Parish of Skibbereen, Rath and the Islands, 1817-1901, Skibbereen Heritage Centre Archive.

Agriculture

Irish agriculture underwent huge changes in the period from 1750 to 1800. In the mid-eighteenth century, Irish farming was primarily pastoral, producing butter and meat, with some oats grown to sustain the poorest farmers. By 1800, however, the use of the potato had expanded until it became the dominant product. This shift to tillage meant that each acre could feed more people and so the land could support a much greater population, and the amount of land under cultivation increased accordingly. By 1780, Ireland was producing more food than ever before and met not only the demands of the rising native population, but also had surplus to export. By the 1840s, approximately three-fifths of all agricultural output ended up in the marketplace.[31]

The Potato Diggers in the West (1903) by Charles McIver Grierson. The shift in land usage from pastoral to tillage farming, alongside the increasing use of the potato, meant that each acre could support more people, enabling a significant increase in population. (Image courtesy of the Crawford Art Gallery.)

In 1845, out of the total Irish population of *c.* 8.5 million, it is estimated that about 4.6 million people relied directly on the potato as their main food.[32] As well as providing for the people themselves, the potato was also used as animal feed, especially for pigs, which were often kept as a means of paying the rent. This single crop, therefore, provided sustenance for the majority of the Irish people and, in many cases, also helped to keep a roof over their heads. In the decades before the Great Famine, as dependence on the potato increased, many better-quality varieties, such as the Apple and Cup, were gradually replaced by the higher-yielding, but inferior, Lumper potato.[33]

The Lumper potato was an old variety that was initially used as animal feed but came into general use because it produced large crops on poor soils. By the 1840s, it accounted for over 90% of the potato crop and was widely used in West Cork. It was watery and kept badly and was very susceptible to blight. Outside times of shortage, it is estimated that a man would consume up to fourteen pounds of potatoes a day and a woman and child about eleven and five respectively. Studies have shown that Irish men were taller than their British counterparts of the time, showing that this diet was healthy despite its monotonous nature.[34]

The potato was an ideal crop for the subsistence farmer. It could be grown on poor-quality land, including boggy and hilly areas, and could be cultivated using only a spade. It was suitable for Ireland's weather conditions and it was also a very nutritious crop. With the addition of some buttermilk or fish, it provided all the requirements necessary for a healthy diet when consumed in sufficient quantities.[35] However, the volume required for sustenance was huge, with daily consumption estimated to have been about fourteen pounds for a man, eleven pounds for a woman and five pounds for a child.[36] The people who were most reliant on the potato as their primary food source had few other resources to fall back on and so were the most vulnerable in times of crop failure.

In the nineteenth century, potatoes were grown using drills known as 'lazy beds'. The name is deceptive, as this was a very labour-intensive method of farming. The potatoes were planted by hand, in raised ridges. Narrow trenches between the ridges facilitated drainage and provided access to tend the plants. This method suited the small field sizes, hilly ground and mountain sides of the Lough Hyne area. Seaweed or animal manure was used to fertilise the plants, which was a vital part of the process. Small fields, high in Glannafeen townland, still show traces of lazy-bed cultivation today and these give an indication of the pressure for land that must have existed in the Lough Hyne area.

There were many periods when the land of Ireland could not sustain its people. There were at least eighteen episodes of famine in Ireland between 1600 and 1845, caused by a combination of bad weather, crop failures, war and conflict. One of the worst was the famine of 1740–41, in which a quarter of Munster's population died.[37] In the first half of the nineteenth century, there were eight general failures of the potato crop prior to the Great Famine and five of these were attributed to potato plant disease.[38] The famine of 1821 and 1822 caused distress, 'horrible beyond description', in and around Skibbereen.[39] The unreliability of this crop was therefore well known and accepted. However, the two plant diseases which had affected potatoes in Ireland to date were nowhere near as destructive as the blight that was to arrive in 1845.[40]

These tiny fields, high in Glannafeen townland, that still show traces of lazy-bed cultivation give an indication of the pressure for land that existed in the Lough Hyne area. Previously uncultivated marginal land was tilled as the population pressure, alongside the lack of alternative means of earning a living, forced people to colonise new areas in the search for land.

The prevailing economic situation in the nineteenth century also had an effect on the conditions of those dependent on agriculture. In the early part of the century, there was a period of inflation in Britain as a result of the Napoleonic Wars. There was increased demand for supplies and the price of foodstuff soared as a result. Cork was a principal centre for the provisioning of the British military during this period.[41] The high prices meant that a farmer could gain a reasonable living from a smaller farm, while the increasing population meant that each farmer had more children to provide for, resulting in subdivision of land. At this time, the linen trade was also providing an additional income, with Townsend, in 1810, describing Skibbereen as 'having very large quantities of coarse linens and yarn [for] sale'.[42]

This increased demand for food came to end with the arrival of peace in 1815 and an economic decline followed. Increases in taxation to repay war debts meant reduced wages for British workers, who could therefore afford to buy less. Lower prices for their goods meant dependence on the potato increased as Irish farmers were forced to sell eggs, butter and grain that they would previously have consumed in their own homes. Farmers also economised by carrying out work themselves that they might formerly have employed labourers to do, thereby adding to the unemployment problem.

Despite the adverse conditions, the increasing population meant there was more demand for land. Rents in Ireland were very high as a result, between 80% and 100% higher than in England.[43] Many rental agreements had been negotiated during the boom period, adding to the inflationary pressure on the cost of land.

Some of the property holdings at Lough Hyne were tiny, some as small as one-sixteenth of an acre, as can be seen from the smallholdings in Ballyoughtera shown here in the Valuation notebooks of the 1840s. Land held in 'commonage' between many people was generally of very bad quality. The people who rented such land together, under a system called rundale, were generally of the same family group, as can be seen here from the dominance of the Burke family name. (Image courtesy of the Valuations Office, Dublin.)

Despite a vulnerability to adverse conditions and the monotony of their diet, the people of early nineteenth-century Ireland fared better than many of their European contemporaries. Studies have shown that life expectancy here was greater than in most European countries and that an Irishman's height was greater than that of his English counterpart of the time.[44] The potato provided them with sustenance if eaten in sufficient quantities. There was access to fuel, in the form of turf, and there was a strong community infrastructure in rural Ireland to provide support. Neighbours were considered to be the closest thing to family and, indeed, quite often were family members. As farms were repeatedly divided up, large extended families quite often lived together in the same area.

Lough Hyne's robust pre-Famine population included many clusters of extended family units living together in small groups of houses, known as claháns. They were scattered all around the lough; for example, in Balloughtera, Ballinard, Glannafeen, Dromadoon and Highfield townlands. On the eve of the Great Famine, the Lough Hyne area was full of people and must have been a lively and sociable place to live.

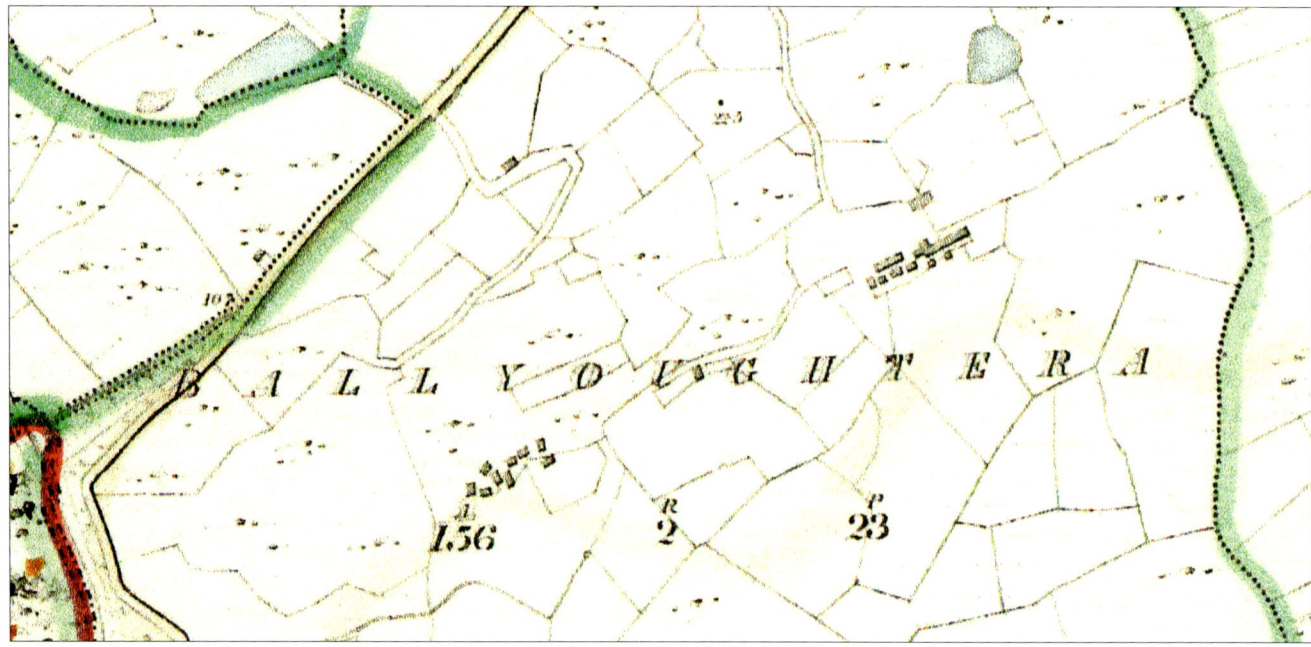

The 1842 map of Lough Hyne shows two clusters of houses in Ballyoughtera, one of eighteen houses, the other of fourteen, the latter known as *Bothárin na* 'Barracks'. Other clusters of houses were scattered all around the lake; for example, in Glannafeen, Ballinard and Highfield. The Lough Hyne of the early 1840s must have been a lively and sociable place to live in. (OSI Map permissions: © Ordnance Survey Ireland/Government of Ireland Copyright Permit No. MP 000714.)

The Poor of Lough Hyne

The poorest of the agricultural workers were known as 'labourers'. The 'landless labourer' category of worker had been part of Irish life since medieval times but their numbers increased exponentially from around the mid-eighteenth century onwards.[45]

A labourer was a worker who sublet a cabin and a small amount of ground from the tenant farmer to grow potatoes. He paid for this by performing labouring work, either for the farmer himself or by casual employment. When exchanging his labour with the farmer as a bound worker, the labourer was known as a 'cottier tenant'.[46] Given the intense competition for land, many cottiers agreed to high rents while putting a very low value on their labour. As much as 250 days of labour, plus the regular provision of poultry and eggs, were required as payment for a cabin and an acre of manured potato ground.[47]

Many labourers were forced to rent their land without an exchange of labour agreement and so relied on casual employment to pay the rent under a system called 'conacre'. This was the practice generally used in the Lough Hyne area. In the words of Rev. McCartney of Creagh in 1836, 'they live on [conacre], or on credit, until employed again; very often half starving'.[48] There was a high rate of unemployment, with McCartney testifying that just 55 out of 341 were in constant employment and that they were 'thankful for work, at any time, for 6d [six pence a day] without food'.[49]

The labourers and their families were the tenants of the most basic housing in Ireland. In the 1841 census, houses were divided into four categories. The poorest of these, categorised as '4th-class' houses, consisted of one-roomed cabins. These accounted for 47% of the housing in the Creagh and Tullagh parishes (which included Lough Hyne) in 1841. Even in the town of Skibbereen, these cabins were prevalent, with a visitor of the early 1800s remarking that 'we found whole streets ... formed of cabins without chimneys, situated at the bottom of a deep trench or ditch'.[50]

Sketch of Skibbereen town as featured in the *Illustrated London News* (*ILN*).

The pre-famine living conditions of these poor cabin dwellers were described by Rev. M. Power, Parish Priest of Tullagh and Creagh, in the Poor Law Inquiry of 1836:

> Most filthy, smokey, sooty hovels, badly built and worse finished; a small stool, a broken chair or two, a box without lock or cover, a miserable dresser under which the pig lies, on its top the hens roost, the middle is occupied by a few broken plates and basins.[51]

Asked if he thought that their condition was improving or getting worse, he replied:

> The condition of the poor has become worse since 1815; they had then more demand for their labour: a considerable number of [linen] weavers were then employed who are now starving almost … The population is, I understand, increasing.[52]

He went on to testify further about the labourers, the occupants of these small cabins:

> Their ordinary diet, when employed by farmers, is potatoes and salt fish, occasionally a little milk; when dieted by themselves, potatoes and a little salt diluted with water, in which they dip the potato.[53]

Asked how many labourers there were in his parish, he replied:

> 600 labourers, professionally so. About 200 of them are constantly employed; there are 400 more, who are holders of small portions of ground; they act as labourers in spring and harvest.[54]

Daniel McCarthy, who lived in Lough Ine Cottage, when asked by the same Commission whether their conditions were improving, replied 'they are considerably deteriorating' and described their condition as 'wretched'.[55]

Yet, despite their appalling living conditions, there are accounts of their daily life that show that things were not all miserable for the poor:

> The inhabitants of these hovels were healthy and cheerful; and, in the evening, we saw numerous groups of girls singing and dancing with uncommon vivacity and regularity, amidst the clouds of smoke which issued from the doors.[56]

A contemporary image from the *Illustrated London News* newspaper, showing the village of Meenies, near Drimoleague, which was also in Skibbereen Poor Law Union, featuring the one-roomed cabins of the labourers.[57] These cabins were about between 3.6m (12 feet) and 4.5m (15 feet) wide internally and of varying lengths. The poorest had no chimneys – the smoke escaped via the thatched roof – and the floor was of beaten earth. Windows were small and some cabins had a door only. In these dark, cramped conditions, the family generally shared their living space with an animal, which was usually a pig.

Almost 47% of the houses of Creagh and Tullagh parishes in 1841 (which included Lough Hyne) consisted of these one-roomed cabins.[58]

The labourers had only a tenuous grip on the land on which they so depended, with eviction being a constant threat. They were particularly vulnerable during the post-1815 recessionary period. More stringent controls on the subdivision and subletting of land were a feature of this period. In 1843, Wrixon-Becher evicted a tenant who had been arguing with his brother over the division of the farm after their father's death.[59] Another tenant was threatened with eviction a few years later, with Wrixon-Becher commenting that 'I am well acquainted with the Widow Cadogan's case, who has to be dispossessed of her farm if she perseveres in subdividing or subletting it contrary to agreement'.[60]

The only refuge available to the poor who were evicted and destitute was the workhouse, which was funded under the so-called 'Poor Laws'.

The Poor Laws

In 1800 Ireland was joined in union with Britain, which was, at the time, the wealthiest country in the world. The Act of Union essentially resulted in Ireland losing its right to self-govern and its policies were dictated directly by the British government. It also meant that the British administration had a vested interest in ensuring that the condition of Ireland, then regarded as a poor backward country, did not deteriorate further. Ireland's poverty was seen as a potential threat to Britain's prosperity. It was feared that, should the disparity between the poor of Ireland and Britain grow too much, Britain would be flooded with Irish paupers as refugees.[61] Various inquiries into the conditions of the poor were carried out with a view to finding a solution. At the Poor Law Inquiry of 1836, Daniel McCarthy of Lough Ine Cottage and Rev. Power gave testimonies on the conditions that prevailed for the people in the Lough Hyne area.

Ireland had been the subject of adverse publicity in Britain for centuries, which had negative effects on how it was perceived. The plantations of the seventeenth century had been justified by portraying Ireland as a degenerate country, inhabited by a lazy, dishonest and backward people. This depiction of Ireland and the Irish people was reiterated thereafter. By the nineteenth century, 'Ireland was considered by Britain an alien and even hostile country'.[62] Ireland needed to be rescued from its agricultural backwardness and habits of lassitude.[63] The solutions proposed for Ireland were all influenced by the popular thinking of the time.

The prevailing economic theories of the period also strongly influenced the government's response to poverty in Ireland. The predominant economic doctrine was that of 'political economy', otherwise known as *laissez-faire*. This proposed the theory that a nation's wealth would be increased if government intervention was kept to a minimum and the market kept free of restraints. Leading economists of the time, including Nassau Senior, regarded poverty as the fault of the individual and considered that it was not the duty of the government to alleviate it.[64] Another prominent economist, Thomas Malthus, believed that overpopulation and the inaction of the Irish landlords were the primary causes of poverty in Ireland.[65] As the landlords had not properly managed their estates in Ireland, relief of the poor was therefore deemed to be their responsibility and not that of the British government.[66] Other economic solutions were proposed by various groups of economists, such as the 'Manchester School', all of which influenced the political thinking of the time.[67] It was fashionable to blame the poor, both in Ireland and Britain, for their own situation rather than the overall system, which locked them into a life of poverty.

Traditionally, poverty in Ireland was relieved almost entirely by private charity, with government intervention taking place only in times of extreme, sustained shortages.[68] In 1838, a new system was put in place under the Poor Law of Ireland Act. The country was divided into 130 units, known as 'unions', each of which was to support a workhouse through rates paid by its landholders.[69] The basic premise underlying the system was that the destitute could get food and shelter in the workhouse in exchange for their labour. It was modelled on the British workhouse system but with two important differences. Unlike Britain, relief was only to be given within the confines of the workhouse, as no 'outdoor relief' was permitted.[70] Secondly, there was no 'right' to relief, so it was dependent on the availability of workhouse spaces.[71] These two clauses caused the deaths of many thousands of people during the Great Famine.

The principle of 'local chargeability' meant that each workhouse had to be supported by local ratepayers. By allocating the financial burden locally, local landowners would be 'encouraged' to take a greater interest in effectively managing their estates, resulting in a decreased demand for relief.[72] This meant that, during the Great Famine, the worst affected areas had to provide financial support to themselves. They were badly hit precisely because they were poor and therefore had only weak sources of revenue. However, in a truly Catch-22 situation, they were still expected to provide their own support.

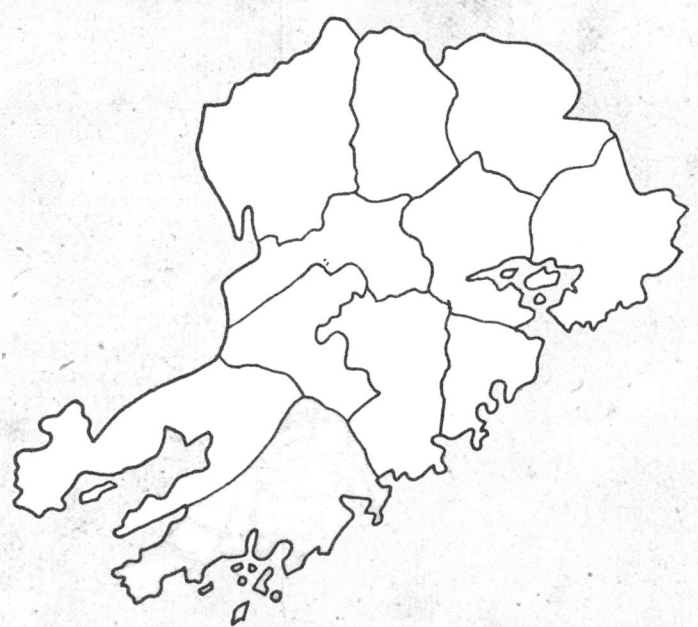

Skibbereen Poor Law Union
Pre 1850

Skibbereen Poor Law Union was one of 130 such Unions in Ireland, each of which was to support a workhouse. It covered the area shown here, which held a population of almost 105,000 people. Skibbereen workhouse, built to accommodate 800 inmates, was to serve the needs of the poor of this vast area, including the people of Lough Hyne.

The conditions within the workhouses were designed to be worse than those experienced in the normal life of a labourer.[73] This was thought to be a necessary requirement in Ireland, with its multitude of paupers. It was feared that, if they found that life in the workhouse was more comfortable than their normal living conditions, the poor of Ireland would be clamouring to get into them. Therefore, restrictions were used to deter admission.

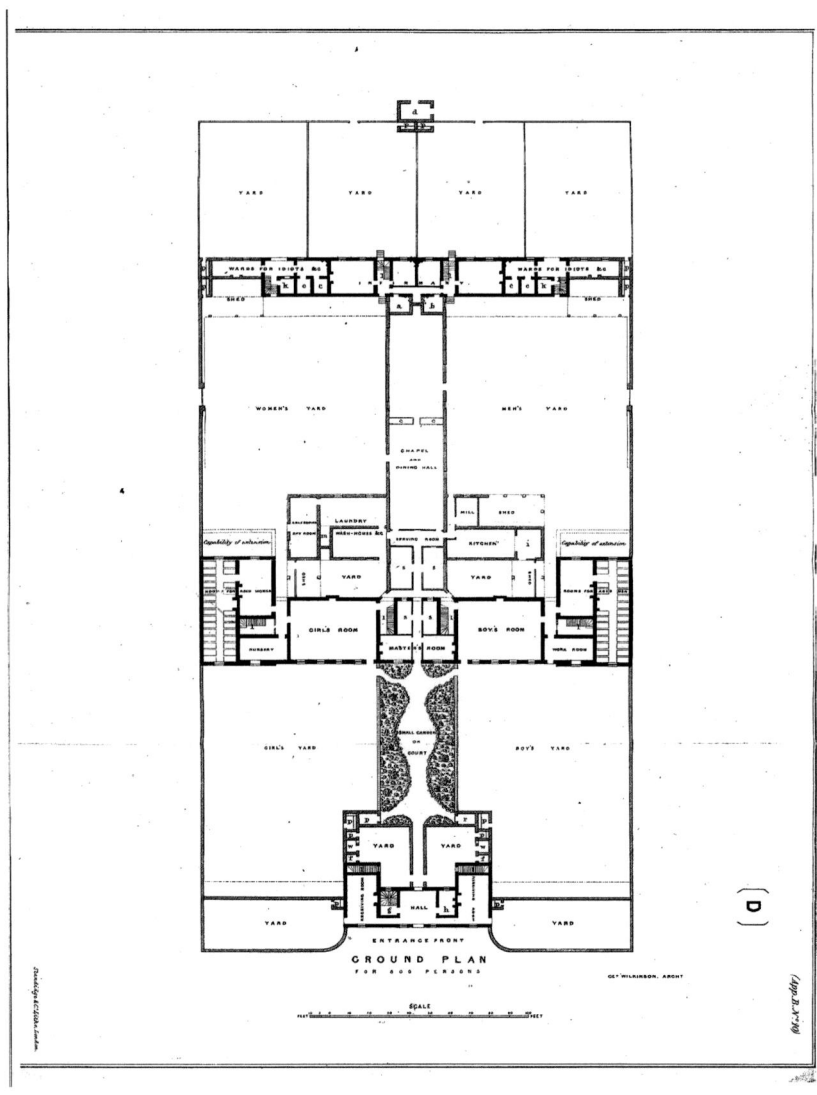

To gain admission to a workhouse, potential inmates had to be destitute rather than simply being poor. Individual people could not enter the workhouse, only entire family units.[74] The rules required that these families be separated on admission, husbands from wives, parents from children.[75] In accordance with the economic principles of the era, the punitive nature of poor relief permeated all areas of life in the workhouse and applied to every inmate, including the elderly, infirm and children.[76] The workhouse system was established to provide support to the poor, but, in its operation, it was closer in nature to that of a prison service.

The interior of the workhouse was divided into sections for men, women, boys, girls and 'lunatics'. Upon entry to the workhouse, families were split up and segregated in these different sectors. Their clothes were taken from them and they were given workhouse clothing. With the strict regime, high walls and punitive nature of the relief given, the workhouse system was closer in nature to a prison than a place of refuge. (Workhouse Collection, Irish Architectural Archive.)

Skibbereen workhouse, which opened in March 1842, was one of the first to be built under provisions of the Act.[77] The workhouse was built to accommodate 800 inmates and was to cater for the Skibbereen Union's population of almost 105,000 people.[78] This enormous building was located on the way into Skibbereen town, where the hospital grounds are today, and dominated the entrance to the town. Hidden behind high walls, it must have appeared alien on the landscape, especially when compared to the modest cabins and cottages that surrounded it, resembling a place of detention rather than one of sanctuary.

This was the only refuge available to the poor of Lough Hyne. Like many other workhouses in the south and west of Ireland, it was totally inadequate for the scale of the poverty that it was meant to alleviate. No one had foreseen, or even imagined, the demands that were to be put on this deficient system during the devastating Great Famine years.

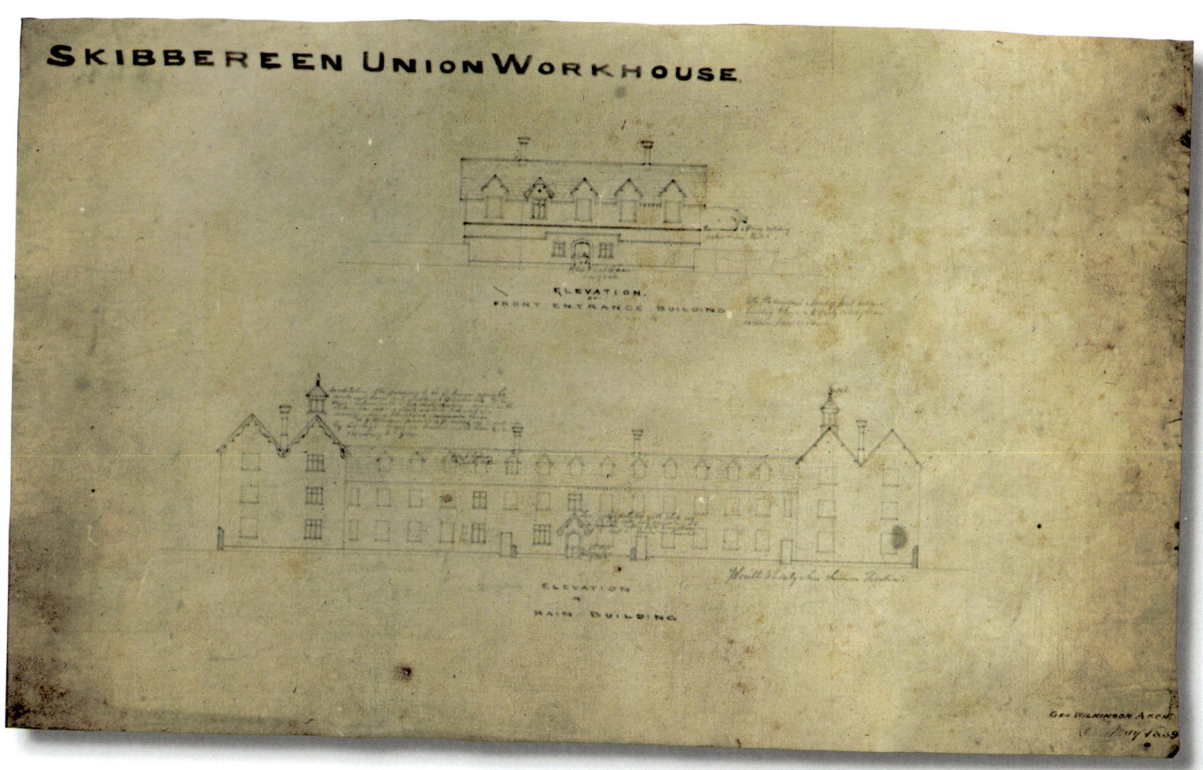

Skibbereen Workhouse was situated in the townland of Coolnagurrane, on the outskirts of Skibbereen town, on the site of the hospital grounds today. This commanding structure would have loomed over the cottages and farmhouses of the area and it must have appeared alien on the landscape, its scale at odds with the other buildings in the town. All that is left of it today are the original high stone walls that once surrounded this imposing building. The workhouse was burnt down on the night of 25 June 1921. (Workhouse Collection, Irish Architectural Archive.)

The Great Famine at Lough Hyne

The Great Famine was a catastrophe that changed Ireland irrevocably. From a population of about 8.5 million, it is estimated that over one million people died unnecessarily between the years of 1846 and 1851.[1] This figure rises to almost 1.5 million when averted births are included.[2]

Emigration offered a chance to escape, and more than a million people emigrated between 1846 and 1851, adding to the decline in Ireland's population.[3] Emigration was already taking place prior to the Great Famine but the scale of the exodus during and after the Famine was unprecedented in the history of international migration, with two million people leaving Ireland between 1845 and 1855.[4] This was more than had emigrated from Ireland in the preceding two and a half centuries.[5]

Some areas of Ireland were disproportionally affected and the Great Famine 'was less a national disaster than a social and regional one'.[6] Of the excess deaths, Munster accounted for 30.3%, Connacht 40.4%, Ulster for 20.7% and Leinster 8.6%, so the south and west were particularly badly affected areas.[7] The average population loss in the Poor Law unions of Cork was 24.2%, and Skibbereen Poor Law Union reported the highest loss in the entire county at 36.1%.[8]

Lough Hyne, as part of Skibbereen Poor Law Union, lost an even higher proportion of its people, with a population loss of over 45% in the decade 1841 to 1851. This figure includes deaths, emigration and migration within Ireland and it reflects the fundamental change that occurred in the demographics of the area. Places with the lowest incomes per capita and the highest rates of illiteracy were those that experienced the highest mortality rates nationally.[9] This is reflected in the Lough Hyne area, where, as can be seen from the census comparisons in Table Two, it was the cabin-dwellers and illiterate who were mostly affected. The Great Famine had a profound impact on the Lough Hyne area from which, as Table Three shows, its population never recovered, as it continued to lose its people into the twentieth century.

The years of the Great Famine caused fundamental social, cultural and demographic changes, the scale of which had not been seen since the seventeenth century. The effects continued to be felt at Lough Hyne long after the years of the crisis itself and cleaved the history of the area into two distinct eras of pre- and post-Famine.

Table Two: Number of first-, second-, third- and fourth-class houses; number of people employed in agriculture; number of people who could read/write, read only and illiterate in the parishes of Creagh and Tullagh in the 1841 and 1851 censuses.

	Creagh 1841	Creagh 1851	Change in %	Tullagh 1841	Tullagh 1851	Change in %	Average % change of both parishes
1st-class	8	9	12	1	1	0	6
2nd-class	55	72	31	42	55	31	31
3rd-class	277	225	−19	274	299	9	−5
4th-class	276	75	−73	303	59	−81	−77
Agriculture	541	304	−44	457	288	−37	−41
Can read/write	387	355	−9	357	323	−10	−9.5
Read only	251	182	−28	173	91	−47	−37.5
No read/write	2447	1525	−38	2356	1472	−38	−38

Source: Census of Ireland, 1911. Area, houses, and population: also the ages, civil or conjugal condition, occupations, birthplaces, religions, and education of the people. Province of Munster BPP 1912–13 CXV [Cd.6050] 152.

Table Three: Populations of the townlands at Lough Hyne from 1841–1911 census records showing percentage change from 1841 base figure, including the area of each townland in acres.

Townland	1841	1851	1861	1871	1881	1891	1901	1911	area
Ballinard	110	44	39	32	32	36	40	42	230
Ballyisland	64	31	36	41	37	20	19	7	101
Ballyoughtera	94	100	63	76	65	56	48	45	156
Barnabah	59	27	8	14	6	3	3	4	47
Coomavarrodig	49	15	18	20	10	15	20	9	81
Dromadoon	82	63	50	45	45	38	31	22	137
Glannafeen	164	100	117	70	49	42	35	35	259
Highfield	266	80	117	96	93	95	60	53	576
Knockanoulty	30	18	21	18	10	13	16	15	64
Knockeencon	65	65	20	22	9	5	6	4	108
Pookeen	66	35	34	21	26	26	25	24	159
	1049	**578**	**523**	**455**	**382**	**349**	**303**	**260**	**1918**
% change from 1841		−45	−50	−57	−64	−67	−71	−75	

Source: Census of Ireland, 1911. Area, houses, and population: also the ages, civil or conjugal condition, occupations, birthplaces, religions, and education of the people. Province of Munster BPP 1912–13 CXV [Cd.6050] 152.

1845 – The Blight Arrives

Phytophthora infestans, commonly known as potato blight, affected the potato crop in north-eastern America in 1843 and 1844.[10] Imports of seed potatoes from the US to Europe carried the disease across the Atlantic and it appeared there in 1845.[11] It was reported in England later in mid-August 1845 and, by the end of that month, it had arrived in Dublin. It was first noticed in Cork city in the second week of September but it was October, when the potatoes were taken out of the ground, that the full extent of the loss was known.[12] The late-maturing Lumper variety, which was widely used in West Cork, was badly affected.[13] Europe had no prior experience of this fungal disease, which was spread rapidly by wind-borne infectious spores. Despite many efforts, no cure was found at the time.

The Times' 'Commissioner', Thomas Campbell Foster, reported from Ireland in its edition of 28 November 1845:[14]

> Amongst the rough hills of West Carbery ... The general topic of conversation everywhere now is the failure of the potato crop ... I am as firmly convinced ... such is the general apathy, want of exertion and feeling of fatality amongst the people ... that unless the Government step forward to enforce these or similar plans for the national welfare, not any one of them will be generally adopted *and nothing will be done* ... The Government ... [should] ... act promptly, decisively, and at once, and not depend on people helping themselves: for, such is the character of the people, that *they will do nothing until starvation faces them.*[15]

Dr Dan Donovan, the dispensary doctor for Skibbereen, showed concern at a meeting of the Carbery Agricultural Show in Skibbereen in October 1845. The *Cork Constitution* of 1 November 1845 reported that:

> Dr. Donovan ... found that the wail all around him was that the potatoes were rotting everywhere.[16]

1845 – Famine Relief

The response of the people of Skibbereen to this crisis was prompt and, on 10 November 1845, 'a large and influential meeting of the inhabitants of Skibbereen and the gentry and landed proprietors of the vicinity was held ... in the Courthouse of that town, for the purpose of considering the state of the potato crop in the district, and of petitioning government to adopt the best measures to alleviate the distress likely to arise from the failure of the crop by affording employment to the labouring classes'.[18] Daniel McCarthy of Lough Ine Cottage was at this meeting. The principle of creating work to enable people to earn money to buy food was a long-established policy in response to Irish food crises.[19] Provision of Relief Work had already been used successfully to alleviate the famine of 1822 in the Skibbereen area.

SKIBBEREEN, FROM CLOVER-HILL.

'A large and influential meeting of the inhabitants of Skibbereen and the gentry and landed proprietors of the vicinity was held on Monday [10 November, 1845], in the Courthouse of that town, for the purpose of considering the state of the potato crop in the district.'[17] Skibbereen Courthouse, shown here to the left, as sketched by James Mahoney in 1847. (*ILN*)

The proportion of potato crop lost that first year was estimated to be somewhere between a quarter and a third, but by early December retail prices had more than doubled.[22] The British government, under Prime Minister Sir Robert Peel, was urged to repeal the restrictive Corn Laws and allow the duty-free importation of grain.[23] These controversial laws only allowed grain importation when the price of homegrown corn reached certain levels, thereby restricting foreign imports to times of scarcity.[24] It was politically impossible for Peel's Tory government to repeal them in 1845 and, instead, his administration made a secret purchase of Indian corn (maize) and meal from the United States.[25] There was no large established trade in this commodity, therefore its interference with private commerce was minimal. This was the *laissez-faire* dogma put into effect in that there would be 'no [government] interference in the ordinary course of trade'.[26] The abundant Irish oat crop of 1845 was simultaneously being depleted by export, which the government refused to stop by citing the same principle of non-intervention in the market.[27]

A central relief commission was set up under Sir Randolph Routh, which was to arrange the efficient distribution of this food via a network of local committees. The main aim of the government was to dampen down the inflationary pressure of rising food prices, not to provide direct relief to the Irish poor.[28] The local committees were to raise funds among landowners of the area and distribute the food at cost price locally. Irish property would have to support Irish poverty.

> The principle of creating work, enabling people to earn money to buy food, was a long-established policy in response to Irish food crises.[20] Provision of relief work had been used to alleviate the 1822 famine in the Skibbereen area. Richard Griffith (who later went on to oversee the Griffith's Valuation) was in charge of a road-building relief scheme that brought a road from Skibbereen to Crookhaven, part of which is now the N71.[21] One of the bridges that was built as part of that project, at Kilcoe (shown here), still stands today.

The creation of work was one arm of the relief effort by the British government during the first year of the Great Famine, the other being the import of Indian corn (maize), which was distributed throughout the country and released at cost price when food inflation reached critical levels. These two measures were to work in tandem: the money earned on the relief work would be used to buy food, the supply of which was guaranteed by the importation of maize. (Image: R. O'Regan.)

It was 24 March 1846 when the divisions for the county of Cork were decided and an immediate preliminary meeting was held in Skibbereen on that very day. Just four days later, the Skibbereen Committee secretary, Thomas Hungerford, applied to the commission in Dublin.[29] The urgency of the local situation was evident from the rapid response of the Skibbereen Committee to the government actions. Another, larger, gathering was held on 2 April, at which Daniel McCarthy of Lough Ine Cottage remarked on 'the frightful state of destitution amongst the people'.[30]

Daniel McCarthy, the owner of a brewery in North Street, Skibbereen, leased Lough Ine Cottage (now Lough Hyne House) from Lord Carbery in 1834. A wealthy man, he was described as 'the largest ratepayer in the Union' and the brewery was 'far and away the most valuable property in the whole Skibbereen district'.[31] McCarthy lived at Lough Hyne during the years of the Great Famine and his twin sons were born there in 1847. Active in relief efforts, he attended all the early meetings of the landowners of the area and later went on to be one of the founder members of the Skibbereen 'Committee for Gratuitous Relief'. The members of this charitable committee opened a soup kitchen in Skibbereen in November 1846, months before the government-run soup kitchens opened in the spring of 1847.

By the end of April, the Skibbereen Committee had begun to intervene in the market and, by 8 May, it was reported that 'the [Skibbereen] Committee ... [sells] Indian meal at 2d per quart ... where potatoes could not be had last week the market is crowded with them now and the famine panic has entirely disappeared'.[32] Additional supplies of meal were supplied to the coastguard stations around the coast. There was a coastguard station at Barlogue in Lough Hyne at that time, which was not supplied; however, the one at nearby Baltimore was.[33]

1846 – Famine Relief

While only a portion of the 1845 potato crop was destroyed by blight, the 1846 crop was almost a total loss. Despite this, the new Whig government, under Prime Minister John Russell, decided in August 1846 to reverse Peel's previous Tory government policy of importing foreign grain in an effort to control food inflation.[34] An exception to this rule was made for a few places only, among them Skibbereen, where government food depots were set up. However, they were to be opened only as a last resort.[35]

This decision, which caused extreme distress in the months to follow, was recommended by a very influential individual, Charles Edward Trevelyan. He was a dominant figure throughout the years of the Famine with far-reaching control over government relief policy, especially during Russell's divided Whig cabinet of 1846–52.[36] In theory, as permanent Head of Treasury, he was subject to ministerial direction, but, in effect, he exercised wide discretionary powers. A strong believer in the doctrine of *laissez-faire,* he was an evangelical Protestant who was insensitive and uncompromising in his actions during the crisis.[37] He believed that the poor state of Irish society was a result of the moral failings of its people and that the Famine had therefore been sent by God.[38] This belief was known as 'divine providence'.

The new policies of 1846–47 were proposed as a revised system of relief by Trevelyan and were accepted by the Whig government.[42] Trevelyan insisted that the government would not interfere with the market and that the emphasis would be placed less on the sale of food and more on the provision of employment. Treasury money continued to fund local relief works, but these would have to be repaid from local rates over a ten-year period. He justified this by explaining that:

> The owners and holders of land … had permitted … the growth of the excessive population … and they alone had it in their power to restore society to a safe and healthy state … The deep and inveterate root of social evil remained, and this has been laid bare by a direct stroke of an all-wise and all-merciful Providence.[43]

Charles Edward Trevelyan, in his position as permanent Head of Treasury, strongly influenced government policy during the Great Famine. He was an ideologically driven workaholic who was a strong supporter of the *laissez-faire* economic doctrine. He believed that Ireland's pre-Famine conditions and 'social evil' were altered by an 'all-merciful' God.[39] In his eyes, the Famine was a punishment sent by God that had to take its course, and any human intervention would therefore be contravening His divine will. He was supported in his beliefs by two other influential individuals who played pivotal roles in Famine relief: Charles Wood, the Chancellor of the Exchequer, and Sir Peter Grey, the Home Secretary.[40] Trevelyan's book *The Irish Crisis* was published in late 1847, just after the British administration halted its relief efforts in Ireland. Trevelyan's policies, which reflected the economic beliefs of the period, exacerbated the effects of the Famine and caused untold suffering and mortality. However, he was lauded by his contemporaries and, in 1848, was knighted for his work in Ireland.[41]

The almost total potato-crop failure of 1846 meant that, by August, all but a few food depots had run out of food.[44] Routh pleaded with Trevelyan to purchase food from abroad, saying that 'you cannot answer the cry of want by a quotation from political economy'.[45] Trevelyan, however, refused. His policy of non-intervention in the market resulted in a fatal delay in the purchase of food. By the time that the government decided that food purchases were necessary, obstacles such as long lead-in times for imports and short supply of American maize in Europe meant that it could not arrive in time to avert deaths from starvation.[46] At this time, food was still being exported from Ireland, with Trevelyan directing Routh 'not to countenance in any way the idea of prohibiting exportation'. This decision, alongside his delay in purchasing food, meant that there was a major shortage of food that winter, only alleviated from December onwards when maize began to arrive from America.[47] The food delivered in December took time to distribute, especially to more remote areas, and the lack of food caused multiple deaths in the Skibbereen area.[48] The desperation of the people was described by an official when he wrote to Routh from Skibbereen Reserve Depot on 20 September 1846:

> The picture of wretchedness and destitution in this Union requires no colouring ... On the 12th inst. (market day here) there was neither meal nor bread for sale in the town at 5 o clock ... On Friday the 18th inst. great numbers of famishing [sic] creatures were following members of the Relief Committee about, begging for food ... On the road to Baltimore, a third application was made by a deputation from Leap for 10 tons, which I most respectfully refused, when they ... said 'Mr Deputy Commissary, do you refuse to give out food to a starving people who are willing to pay for it; if so, in the event of an outbreak this night, the responsibility is yours'.[49]

| Skibbereen Town, 1847. (*ILN*)

The shortage of food resulted in an exponential food price increase. Indian meal in Cork rose from a price of £10 per ton in August to £19 in December.[50] This ludicrous situation arose where the government depots, which had bought the meal for as little as £13 per ton, were selling it to relief committees for £19 as they could not undercut the market cost.[51] This inflation of food prices meant that, by December 1846, in the Skibbereen district a labourer earning the prevailing wage of 8d per day was able to purchase only four pounds of meal a day, resulting in slow starvation.[52] There were a series of riots and disturbances throughout the Skibbereen Union during that autumn and winter.[53] In the closing weeks of 1846, Routh persistently argued that the government depots should be opened before the appointed date of 28 December, but even in Skibbereen, by then achieving an international reputation due to almost daily reports of death by starvation, no exception was to be made.[54] This was subsequently revoked, but at the time Trevelyan explained to Routh:

> These principles must be kept in view in reference to what is now going on in Skibbereen, for if we were to commence a lavish issue there, we might find it difficult to adopt a safe course elsewhere.[55]

The almost complete failure of the 1846 harvest, alongside the British government's reversal of its food importation policy, caused serious food shortages in the winter of 1846–47. (*ILN*)

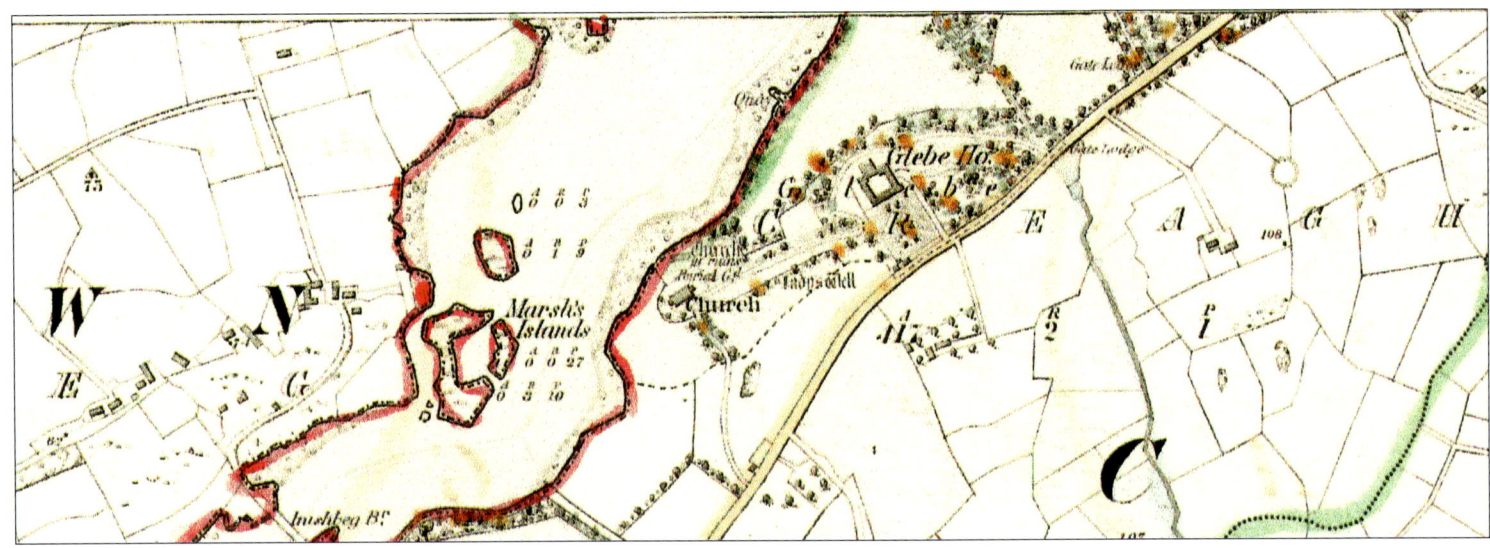

Rev. Charles Caulfeild was rector of Creagh parish during the Great Famine and was actively involved in relief work. Even before the Great Famine, he made efforts to help the poor of the locality by setting up a Loan Fund in Creagh in 1843.[56] He spoke at many of the famine relief meetings and was a member of the Skibbereen 'Committee for Gratuitous Relief', which set up the first soup kitchen in the town. He also dispensed soup from his own house in late 1846, shown as 'The Glebe' on the map here. He travelled to London, with Rev. R.B. Townsend, to seek aid for Skibbereen in the winter of 1846, where he met with Trevelyan personally. (OSI Map permissions: © Ordnance Survey Ireland/Government of Ireland. Copyright Permit No. MP 000714.)

In the Lough Hyne area, Rev. Charles Caulfeild, who was rector of Creagh parish, which encompassed the lough, wrote to Grey on 4 January 1846 that:

> The burial grounds are being changed in appearance: in some cases enlarged ... [and] the bodies were not sufficiently interred. In the small burying ground near Skibbereen, eight bodies were interred within an hour. Very few now attend funerals, which is strange in this country ... the scenes we witness are very terrible ... in a remote district in this parish there are on the property of a wealthy nobleman (munificent in charity) 200 destitute persons, many living in hovels not fit for dogs.[57]

The 'wealthy nobleman' referred to here was Lord Carbery. Part of his estate, including Lough Hyne, was in Creagh parish. The 'remote area' may well have been Lough Hyne, but, even if it was not a direct description of the lough itself, conditions there would have been similar.

Caulfeild was vocal in his efforts and was described by the official forwarding the letter as 'much respected … [and]… energetic in seeking aid for the people of his neighbourhood.[58] Caulfeild continued to push for relief and his actions certainly had material benefits for the Skibbereen Union. In November 1846, Caulfeild went to London to seek relief for Skibbereen and was at a meeting where Trevelyan was also present. Just three days later, Trevelyan suggested to Routh that 'the whole or portion of the Ceylon subscription be given to Skibbereen, where, judging from the number of deaths, the destitution must be frightful'.[59]

1846 – Public Works

As part of the relief efforts by the government, public works were set up so that people would be able to earn money to buy food.[60] This system of work creation had been used in the earlier famines of 1816–17 and 1822.[61] This involved physical labour on construction work, with road-building as the central focus.[62] When adverse weather conditions meant the building work was not possible, the workers were compelled to break stones for a lower wage.[63] The number of people employed on these works steadily increased, reaching a peak of 714,390 nationally in March 1847.[64]

Changes in the system of the relief works, devised by Trevelyan in August 1846, meant that the Board of Works assumed complete responsibility for all public schemes.[65] This resulted in a massive bureaucratic machine, which often led to delays in payment to workers.[66] The revised system had to be entirely supported by local taxation and, from September onwards, a scheme based on task labour, or 'piece work', came into effect, replacing the former method of a daily wage.[67] The amount paid had to be lower than the usual local wage in order to avoid the risk of encouraging unscrupulous conduct.[68] This system pushed those least able for physical activity, such as the ill and the elderly, below the level of subsistence.

Many thousands of people employed on these public works slowly died of starvation in the winter of 1846–47. Malnourished or sick, they were unable to earn enough under the measured task system of labour to buy sufficient food to stay alive.[69] Even when there was money to pay for it, there was often no supply of food available. The works brought together large numbers of malnourished people and thus facilitated the spread of diseases which were, by this stage, reaching epidemic proportions.[70]

1846–47 was an extreme winter, with exceptionally cold conditions setting in between December and April. Severe frosts were followed by heavy snowfalls and many of the public works had to be halted as a result.[71] One of the many adverse effects starvation has on the human body is an increased sensitivity to cold.[72] The impact of this bitterly cold weather was made even worse by the fact that the malnourished workers were often wearing very little clothing. Many people had pawned their warm clothes during the first winter of the Famine and lack of clothing for the poor was repeatedly reported as a major problem.[73]

Contemporary reports on the relief works in the Skibbereen area give an indication of the appalling conditions these poor people had to work under. This account dates to February 1847:

> Women with their red swollen feet partially swathed in old rags, some in men's coats, with their arms or skirts torn off, were sitting by the roadside, breaking stones … Men, once athletic labourers, were trying to eke out a few miserable days to their existence, by toiling upon these works. Poor creatures! Many of them are already famine stricken … The plague spot of famine is on their foreheads … Still they go forth uncomplaining to their labour and toil, cold, and half naked upon the roads.[74]

Leitry Bridge near Drimoleague, also in Skibbereen Union, was built as a relief effort during the Great Famine. Many people died of starvation and 'road sickness' while working on such schemes. In a malnourished and weakened condition, they were extremely susceptible to disease. The relief works brought large numbers of these people together, thereby facilitating the spread of the 'fever'.

There are only a few occasions when Lough Hyne has frozen and this 2010 photo captures one such rare occurrence. Similar conditions would have been experienced during the bitterly cold winter months of 1846–47 when the wall on the western side of the Rapids in Lough Hyne was built as a relief scheme. To build the wall, the workers would have had to stand in the freezing waters of the lough, many of them wearing insufficient clothing. Poor people pawned what little they had, including their clothes, in the early years of the Famine and lack of clothing was frequently mentioned as a problem during the cold Famine winters. To add to this, one of the many adverse effects that starvation has on the human body is an increased sensitivity to cold, so these workers at Lough Hyne would have suffered terribly in the freezing conditions.

Rapids Wall

The wall at the western side of the Rapids at Lough Hyne was built as a famine relief scheme, as an 1848 letter records:

> On the west side of the strait, a warping wall consisting of dry rubble masonry had been in course of construction, under the 'Relief Acts' by Mr Treacy, county supervisor, but owing to stopping of the work, it was not completed.[75]

We do not know the exact date that the work was carried out, but an examination of the overall numbers nationally will give an idea of when it might have been done. By the end of April, 29% of the schemes had been stopped with a further 15% by the end of May, and by June 1847 all but 4% of the public works had been closed.[76] This Lough Hyne relief work was probably carried out towards the end of the scheme, as the letter's 'owing to the stopping of the work' remark suggests. The Rapids wall was therefore probably built in the first six months of 1847.

As there are no contemporary descriptions of the work at Lough Hyne, we can only imagine the conditions under which it was built. As it was impossible to carry out the work from the land above, the workers must have stood in the water at the Rapids to build the wall's foundations. This would have meant that they would have been partly immersed in the water of Lough Hyne during those bitterly cold months in early 1847. The stones for the wall would have been carried to the site by hand, probably using baskets.

The 1847 project was a huge undertaking, bearing in mind that a reconstruction of this same wall at the Rapids took two months to complete in 2006. This was achieved with the use of modern machinery, including a digger, low-loader and a barge to transport the materials.[77] The 1847 work would have been carried out without the benefits of mechanism and must have employed a considerable number of people. The 1842 Ordnance Survey of Ireland map does not show any evidence of a pre-existing wall at the site, so it would have been built from foundation level in 1847. There is no doubt that many people died while working on the Rapids Relief Scheme in those bitter months of early '47.

By the end of 1846, the administration was forced to acknowledge that the public works schemes were not effective and, in early 1847, pressure mounted on the government to meet and to resolve the crisis. A new method of relief would have to be found, one that was cheaper and more effective, and one that was already in place in the Skibbereen Union.

The original western Rapids wall, which was built in 1847 as a famine relief effort, photographed just before its replacement in 2006. Even with the benefit of modern machinery, the reconstruction of this wall took two months to complete. Using this as a measure of the work involved, the building of the original wall in 1847 was, therefore, a considerable undertaking and must have involved a substantial workforce. (Photo: R. McAllen.)

1846 – Soup in the Skibbereen Union

In late 1846, the appalling conditions in Skibbereen prompted local action and a group of people came together in an effort to supply relief to the poor. The 'Committee for Gratuitous Relief' opened a soup kitchen in Skibbereen on 7 November 1846, months before the government-run soup kitchen scheme started. Daniel McCarthy of Lough Ine Cottage and Rev. Caulfeild of Creagh were members of this committee. The Skibbereen soup kitchen, located in the steam mill on Ilen Street, supplied relief on a massive scale. It is estimated that it fed up to 8,600 people per day in early 1847.[78] A witness account from February 1847 gives us a description of the soup kitchen:

> The soup house was surrounded by a cloud of these famine spectres, half naked, and standing or sitting in the mud, beneath a cold, drizzling rain ... [there were] ... young and old of both sexes, struggling forward with their rusty tin and iron vessels for soup, some of them upon all fours, like famished beasts.[79]

The 'Committee for Gratuitous Relief' set up a soup kitchen in Skibbereen in November 1846, months before the government-run soup kitchen scheme started. Run from the steam-mill building in Ilen Street, shown here as it appears today, it fed up to *c.* 8,600 people per day. Daniel McCarthy of Lough Ine Cottage and Rev. Caulfeild of Creagh were members of this committee.

As well as direct provision of soup, the Skibbereen Committee also distributed food daily to areas outside of the town in an effort to stop the influx of people into Skibbereen in search of relief. In February 1847, the Relief Committee estimated that over 3,000 people seeking relief had migrated into Skibbereen.[80] As Lough Hyne was within walking distance of the town, some of the people of that area were surely part of this number. In an effort to control the flood of people into the town, many of them disease-ridden, the committee sent soup and rice 'in closed barrels, by carts, distances of 3, 4, 5 miles to the country in different directions [as well as] rice milk daily sent round to the sick'.[81] It is impossible to know if Lough Hyne was one of the areas covered. However, Daniel McCarthy served on the committee and was living in Lough Ine Cottage at the time, so he would have been aware of the awful conditions in the area.[82] However, as an official wrote to Routh on 7 January 1847:

> It cannot, however, be too carefully borne in mind … [that] … it is as a 'drop in the ocean'. Hundreds are relieved but thousands still want.[83]

Soup was also being given as relief in Creagh, just a few miles from Lough Hyne. Rev. Caulfeild of Creagh told Trevelyan in London on 2 December 1846 that '50 or 60 people were fed daily from the soup cauldron at his house, who would die if this means of support were discontinued'.[84] The glebe house at Creagh as it appears today. (With thanks to the current owners, Mark Benson and family.) (Photo: R. O'Regan.)

In the written accounts of the time, the desperation of the people is tangible. Hoards of starving people were reported as roaming around in search of food, with none to be had. The situation was worsening by the day and reports of the suffering of the people of the Skibbereen Poor Law Union began to appear in the media. The *Cork Examiner* and another Cork newspaper, the *Southern Reporter,* carried extensive coverage of the Famine in the Skibbereen area under such headlines as 'Death by Starvation', 'More Deaths from Starvation!!!', 'Another Death by Starvation', 'More Deaths by Starvation', 'Deaths from Starvation', The Deaths from Starvation at Skibbereen – The Inquests', 'Horrible Distress in the West – Another Death from Starvation', 'Awful State of Skibbereen District – Destruction of the People – Famine, Disease and Death'.[85] Extracts from these provincial newspapers were carried in the 'Ireland' column of *The Times*, reaching a huge international readership.[86] The name 'Skibbereen' was becoming a byword for famine.[87] By this stage, the poor of Lough Hyne were suffering terribly.

1847 – Government-Run Soup Kitchens

Pressure was mounting on the British government to take action and, in early 1847, it established an alternative system of relief which would deliver cheap food to the masses via soup kitchens while simultaneously winding down the public works. The so-called 'soup kitchen act' was hurried through parliament in late January and early February, but the massive administrative machinery for its actual operation took some months to establish.[88] This system of relief was intended to be only a temporary measure, lasting until the harvest season of 1847, when a revised Poor Law system would come into place.[89]

The soup kitchen system was much cheaper to run than the public works; nevertheless, the emphasis was, at all times, on cutting down costs and the possibility of abuse.[90] As the public works wound down, people were reliant on the soup kitchens, although many who were eligible for the relief works were ineligible for the new system. The numbers of people in receipt of soup steadily increased as the Famine wore on, with over three million people receiving rations from the soup kitchens by July 1847.[91]

The recipe used in the government-run kitchens was created by Alexis Soyer, who was then chef at the Reform Club in London, who said that it 'had been tasted by numerous noblemen, members of Parliament and several ladies ... who have found it very good and nourishing'. One meal of 'Soyer's Soup', however, provided just 10% of the calorific requirements of an adult for a day. Millions of Irish people were fed by the government soup over the following months, which provided them with only a fraction of what was required for proper nourishment.

Soyer's Soup Recipe Number 1

2 gallons of water

Quarter pound of beef

2 oz of dripping

2 onions

Half pound of flour and half pound of pearl barley

3 oz of salt and 1/2 oz of brown sugar

THE CORK SOCIETY OF FRIEND'S SOUP HOUSE.

The soup served in the Quaker kitchens had six times the amount of meat of that served in the government-run soup kitchens. The government soup recipe, known as 'Soyer's Soup' after its creator, contained just 10% of the daily calorific requirements of an adult. (*ILN*)

In the summer of 1847, while millions of Irish people were being kept barely alive by the soup kitchens, the Whig government was making arrangements to close them down. The government had always considered the soup kitchen act to be a temporary measure, lasting only until the harvest of 1847. There was no blight in 1847, nevertheless the Famine continued unabated. Because of the lack of food in 1846, no seed potatoes had been kept to plant for the following year's harvest. Therefore, despite the lack of blight, there was no food to harvest in 1847.

By this stage of the Famine, sympathy for Ireland was wearing thin and the British media reports of the time reflect this 'famine fatigue'. Attacks on Irish landlords and the Irish land system were widespread and, according to the critics, Irish landlords had been so neglectful of their duties that they had created the conditions that led to the Famine.[92] Worse again, they were dumping their evicted pauper tenants on the shores of England, Scotland and Wales.[93]

The relief measures at Lough Hyne under the 1847 Temporary Relief Act spanned two parishes, Creagh and Tullagh. Table Four shows the numbers in receipt of soup in these areas. Over 70% of people in Creagh and Tullagh received relief on the busiest day, demonstrating the high level of dependence and necessity for the relief measures.[94] There were still 916 people on this list in Creagh and 561 in Tullagh when 'the supply of rations ceased'.[95] The last report of the Relief Commissioners notes that during the period of relief:

> The orderly and good conduct of the peasantry and even the people generally, notwithstanding the great influx of paupers into towns, is highly to be commended. All admit that resignation and forbearance of the labouring classes was astonishing.[96]

Table Four: 1847 relief figures for the parishes that included Lough Hyne.

	Population in 1841	Max. number of people given relief in any one day	Date relief started	Date relief finished	No. of people on the list when relief measures stopped
Creagh parish	6415	4864	26 May 1847	12 Sept. 1847	916
Tullagh parish	4742	3531	27 May 1847	2 Sept. 1847	561

Source: Supplementary Appendix to the Seventh and Last, Report of the Relief Commissioners Presented to Both Houses of Parliament by Command of her Majesty, Abstracts District Electoral Divisions, No. 117, Skibbereen Union, Cork County, British Parliamentary Papers, Vol. 8, p. 351.

(ILN)

New Poor Law System

In 1847, the crisis continued and on such a scale that it became known as 'Black '47'. Despite the deteriorating situation, the government officially declared the Famine to be over because of the lack of blight that year. As a result, all relief measures by the British administration in Ireland were ceased. When the soup kitchen scheme was terminated in September 1847, the government resorted to the Poor Law system to give relief to the destitute.[97] The Poor Law Amendment Act would shift the burden of relief completely from the British Treasury on to the Irish landlords and tenants.[98] However, by this stage of the Famine the finances of the landowners of Ireland were in no condition to provide relief to millions of starving people.

An insight into the thinking of the official administration of the time comes from Trevelyan's book, *The Irish Crisis,* published in autumn 1847:

> In the west and south of Ireland ... the owners and holders of land ... had permitted or encouraged the growth of the excessive population which depended on the precarious potato ... [the blight was the hand of God as] ... Supreme Wisdom had educed permanent good out of transient evil.[99]

The Famine was seen to be a judgement sent by God to sort out Ireland's longstanding problems. The way in which the Irish landlords were treated by the British press and parliament during this time displays the telltale features of scapegoating and, with God's judgement added to the equation, it helped to resolve any British middle-class guilt about the mass deaths.[100]

The government decision to throw the whole burden of relief on to Irish landlords, who were already in a crisis state, was a death sentence for thousands of Irish people.[101] The success of the soup kitchens proved that widespread relief was possible, when there was the will for it. However, feeding the poor was not the government's main concern, as its expenditure in Ireland during the period shows. The British Treasury spent a total of £9.5 million on relief efforts during the Famine.[102] The cost of keeping the military in Ireland for the same period was over £10 million, with an additional £4 million spent on the constabulary police.[103] The British administration seemingly prioritised expenditure on maintaining law and order over the provision of relief in Ireland.

In 1847, the British government officially declared that the Famine was over and halted its relief measures in Ireland. The only relief available from the autumn of 1847 was via the workhouse system. These institutions were funded by the ratepayers of the locality, many of whom were in dire financial straits by this stage. All that remains today of the Skibbereen Workhouse are its walls, seen here encircling the current hospital grounds just outside the town in Coolnagarrane townland. Underfunded and grossly overcrowded, this deficient and punitive institution would have been the only place of refuge available to the poor of Lough Hyne.

The sole system of relief from then on was through the workhouses, which were hopelessly underfunded and overcrowded. Skibbereen Union Workhouse, designed to house 800 people, contained 4,221 inmates in December 1848.[104] Even as late as 1850, when A.G. Stark visited Skibbereen he recorded that:

> In the main workhouse and about twenty auxiliaries ... there are upwards of 4,000 paupers fed, lodged and clothed in idleness at the public expense.[105]

The percentage of those in the Skibbereen Union receiving relief was 31.4% in 1847–48, 56.6% in 1848–49 and 22.1% in 1849–50.[106] The drop in the number of smallholdings of less than six acres was a shocking 62.1% between 1841 and 1851 in the Skibbereen Union.[107] The landscape and society of the area were fundamentally changed, including that of Lough Hyne.

Eviction – Disease – Emigration

As the Famine wore on, more and more people fell into rent arrears. The new Poor Law of 1847 included a provision which offered a method of clearing such unwanted tenants from the land. Under the so-called 'quarter-acre clause', any tenant who occupied more than a quarter-acre of land could not qualify for admission to the workhouse.[108] Also known as the 'Gregory clause', because it was proposed by Lord William Gregory, it enabled land clearances by forcing people who were desperate for aid to give up their land. It also deemed the landlord to be liable for the rates of any tenant whose holding had a rateable valuation of under £4.[109] This was another incentive for landlords to clear their land of tenants who were not paying rent. Some of the largest estate clearances in Cork took place in the Skibbereen Union with, newspapers reporting that evictions were more numerous there than in any other district.[110]

As can be seen from the population figures in Table Two, the steepest drop in numbers in the Lough Hyne area was in the townland of Highfield. Robert Delacour Beamish was a middleman on the estate of Wrixon-Becher.[111] In Highfield townland he had 21 families evicted, with a total of over 100 people made homeless in May 1847.[112] The *Cork Examiner* carried extensive coverage of the event, giving a list of the those evicted which included farmers, labourers and the widow Ganey with her seven children whose subsequent fate the reporter poignantly describes:

'Eviction Scene' by Daniel McDonald. (Courtesy of the Crawford Art Gallery.)

> [the agent] ascended the roof and [stripped] off the thatch ... The fever-stricken mother ... followed him for about a mile ... [and] endeavoured to crawl back but ... had no recourse but a ditch, where I saw her this day, apparently lifeless. I imagined she was a corpse ... but discovered she breathed slowly ... and discovered a child dying by her side. [113]

He created a 'sort of shed' with some broken furniture and left her and her child to die.[114] His report of the following week says:

> She expired in the open air, with the exception of the few sticks before mentioned ... her death has occasioned considerable alarm in the locality.[115]

O'Callaghan reports that, on his first visit, he

> Proceded [sic] through the deserted village to where the rest of her family lay ... laboring in all the agony of fever ... a female spectre just risen from fever was bringing water to quench their thirst.[116]

Excerpt from the *Cork Examiner* of Monday evening, 31 May 1847

"The townland of Highfield, in the parish of Creagh, is the property of Robert Dalacour Beamish Esq. of Cork. A few days since these proscribed victims were visited by the Rev. Summerset Townsend and Mr Lovel, agent and under agent to Mr. B., for the purpose of clearing these lands of the tenants. On that day, and some time prior, they succeeded in turning out the following persons with their families:

Daniel Whoulahane, farmer, with six in family.

Thomas Whoulihane, farmer, with six in family.

Michael Whoulahane, farmer, five in family.

Michael Ganey, labourer, three in family.

Widow Burke, five in family,

Denis Cartny, farmer, eight in family.

John Collins, farmer, eight in family.

John Sullivan, farmer, eight in family.

Florence Sullivan, farmer, seven in family.

Florence Carthy, farmer, three in family.

William Leahy, farmer, six in family.

Jeremiah Toomy, labourer, nine in family.

Michael Wholahan, farmer, ten in family.

Tom Croston, labourer, eight in family.

James Murphy, labourer, four in family.

Denis Cahalane, five in family.

Daniel Carthy, five in family.

Widow Donovan, five in family. At the moment of extermination, this ill-fated woman was preparing a little Indian Meal in a pot, which Lovel and Hosford threw out on the dung.

John Collins, labourer, died in the ruins of his own house.

The Widow Regan, four in family, subsequent to receiving notice to quit, had her husband and daughter laid out on the same table.

The Widow Ganey with seven in family.

Disease was the major cause of death during the Great Famine and, even before this catastrophe, the pattern of disease following food shortages was well known.[117] It was during 1847 that famine fever, dysentery and diarrhoea caused most deaths but they also persisted at extremely high levels throughout 1850.[118] An epidemic of Asiatic cholera occurred in 1849, while deaths from measles tripled between 1845 and 1849; consumption deaths doubled between 1846 and 1847 and smallpox deaths tripled in 1849 compared to previous years.[119] But typhus and relapsing fever were the big killers; the latter was prevalent among the poor, while typhus also affected the higher social classes, particularly those who were engaged directly in relief work.[120] Rev. R.B. Townsend, who had visited London with Caulfeild in 1846, contracted typhus at Skibbereen Workhouse and died from it in 1850.[121]

Emigration was another factor in Ireland's population decline, with over 1.2 million people fleeing Ireland between 1845 and 1851.[122] In West Cork, where deaths were high, emigration was relatively low.[123] However, emigration figures from Baltimore port show an exponential increase from 901 in 1845, to 2,122 in 1846.[124] The *Wanderer* sailed out of Baltimore on 23 December 1846 with '113 destitute passengers' and finally arrived in Wales on 1 February 1847, with 26 'men, women and children … in a dying state stretched upon a scanty portion of straw'.[125]

The *Wanderer* report from 'Wretched Condition of Emigrants', *Monmouthshire Merlin*, 6 February 1847. (Courtesy of John Sweeney, Chairman of the 'Wales Famine Forum', publishers of the *Green Dragon*.)

225

£10 REWARD.

THE above Reward will be paid to any Person or Persons who shall give such information to the undersigned, as will lead to the conviction of any COMMANDER of a VESSEL, who shall illegally

LAND ANY IRISH PASSENGERS

on the Coast between Aberthaw and the River Rumney.

By Order of the Board of Guardians of the Cardiff Union,

T. WATKINS,

CLERK.

CARDIFF UNION,
2nd JUNE, 1849.

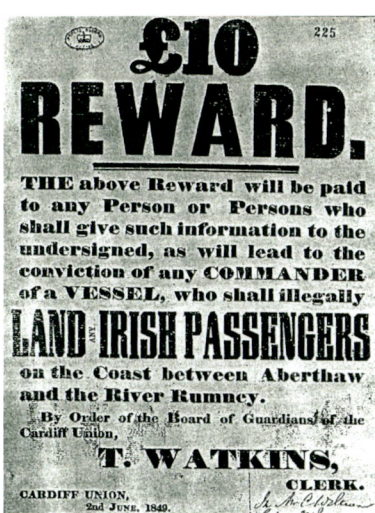

As the Famine wore on, emigrants to Britain who were destitute on arrival and in need of relief were classed as vagrants and deported back to Ireland. As this poster from the Cardiff Union shows, a reward was given for information on ships that landed such desperate migrants illegally.

There were many emigrants who left the ports of West Cork on small ships during the Great Famine. 'Emigrants Awaiting Embarkation West Cork' by Robert Richard Scanlan. (Courtesy of the Crawford Art Gallery.)

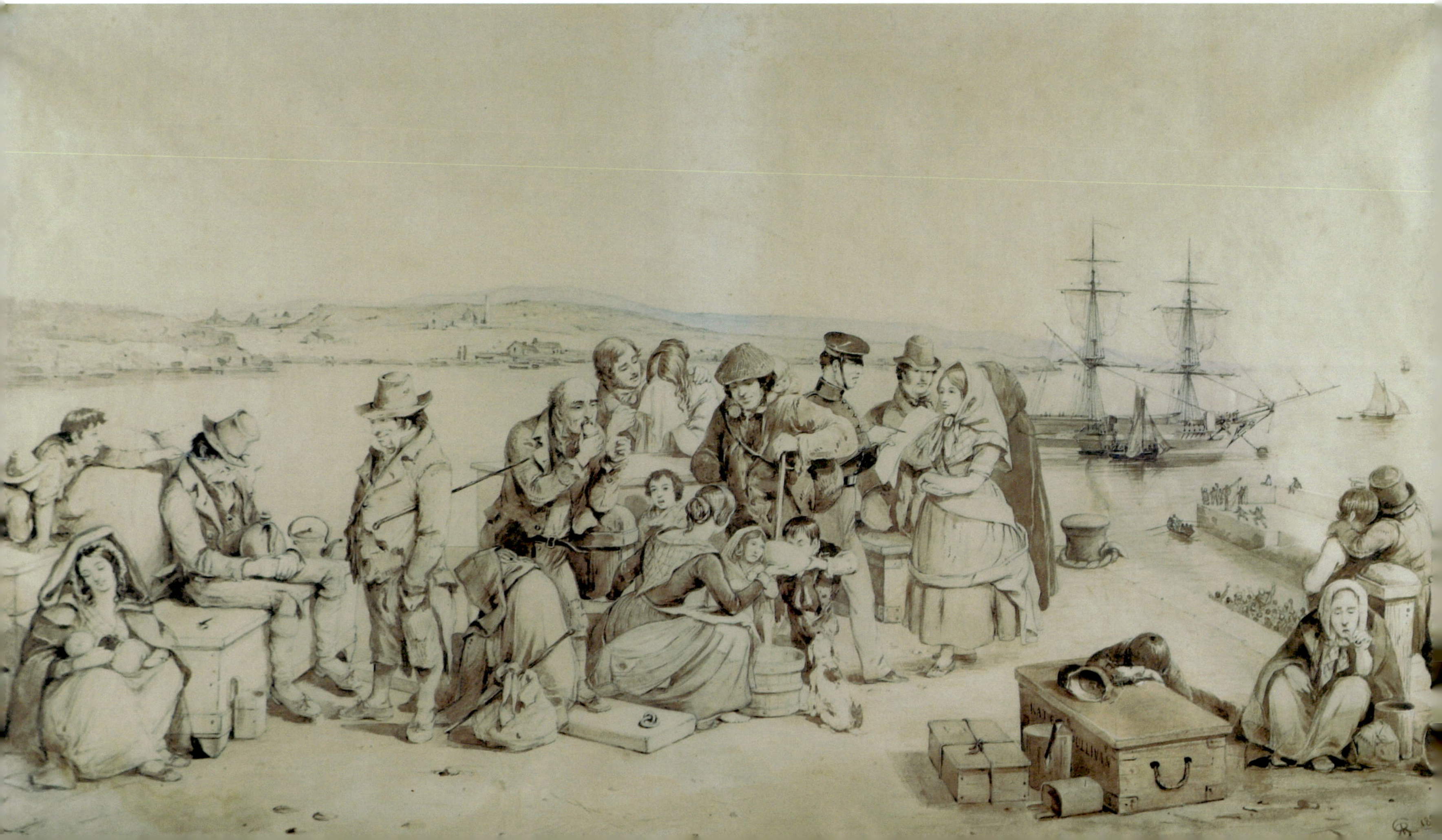

The Effects of the Famine on Lough Hyne

By comparing the 1841 and 1851 census records we can see the impact that the Famine had on the Lough Hyne area (see Table Two). The comparison shows a staggering population loss of over 45%. This figure would be even higher if the increasing birth rate between 1841 and 1844 is factored in (see page 81).

The census records also give an indication of who was worst affected by the Great Famine. The 1841 census shows that 48% of the houses in the Creagh and Tullagh parishes, which included Lough Hyne, were fourth-class houses or 'cabins'. By 1851, a shocking 77% of these were gone. The poor occupants of these houses had few resources in the event of crop failure or distress. They lived close to subsistence level with no surplus money or goods that could be sold. The Census Commissioners of 1851 remarked that 'the population removed from us by death and emigration belonged principally to the lower classes'.[126] The census records show that the worst affected were those who were unable to read or write, reflecting the trend nationally.[127] It was the poorest people, the labourers, who were the most dependent on the potato and lacked the money to buy alternative food. These made up the bulk of the people who died or left Lough Hyne during the Great Famine.

It is impossible to know how much of this drop in Lough Hyne's population is attributable to death, emigration or migration within Ireland. Records to accurately calculate such data simply do not exist. Foynes estimates a figure of between 8% and 25% for emigration in the Skibbereen Poor Law Union overall.[128] A poll exists for six parishes of the Skibbereen Union (not including Creagh or Tullagh) which covers the period September 1846 to September 1847.[129] This found that, while 7,332 people died, only 997 emigrated, which accounts for just 2.5%. This follows the general pattern in Ireland. The destitute simply did not have the means to emigrate. If this correlation were to be applied to Lough Hyne, with its low relative valuation, it would suggest a low emigration rate. Migration within Ireland was certainly a factor too, as 'misery and wretchedness ... flowed into Cork from the western parts of the County'.[130] We can only say with certainty that it was the poor people of Lough Hyne that 'disappeared', however that came about.

This ruin is all that remains today of the pre-Famine village of eighteen houses known as *Bothárin na* 'Barracks' in Ballyoughtera (see page 86).

Table Two shows that the number of people dependent on agriculture dropped by 41% in the parishes encompassing Lough Hyne between 1841 and 1851. This would reflect the changes in the patterns of land ownership in Ireland generally. Plots of under five acres dropped by 25% in the Skibbereen Union between 1845 and 1852; those of between five and fifteen acres dropped by almost 38%, while there was an increase of 63% in holdings of over thirty acres in size.[131] The landscape was utterly transformed.

The evictions at Highfield in 1847 were not the only evictions carried out at Lough Hyne. As the poverty of the area had to be supported, the Poor Rate increased accordingly, giving landlords a further incentive to evict tenants, particularly those with holdings valued at under £4, as the landlord was liable for their rates under the quarter-acre clause.[132] Evictions were regularly carried out in West Cork. Archibald Stark, visiting in 1850, gives us a description of the Lough Hyne townlands of Highfield and Ballinard:

> The landlords, each of whom aims at removing the burden of supporting the poor from his own shoulders … [takes] the roof from the houses … The outcasts either die on the road side or wander to another electoral division … [reducing] the poor-law-rating for his own district … [In] Tallagh [sic] the property of Sir William Beecher [sic], the clearance system has been carried out to an alarming extent … [He] lives quietly on his estate in his mansion, near Mallow … his agent … expected the rent … as if the famine had never been felt … In North and South Ballinard, in the same electoral division of Tallagh [sic]… the clearances have been numerous … [there is] not a soul to be discovered in Highfield, a townland once densely populated.[133]

Who were these poor people that 'disappeared' from Lough Hyne? We have a list of those evicted in 1847, alongside the widow Ganey, but the rest are nameless. Without doubt, many people died while working on the relief scheme at the Rapids in the bitterly cold months of early 1847; however, no documentation exists to record their deaths. From the Baltimore Loan Funds records, we know that Daniel Casey of Ballinard emigrated to America and that Andy Sullivan, a labourer from Pookeen, died in the winter of 1849.[134] The poor people of Lough Hyne were not worthy of note either in life or in death.

The absence of documentation relating to those lost during the Great Famine at Lough Hyne is inexplicably mirrored by a comparable lack of folklore. Despite its catastrophic effect on the area, it seems that the Great Famine was little spoken about afterwards. Perhaps it was just too painful for those who had to live out the remainder of their lives with its consequences. The survivors carried within them the horrors of what they had experienced and witnessed, while the ruined houses all around were constant reminders of lost family and friends. They also had to carry out their mourning at mass graves, where their loved ones had been buried in a way that would have been considered abhorrent, the complete antithesis of normal Irish custom.

The Irish philosopher Edmund Burke says that a society is a continuing conversation between three generations: the dead, the living and those yet unborn. Yet for over a hundred years the Great Famine was followed by a Great Silence in Ireland. It is only in the last few decades that Irish society has really begun to talk about this extraordinary human tragedy. And we can do the same for the people of Lough Hyne. By remembering those who died there during the Famine, and telling what little we know of what happened to them, we can offer them the respect that was so lacking to them in life, and grant them peace.

At Lough Hyne, where so many died within sight of the sea, it seems fitting to remember them with an old prayer in their everyday language: *I líonta Dé go gcastar leo* – 'May they be gathered up in the nets of God'.

Marine Research at Lough Hyne

Lough Hyne has a long association with marine research. The first biological observations were made within the lough in 1886 and research has been ongoing there on an almost continuous basis since the 1920s. It is now one of the most-studied marine sites of its size in the world and was designated as Europe's first Marine Nature Reserve in 1981.

In addition to Lough Hyne's unique hydrography and diverse habitats, its geographical position also contributes to the wide variety of life present within the lough. It contains species from the northern boreal region as well as warm-water Lusitanian, and even Mediterranean, species. Because of its small size and sheltered position, these can be monitored in a safe and accessible environment throughout the year. This 'natural laboratory' has attracted researchers from around the world and there are hundreds of published scientific papers based on studies carried out at the lough. This small lake in West Cork has become known to the scientific community internationally.

Many scientists have returned to work at Lough Hyne year after year, over a period of decades. Today, there are researchers working there who first came to the lough in the 1960s and '70s, as well as students from overseas who are visiting it for the first time. Lough Hyne is a microcosm of the general marine environment and is as 'worthy of examination' now as it was in the nineteenth century when it was first encountered by the scientific community.

| Photos: C. Trowbridge

Lough Hyne's Habitats and Hydrology

Although it is less than one square kilometre in area, Lough Hyne contains a wide variety of marine habitats. These include: the Rapids, where powerful currents travel at up to 3m per second; the Western Trough, which is *c.* 48m deep; a 97m-deep cave on Bullock Island; as well as both sheltered and wave-blasted rocky shores.[1]

The lough also has a number of unique hydrographical features, including an asymmetrical tidal cycle which takes *c.* 4 hours to flow into the lake and about 8.5 hours to drain out. This affects the tidal range, so that the difference between high and low tide is just one metre within the lake, compared to almost 4m in the sea outside. Unlike most other salt-water lakes, it has no significant fresh-water source flowing into it, so it is almost a completely marine environment.

These physical and hydrograpical features contribute towards the wide diversity of marine flora and fauna found within the lake, which include a number of rare species. These can be studied in a safe and controlled environment within Lough Hyne.

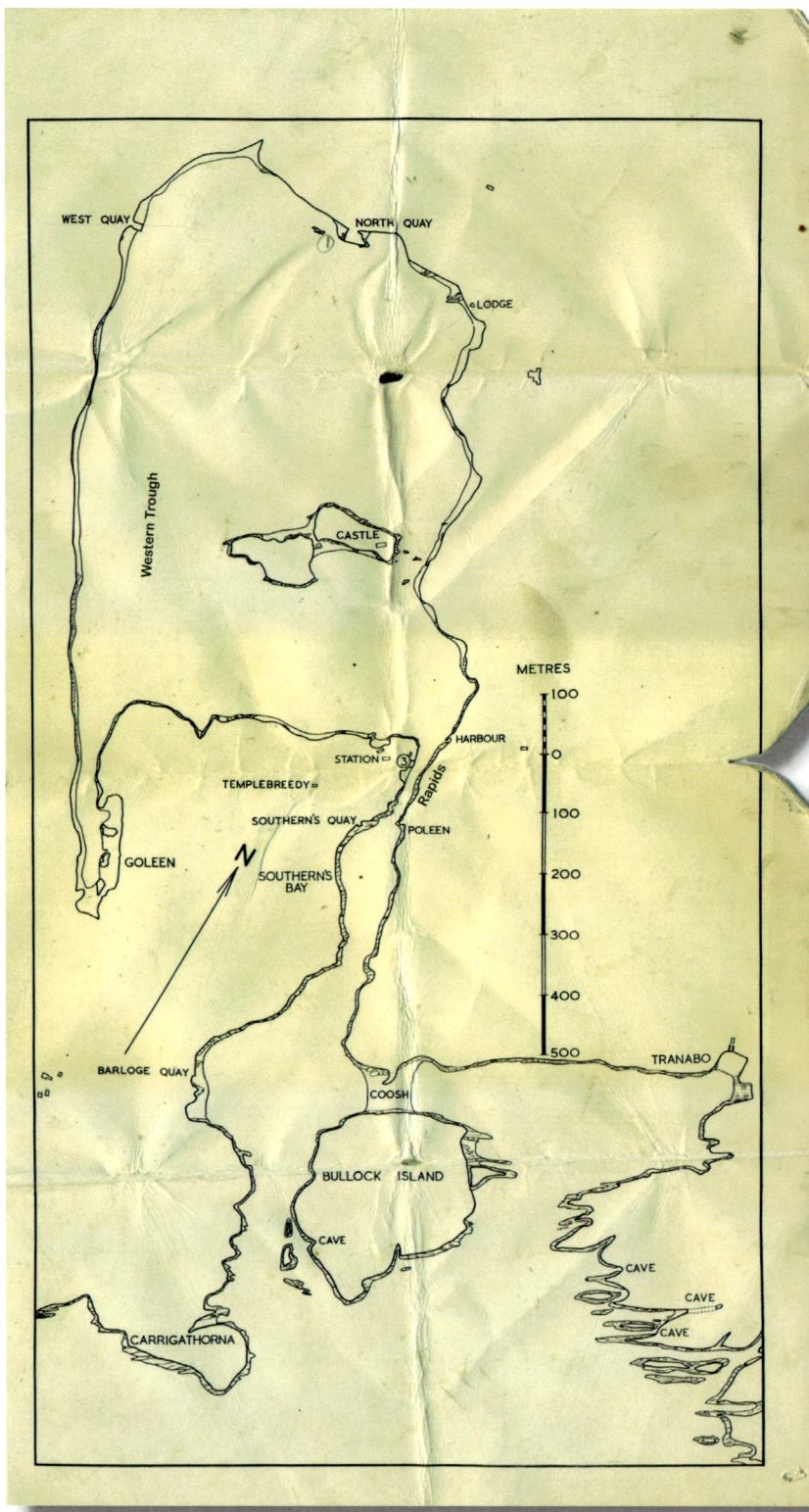

Marine Research in Ireland

The first observations in marine science in Ireland were made in the seventh century on coastal erosion and it was a thousand years later, in the seventeenth century, that the first experimental observations on migrating salmon were recorded.[2] The Royal Dublin Society commissioned some fisheries research in the eighteenth century and, in the late nineteenth century, published on the subject of fish and the fishing industry as well as carrying out surveys.[3] Around the same time, the Royal Irish Academy (RIA) organised a series of deep-sea explorations, one of which included a visit to Lough Hyne.

Sustained systematic marine studies began in 1900 when the national fisheries service was established, which employed W.S. Green and others who had taken part in the RIA cruises.[4] The development and maintenance of the fishing industry was the primary driving force behind this marine research.[5]

In 1908 a group of Irish naturalists set up a committee, with Robert Lloyd Praeger as secretary, to carry out a thorough biological survey of Clare Island, off the Mayo coast.[6] The result, a multidisciplinary study of Clare Island in 1909–11, was the most ambitious collective scientific project undertaken in Ireland up to that time.[7] A total of 8,488 species were recorded and, for the first time, many of the studies focused on the ecology of the area and how the species interacted with each other.[8] Most notable of these studies is the work of Robert Lloyd Praeger and the papers on marine life published by Rowland Southern.[9] Both of these influential men, and others involved in the Clare Island survey, including the research vessel *Helga II*, would later play a part in the research at Lough Hyne.[10]

The studies of hydrography and plankton in Irish coastal waters continued on a considerable scale until the outbreak of the First World War in 1914.[11] However, there were only a few scientists who continued their research through the early decades of the twentieth century.[12]

Over the following decades, work on the marine environment was minimal, with a 'notable exception [being] the study of Lough Hyne'.[13]

Robert Lloyd Praeger was a renowned Irish naturalist, an authority on Irish botany and also recognised for his contributions towards Irish archaeology, geology, ecology, history, travel and zoology. Praeger took part in the Clare Island survey and would later play a role in the establishment of Lough Hyne as a 'biological station'.[14] (Photo courtesy of the RIA.)

Lough Hyne is 'Discovered'

The first recorded biological observations were made within Lough Hyne in 1886 when the paddle steamer, *The Lord Bandon,* was on an RIA dredging expedition along the coast of Cork and Kerry.[15] This was the second cruise, led by the Rev. William Spotswood Green and Professor A.C. Haddon, to explore the marine fauna off the south-west coast of Ireland.[16]

With a team in place and provisions secured, the cruise party set off on 5 July 1886, 'as soon as the garments of civilization were cast aside for those of a more nautical cut'.[17] Working its way from Queenstown (now Cobh), the cruise travelled along the coast, taking shelter in Glandore Bay on the night of 6 July because rough seas had 'disabled' the staff.[18] On Green's suggestion, the party entered Lough Hyne the following day and took specimen samples and depth soundings.[19] When they attempted to leave the lough, the scientists found that they had to haul the boat out by rope through the Rapids against the incoming tide. The final comment relating to Lough Hyne on the expedition's notes states that 'this beautiful lake is worthy of a detailed investigation, both from a physical and biological point of view'.[20]

Standing (left to right): W.S. Green, John Day, J.H. Poole, Sir C.B. Ball and R.L. Praeger; (above) Joseph Wright; (sitting) W.F. de V. Kane.[21]

The RIA 'Dredging Committee' held a meeting in early 1886 where it was decided that Green would have sole control of the boat, crew and commissariat, while Haddon would direct the scientific aspect of the operations. Other scientists and naturalists on the voyage were there to make drawings of the animals, to take soundings and temperature readings and to examine fish for parasites and preserve the samples.[22] (Image courtesy of the RIA.)

(This photo is captioned as 'Deep Sea Dredging Party, 1886' in Praeger's book *Some Irish Naturalists* but it actually features the members of the 1888 expedition. Praeger took part in the later expedition but not the 1886 cruise; however, Green, Ball and Wright participated in the 1886 cruise.[23])

Rowland Southern

The next biological recordings from Lough Hyne were taken in November 1912, when Rowland Southern, of the Fisheries Branch of the Department for Agriculture and Technical Instruction for Ireland, was marooned in Barlogue Creek by foul weather.[24] He spent five days collecting specimens and making observations with an Able-Bodied Seaman and a hand dredge. The collections were so rich that the RIA 'ear-marked the lough for a full survey as soon as conditions should allow'.[25] The outbreak of World War One and the events of 1916 'altered the outlook' and the 'matter was shelved'.[26]

Rowland Southern, who visited Lough Hyne in 1912, is recognised as one of the most thorough investigators of Irish natural history.[27] His report, alongside that of the 1886 expedition, meant that the lough was 'ear-marked' for further investigation by the RIA. (Image courtesy of the RIA.)

The *Helga II* was the fisheries vessel that brought Southern into Barlogue Creek in 1912, where he was 'marooned' for several days. This was the same ship that had been used on the Clare Island survey of 1909–11.[28] Just a few years later, on the outbreak World War One, all scientific work at sea ceased and the *Helga II* was taken over by the Admiralty in 1915.[29] Renamed as the *Helga,* she was re-equipped and fitted with two naval 12-pounder guns to carry out anti-submarine and escort duties on the Irish Sea.[30] In the Republican Rising of 1916, the *Helga* provided military support to the government forces as she fired shells on Boland's Mills, Liberty Hall and the Dublin Distillery from her position on the Liffey.[31] Because this shellfire hastened the end of the Easter Rising, the HMS *Helga* was subsequently the focus of much hatred from the Republican side.[32] (Image courtesy of the RIA.)

Professor Louis Renouf

In 1922, Praeger met Louis Renouf, who had just been appointed Professor of Zoology at University College Cork (UCC). Praeger recommended that Renouf visit Lough Hyne, as it warranted investigation and was within easy reach of Cork city. Renouf first visited the lough in February 1923 during three days of 'incessant rain' and made arrangements to return that Easter, booking the nearest available accommodation in Baltimore village.[33] This was a volatile period in West Cork, as there were still deaths occurring as a result of the Civil War, but this did not deter the English-born professor from planning future excursions.

> In 1922, the Irish naturalist Dr Robert Lloyd Praeger introduced the subject of Lough Hyne to Professor Louis Renouf of UCC. Praeger was a Member of the RIA and would have been aware of Southern's 1912 report on the lough, as the Academy had 'formed the intention of investigating it in detail, as soon as times were normal again'.[34] On Praeger's suggestion, Renouf visited the lough the following February.[35]

During the fortnight of his Easter stay, Renouf secured more or less 'permanent quarters' at Baltimore for the 'summer vacation' and he found 'how ideal the whole district is from almost every biological aspect: marine, fresh-water, terrestrial, agricultural, sociological'.[36] In 1924, a bequest was given by Miss E. Crawford-Hayes for the promotion of biology and Renouf secured part of this from the Governing Body of UCC for use at Lough Hyne. With this funding, in March 1925, he rented a large room in Baltimore for use as a laboratory and 'a really serious start was made'.[37] Renouf walked every day between Lough Hyne and Baltimore carrying his equipment and samples.

Frequent visits by Renouf to the area 'broke down suspicions consequent on the civil war' and Renouf secured short stays at the O'Donovan farm at Lough Hyne.[38] Once 'the shyness of the farmer was overcome', Renouf was able to rent permanent living accommodation at Barlogue.[39] In 1926, permission was granted for the installation of a large packing case 'in a sheltered position alongside the Narrows [the Rapids]' and this was used as a field station, while the headquarters remained at Baltimore.[40]

Lough Hyne's first field station was a packing case 'placed on its side against a stone dyke near the Rapids to act as a field laboratory and store. In it were kept a few essential reagents and vessels. When it was in use, its hinged lid was supported on two columns of large stones and with the upper side provided an open air bench during fine weather [and] protection during rain when we worked face downwards with our upper half in the case'.[41]

The first laboratory at Lough Hyne. In 1928, the Crawford-Hayes fund allowed for the purchase of an 'army-hut type of building', which was fitted out as a laboratory and aquarium at the Rapids on leased land, and an 'intensive study ... was started'.[42] (This hut remained at that site until March 1962, when it was washed into the water by a tidal surge.[43] It was subsequently retrieved by John Bohane and is still used on the family farm today.[44])

In 1928, 'an army-hut [was] fitted out as a laboratory and aquarium alongside the Narrows [the Rapids]'.[45] That same year, following published accounts of his work at Lough Hyne, Renouf was contacted by Professor Tattersall of Cardiff University, who proposed a visit to Lough Hyne. Renouf used this enquiry to obtain further funds from the Finance Committee at UCC and a second hut was erected, with 'essential amenities and equipment', to carry out research at the lake, with another added some years later.[46] Facilities were now in place to establish Lough Hyne as a 'biological station' and, during Easter 1929, Tattersall brought the first students to Lough Hyne.[47]

The First Visitors', Easter 1929: Renouf and Professor W.M. Tattersall, at centre of picture, surrounded by students.[48] Tattersall had worked in Ireland before on the Clare Island survey of 1909–11.[49] His Easter 1931 entry in the Visitors' Book records that 'I am myself so charmed with the station and its wonderful fauna that I have rented a cottage on the shore of the Lough ... [where I hope to] spend a great part of my vacations investigating the varied aspects of the marine fauna of the district'.[50]

Renouf continued to promote Lough Hyne as a research station and carried out a series of lecture tours at British universities in the 1930s to raise awareness about the area.[51] In August 1931, Renouf published a guide to carrying out research at the lough in the *Journal of Ecology* entitled 'Preliminary Work of a New Biological Station (Lough Ine, Co. Cork, IFS)'.[52]

The lecture tours and publication drew many of the eminent scientists of the era to carry out research at Lough Hyne. Some of their work is still being referenced today. For example, Kenneth Rees from Swansea conducted an in-depth study of the seaweeds that has provided a baseline for more recent studies.[53] The 'Visitors' Book' records that researchers from the Universities of Liverpool, Swansea, Aberdeen, Hull, Nottingham, Reading and London worked at Lough Hyne in the 1930s as well as visitors from the Cambridge Botany School and the Temperature Research Station at Cambridge.[54] All record their appreciation of the hospitality of Professor Renouf and his wife Nora, who also played a crucial part in establishing Lough Hyne as a 'marine station'. She helped with the logistics and challenges of working at this remote station and her letters to the researchers show that she provided advice as well as practical help, even providing sheets and bedding for some of the visitors. Renouf's family stayed with him at Lough Hyne every year for a month at Easter and three months in summer. He carried on with his scientific work while the children amused themselves at the lough and they saw each other only at mealtimes.[55]

T. Kenneth Rees visited Lough Hyne in 1930 and 1931 and published three papers on Lough Hyne in the 1930s.[56] His 1930 Visitors' Book entry says that 'A lecture given by Professor Renouf at the University College of Swansea early in 1930, first turned my thoughts to consider a visit to Lough Ine … I shall always remember my stay – the great kindness of Professor and Mrs. Renouf for whom no trouble seemed too great'. His research provided a baseline for more recent studies on seaweeds in Lough Hyne.

Nora Renouf, Louis' wife, played her part in establishing Lough Hyne as a marine station. She spent a lot of time there with Renouf and the children and provided support to visiting researchers. She is shown in the centre of this photo (to the rear) at one of the many picnics of the era. In the foreground are Julian Huxley (wearing glasses) and his wife (with beret), who visited Lough Hyne in 1933. Renouf and Huxley were born in the same year, 1887, and Renouf later referred to Huxley as 'a friend for whom I have a real affection'. Both men strongly supported the theory of evolution. Huxley was later knighted and became well known for his interpretation of science in books, articles, TV and radio. He was the first director of UNESCO and a founding member of the World Wildlife Fund.

Renouf continued to visit and work at Lough Hyne until his retirement in 1953. He died at his home in Cork in 1968.[57] The new UCC laboratory, built in 1987, was officially named 'The Renouf Laboratory' in honour of his work at Lough Hyne. His long association with Lough Hyne is continued today through his family's close ties with the area.

Professor Jack Kitching and Professor John Ebling et al.

The Bristol University Zoological Society was one of the many scientific groups that visited Renouf's 'biological station' in the 1930s. The Bristol group's visit of 1937 was to prove to be an important one for one of its members, John Ebling, who was then a 19-year-old student.[58] This was to be the first of many visits for Ebling, as he continued to return and carry out work at Lough Hyne until 1976.[59]

The Bristol University Zoological Society visited Lough Hyne in 1937 and this was the first visit of many for John Ebling (extreme left back row), who continued to carry out scientific studies at Lough Hyne until 1976. Ebling co-authored many published scientific papers based on studies carried out at the lough over the decades of his research there. Peggy Bowman (second from right, back row) has a site named in her honour at the lough which is known as 'Peggy's mark'.

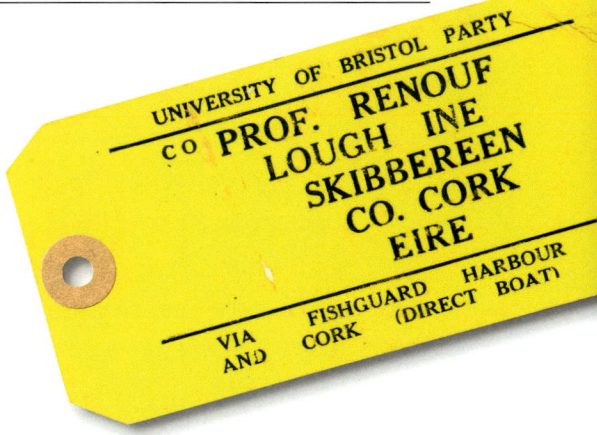

When the Zoological Society returned to Lough Hyne in 1938, a newly appointed university lecturer at Bristol, Dr Jack Kitching, joined the expedition.[60] This was to be the start of Kitching's lifelong commitment to Lough Hyne. He returned annually to the lough to carry out scientific studies up until 1986, only missing the years of World War Two.[61] His move to the University of East Anglia in 1963 saw him make no change in his annual visits to the lough. Kitching and Ebling co-authored, with other scientists, 'The Ecology of Lough Ine' papers, a series of thirty-four scientific papers published over a period of forty years in various journals.[62] Kitching would go on to build two laboratories at Lough Hyne, one at Dromadoon and one at Glannafeen, the latter named in his honour.

Jack Kitching was a 30-year-old newly appointed lecturer at Bristol University when he first visited Lough Hyne in 1938. He continued to return to the lough every year (outside the years of World War Two) up to 1986 and published 34 scientific papers over a period of 40 years based on studies carried out there in association with Ebling and others. He built two laboratories at the lough, now under the ownership of UCC, and one of them is named 'The Kitching Laboratory' in his honour.

The exploration of the Rapids was the prime objective of the first parties to visit Lough Hyne from the University of Bristol. Kitching first recognised the value of the Rapids and its currents for field experiments during his 1938 trip and, at the invitation of a group of students, planned and directed the 1939 studies there. In 1939, Ronald Bassindale, a new member of the Bristol University Zoology Department, joined the group at Lough Hyne, continuing to visit into the 1950s. Richard Purchon, a research student at Bristol, came in 1938 and 1939, and Gerald Walton, then a medical student, also joined the group in 1939.[63] Both Purchon and Walton returned many times to the lough, the latter up to the 1980s.[64] World War Two interrupted the visits (Kitching was awarded an OBE for his work during the period) and it was 1946 before Bassindale, Kitching, Ebling and Purchon jointly co-ordinated the next trip and co-authored the first two published papers on their work at the Rapids.[65] Jock Sloane (another lecturer at Bristol) and Sylvia Lilly were other integral members of the early visits and were co-authors of the 'Ecology of Lough Ine' papers. Mike Sleigh (Bristol University) and Louise Muntz also repeatedly returned to the lough and contributed to many of the papers, as did Liz Davenport.

Kitching selected a group of first-year undergraduate students to go to the lough annually as part of the research team. While there, these students worked together as a group and formed strong friendships, many of which lasted for many years. Kitching and Ebling involved the students in the planning stage of the experiments at the lough, as well as their execution. The design of an experiment might involve many hours of planning and debate before a final version would be agreed upon and the students felt responsible and involved in the work. This practical grounding in experimental studies meant that Lough Hyne was an excellent training ground for these young scientists. Many of the people who worked there as students have since gone on to excel in their specific fields of science.[66]

Many of those who came to Lough Hyne as students went on to excel in science. Malcolm Penny, shown here with his wife Mary in 1964, is now a zoologist, well known for his ornithological fieldwork on Aldabra and the Seychelles. He went on to lead scientific expeditions to Aldabra and the Seychelles in the Indian Ocean and also travelled to Africa, India and the Arctic. He acted as a conservationist for the Wildfowl and Wetlands Trust in England and, since 1994, has worked as a freelance writer for television companies like the BBC and the ZDF. Another example is Professor Geoffrey Parker FRS, also a student at Lough Hyne in the early 1960s, who is now Chair of Zoology at Liverpool University, Fellow of the Royal Society, holder of the Darwin Medal of the Royal Society and is considered to be one of the greatest living theoreticians in evolutionary biology. Lough Hyne has proved to be an excellent training ground over the decades of research and many eminent scientists around the globe today spent time there in their student years.[67]

Pumping air to the diver was an arduous task generally given to students. Ronald Bassindale (Bass), shown here at the Rapids, is speaking to the diver on the telephone, while an unidentified student operates the pump in the background.

The Research Work of Kitching et al.

Marine ecology involves studying the factors affecting the distribution and abundance of marine organisms and the Lough Hyne Rapids offered the opportunity to isolate one ecological factor – the current. The task of these early studies, therefore, was to carry out quantitative surveys of organisms, to measure the currents, and to relate the two.[68]

Currents are very important in marine ecology because many marine species are sedentary as adults, catching their food from the surrounding water, but are motile as larvae; that is, they depend on currents to bring them food and oxygen as well as distribute their larvae. Current is also an important factor in sediment distribution because, when the current slows, particulate matter begins to drop out of the water column, with coarser, heavier material falling first and finer material later. So the sediment type on the lake floor is related to the current regime at that point and the distribution of many marine species is related to sediment type. Some species cannot survive because sediment blocks their feeding structures, while others are tolerant and can survive in areas of lower current. Therefore the presence of certain community types at a particular place is related to currents.[69]

Measuring water speed was one of the early undertakings carried out by Kitching et al. This 1950 photo features Ronald Bassindale (left) with Jack Kitching (to rear), Sheila Lodge (back to camera) and Pat Scholes (recording) at the Rapids using a Pitot tube and manometer.[70] (Note the 'Irish Free State' stamped on the wooden butter boxes at left of photo.)

As the research continued, the scientists found that, in addition to the direct mechanical effects of current in the Rapids on the distribution of organisms and the indirect effects on sedimentation, the water temperature and water chemistry, which also influence the flora and fauna, could be affected by the currents.[71] This led to further experiments measuring sediment and also chemical and physical conditions, including temperature. The research was expanded from the Rapids area in the early 1950s, as the scientists measured current flow and water temperatures to see how the inflow and outflow of the Rapids affected the movement and mixing of water in the whole lough.[72]

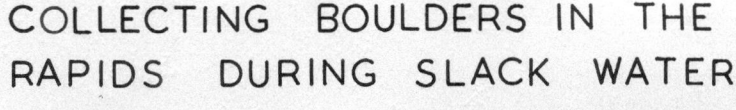
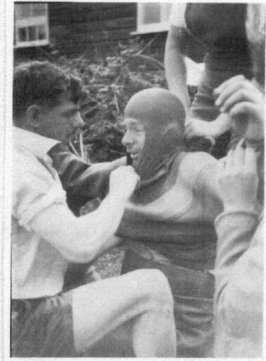

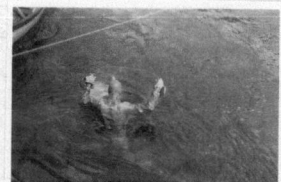

Collecting boulders and counting the species that lived on and under them was a way of determining what survived in the different areas of the Rapids. Jack Kitching's 'leaflet' on boulder collection shows him in the 'frog man suit', while Dick Purchon assists him.

As the work progressed, Kitching, Ebling et al. found that, although a number of species were distributed in relation to current, this effect could be indirect, since the overriding determinants were often predation, grazing and other interactions between marine species.[73] For example, mussels (*Mytilus edulis*) were only found at the Sill area of the Rapids, where the current is fastest. The reason was because their main predators, the velvet swimming crab (*Liocarcinus puber*) and the green shore crab (*Carcinus maenas*), cannot withstand the current at the Sill and therefore the mussels survived there.[74] The researchers concluded that, despite the fact that mussels were physiologically capable of surviving in a wide range of marine environments, the effects of predation confined them to areas such as exposed rocky coasts and vertical surfaces in still waters, etc.

The other studies carried out by Kitching, Ebling and the many other scientists who worked with them over the years covered species distribution in relation to shelter and wave exposure. Here, again, Lough Hyne and the surrounding area was the perfect 'laboratory', with both sheltered and wave-washed shores. They also studied the effects of zonation; i.e. the restriction of each species to its own tidal zone area. Changes in physical conditions, such as exposure to the air, are important in determining this zonation, but biological interactions are also of paramount importance, and zonation patterns can be altered by such factors as wave action, aspect and substrate.[75]

The researchers also studied the importance of biotic factors in influencing zonation by examining the effects of predation, grazing and competition on the communities.[77] They analysed the ecological interrelationships between different organisms, examining the ways in which these organisms contributed to food webs, and the cyclical and causal changes in the populations of organisms within these communities.[78] Kitching was among the first marine ecologists to experimentally manipulate seaweeds and invertebrates to tease out the causal factors of observed patterns of marine biota.[79] While not the first to carry out such work, he would be considered to be one of the leaders in this field of experimental research.[80]

Stripping *Paracentrotus,* Curlew Bay, 1959. The scientists cleared sea urchins from a part of the lough to see what effect this would have on algae and the general community structure in the area.[76]

Jack Kitching was probably the first professional biologist to undertake undersea scientific research using a diving helmet [(in 1931 near Plymouth)].[81]

These studies brought Lough Hyne to prominence worldwide and many eminent marine biologists in Britain and Ireland have spent time researching at the lough.[82] One of them, Professor Trevor Norton, first visited the lough in 1964 as a research student from Liverpool University. This algal specialist continued to carry out work at the lough until 1977, concentrating particularly on seaweeds. He co-authored some of the 'Ecology of Lough Ine' papers, including those covering the biology of the cave on Bullock Island and the dynamics of the Western Trough. He later wrote a book about his experiences at Lough Hyne, *Reflections on a Summer Sea,* which was published in 2001. This is a memoir of his time spent there with Kitching, Ebling and others and covers both the scientific and social aspects of his visits to Lough Hyne.

John Ebling modestly said that their 'work ... kept in parallel with, and perhaps on occasion heralded, developing ideas of behavioural interactions in ecological relationships' and he credited Kitching's contribution by saying 'most of the ideas ... emanated from him in whole or in part'.[83]

Kitching and Ebling both worked at Lough Hyne over long periods, 48 and 39 years respectively, and it became a huge part of their lives. They made many friends locally and maintained these friendships even after they no longer returned to the lough. Many of the scientists who came with them over the years also returned repeatedly to the lough and all appear to have enjoyed their time there.[84] From their writings, it is clear that Lough Hyne meant more to them than just a place to carry out research.

Kitching and Ebling wrote that their 'memories of Lough Ine are many and varied: groping by boat in the darkness of a sea-cave, and the crunch of the swell on the shingle at its head; fishing at night off the coast, with the Fastnet light flashing on the horizon … gannets in flight circling and searching, and one after another hurtling into the water after fish; the curlews crying over the undisturbed waters of Lough Ine in the very early morning, and the soft whir of the nightjars at evening. And always in our ears, like the echo in a shell, is the subdued roar of the Rapids.' [85] (Photo: R. O'Regan.)

UCC and Lough Hyne 1950s–1987

After Renouf's retirement, his successor Professor Fergus O'Rourke put forward proposals for development of the 'Lough Ine Biological Station'.[86] However, lack of funding alongside the low number of students of zoology resulted in very little UCC involvement at the lough in the 1950s.[87] Renouf's assistant, Marjorie Murphy, who had helped him 'particularly in his experiment of founding a Marine Biology Station at Lough Ine', retired in 1965.[88] The UCC huts deteriorated, with two destroyed by a storm in 1962 and the remaining laboratory unusable by 1976.[89]

It was the latter part of the 1960s before UCC staff and students began to return to Lough Hyne. Dr Gerard Walton, who had first visited Lough Hyne as part of the 1939 Bristol party, took up a post in the Zoology Department at UCC in the late 1960s.[90] Máire Mulcahy, who had also visited Lough Hyne as a student, started to act as a demonstrator and accompanied O'Rourke, Walton and UCC students on Easter field trips to Lough Hyne, with the Crawford-Hayes fund providing funding for the trips and the necessary equipment.[91]

The UCC link to Lough Hyne continued into the next decade as the lough once again became the focus of research. Dr Alan Myers came to UCC in 1972 and supervised the first PhD students whose studies were wholly based on research carried out at Lough Hyne.[92] Mark Costello, a PhD student under Myers, published several papers on studies carried out at Lough Hyne and later helped to set up a monitoring scheme there with Dr Colin Little from Bristol.[93] From the early 1980s, UCC's involvement at the lough intensified further, with the Crawford-Hayes fund being used for the purchase of equipment. Two demonstratorships a year were offered to postgraduate students who were carrying out research at the lough, the first consistent commitment made by UCC to Lough Hyne since Renouf's retirement in 1953. A bibliography of literature relating to Lough Hyne was compiled by Keith Wilson and published in 1981.[94] Also supported by the Crawford-Hayes fund, this was the first bibliography that collated both published and unpublished documentation relating to the area.[95]

UCC reiterated its commitment to the lough when President Tadhg Carey approved funding for a new laboratory at Lough Hyne, which opened in 1987. This was named the 'Renouf Laboratory' in recognition of Renouf's significant contribution to research at the lough. That year Kitching also signed over ownership of his land at Lough Hyne to the college and all three laboratories there became the property of UCC.[96]

Máire Mulcahy brought groups of UCC students to Lough Hyne in the 1960s. She is shown here (in pink) in the boat with John Bohane of Dromadoon and the students, some of whom were nuns dressed in their full habits.

5 - Marine Research

Lough Hyne | *From Prehistory to the Present*

Pictured at the official opening of UCC's Renouf Laboratory in 1987 (left to right): Noel Treacy (government Minister), John and Philomena Bohane, Alec Gibson (Department of Fisheries), Mrs Kitching, Prof. Jack Kitching, Prof. Tadhg Ó Ciarda (UCC President), Prof. Máire Mulcahy (UCC), Alan Myers (UCC), Michael Kelleher (UCC) and Ruth McDonnell.

Designation as Europe's First Marine Nature Reserve

The suggestion that Lough Hyne should be protected as a marine reserve was first made by the Cork branch of An Taisce in 1975.[97] An Taisce, also known as the National Trust for Ireland, was founded in 1948 with similar objectives to other National Trusts worldwide. Its first president, Robert Lloyd Praeger, had introduced Renouf to Lough Hyne in 1922.

An Taisce became interested in Lough Hyne in 1973 when accounts of extreme exploitation of its fish stocks by divers were brought to its attention.[98] The Cork branch of the organisation was active in conservation efforts at the time and had a full-time employee and branch office facilities to enable its work.[99]

A board member of An Taisce, Dr Conor Duggan, approached Kitching with the suggestion that the lough should become a reserve.[100] Duggan had first encountered Lough Hyne as a student of zoology in UCC. Kitching was enthusiastic about the idea and agreed to produce a report on the scientific value of Lough Hyne to support the proposal. This was published in 1975 as part of the An Taisce report entitled 'Lough Ine, Ireland's First National Marine Research Park?'.[101]

AN TAISCE STATEMENT ON LOUGH INE

The Cork branch of An Taisce some time ago issued a formal statement of their reasons why Lough Ine should be designated as a Marine Research area. It reads—

"An Taisce, Cork, seeks to have Lough Ine and its adjacent waters i.e., The Rapids, Carrignathorne and Barloge Creek, designated by the Authorities (i.e. Cork County Council and/or the Government) as a special Marine Research Park.

"Lough Ine offers the marine biologist an unique opportunity to investigate the marine ecosphere because of its special topographical features. For instance (a) its tidal pattern is such that one can make a daily examination of organisms in Lough Ine which under normal conditions are only accessible at the short period of low water at the fortnightly spring tides; (b) for a marine body of water, it is very compact; (c) its catchment area is so small that the water and conditions obtaining in the Lough are almost totally marine.

"The Lough also contains many unique associations of plants and animals. Since 1925 several marine biologists have availed of this opportunity, and many scientific papers have been produced regarding the effects of the conditions on the flora and fauna in the Lough, as well as dealing with the interactions among the organisms themselves. Thus, this 'giant marine aquarium' (Preager) has been the site of 50 years continuous scientific investigations, and has thereby become an important source of marine ecological information. In that context, the area is of international importance.

"Mindful of the many new pressures to which marine waters are now subjected, e.g., offshore drilling, mining, dumping, etc., An Taisce sees a great need to develop our knowledge of this largely unexplored realm with its own special natural fluctuations, so that the consequences of man's interference with the natural order can be assessed and controlled.

"Having regard to the great deal of information already gathered from Lough Ine in this respect, An Taisce urges the relevant Authority (ies) to embark on a graduated programme of action, guaranteeing that the area will continue thereby, to be the site of original marine research. Initially, this would involve (I) A prohibition against any future building around the Lough; (II) A further prohibition against some water sports on the Lough, and (III) A need to guard against any further additional exploitation of the fish and other marine stocks, either for research orgastronomic purposes. Later on, more ambitious schemes could be contemplated including, say, the use of educational displays, foundation of field courses, organising and financing research, and so on. One must stress again, however, that the initial activity as outlined above will cost nothing, but it will ensure that the scientific work on the natural fluctuations in animal and plant populations will continue."

An Taisce, Cork, is anxious to further the above aim for the reasons stated, and will work with, lobby and assist any local interests who share the same desire to have Lough Ine designated as a Marine Research Park.

SOUTHERN STAR, SATURDAY, NOVEMBER 8, 1975. 15
SPECIAL 'STAR' REPORT

[102]

Because of changes in legislation and planning laws, the 1975 report was revised and reissued by An Taisce Cork in 1979. The revised report was put before the board of the Wildlife Advisory Council (WAC), which accepted the proposal.[103] The WAC would have been aware of Lough Hyne, as Dr Máire Mulcahy, by then a lecturer at the Zoology Department of UCC, was a board member of the Council. The Chairman of the WAC, Arthur Went, also knew Lough Hyne. The Department of Agriculture and Fisheries had been carrying out research at the lough for some years and Went was the Scientific Advisor to the Fisheries Division of this government department at the time. The WAC made a recommendation to the government that the lough should be designated as a marine reserve.[104]

Dr Dan Minchin, a marine biologist with the Department of Agriculture and Fisheries, had been working at Lough Hyne since 1975 studying the biology of the young stages of the scallop *Pecten maximus*. This was an initiative carried out in order to understand how they might be cultivated. Minchin then went on to work with the Forest and Wildlife Service, the department which would subsequently take control of the Lough Hyne Marine Reserve, in order to further the reserve proposal.[105] A seminar to 'provide a forum for the discussion of the future of Lough Ine' was held in Skibbereen in August 1976 at which the proposal gained local support.[106] Further open meetings were held in Skibbereen, Old Court and Baltimore and the by-laws for the reserve were based on concerns raised at these meetings and follow-up discussions with interested parties.[107]

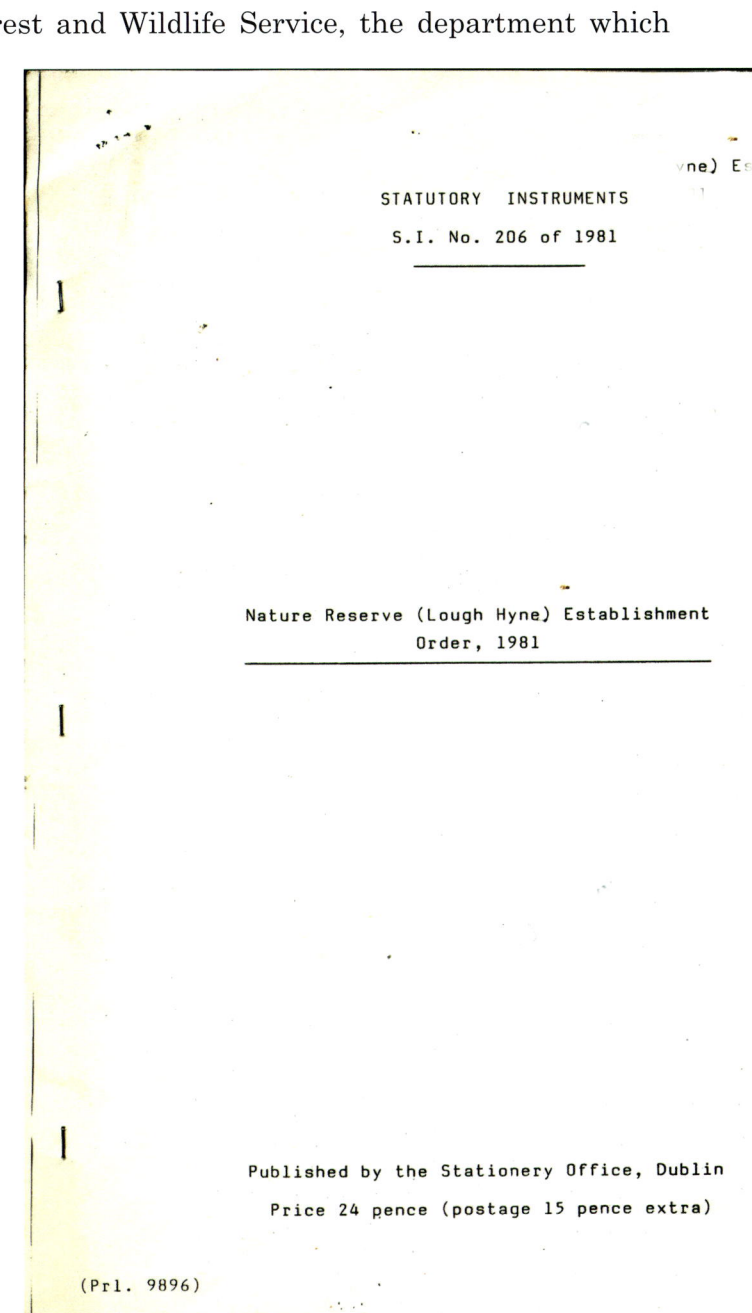

Lough Hyne was established as a marine reserve in June 1981 by the Minister for Fisheries and Forestry, and it came under the ownership of the Irish State.[108] The WAC made further proposals regarding a management plan for the reserve which was subsequently developed by Minchin and Dr Martin Speight.[109]

Declan O'Donnell was appointed as Lough Hyne's first Conservation Ranger in 1984 by the Forest and Wildlife Service. He was Ranger at Lough Hyne until 2004 and took a great interest in the area. He was responsible for ensuring that the legislation relating to the reserve was adhered to and he was helped in this regard by the appointment of John and Neily Bohane of Dromadoon as Wardens of Lough Hyne. As the first Ranger, his role involved interacting with universities, fishermen, local people and other users of the lough in order to monitor and control activities within the reserve area under the new regulations. This was an ongoing process and later involved applying a reviewed management plan which regulated scuba diving at the lough in response to a sudden increase in demand. The greater Lough Hyne area came under increased protection when it was listed as a Special Area of Conservation (SAC) in May 1998 under the European Union's Habitats Directive. O'Donnell's successor, Patrick Graham, took over the role of Conservation Ranger in 2004 and the Lough Hyne Marine Nature Reserve is now managed by the National Parks and Wildlife Service on behalf of the Irish State.[110]

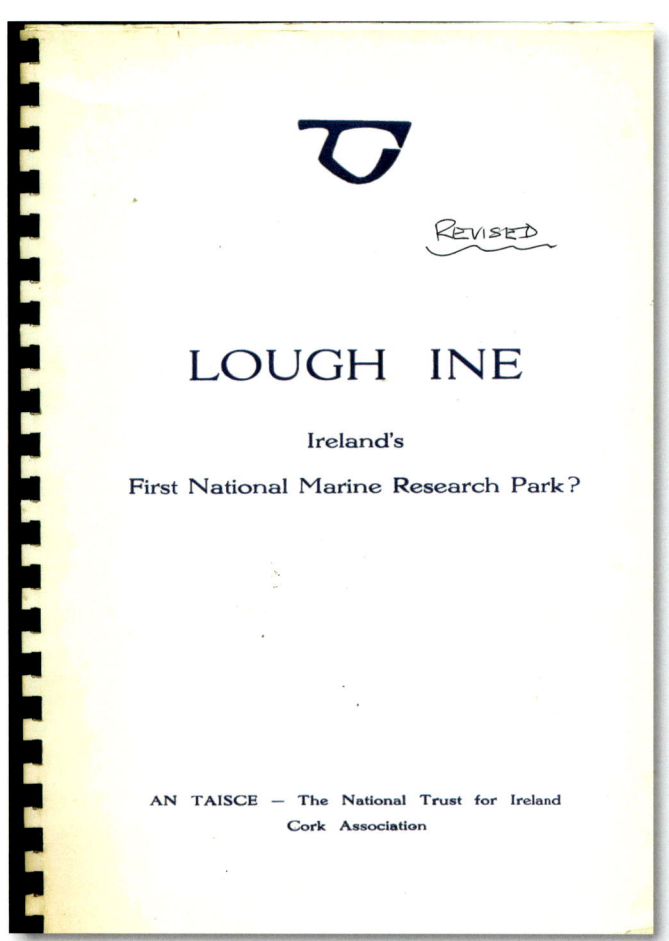

The revised 1979 An Taisce Report, which was ultimately successful in getting Lough Hyne designated as a Marine Nature Reserve.

Dr Colin Little et al.

Dr Colin Little of Bristol University first visited Lough Hyne in 1979 as Kitching's guest and, since then, he has worked at the lough every year, with Penny Stirling and others.

> Little, on his 1979 trip. 'As anyone who has been to the lough will understand, I fell in love with the place immediately, and went home to rave about it. While I was lying in the bath trying to remove the dust of three days' travel, Penny pointed out to me that I had gathered not just one, but a whole family of extremely well-fed ticks. Even that didn't deter me from going back and dragging everyone I could with me.'[111]

Little, Stirling and a team of helpers studied the movements of limpets for sixteen years and published five papers on the subject between 1985 and 1999.[112] Most of the study team were members of the Severn Estuary Research Group, at Bristol University. They discovered that, while some populations of limpets feed at night out of water, others feed during the day under water. Individual limpets can move as far as a metre when feeding, but they all return to their own individual 'scar' on the rock before the tide turns. Why different populations have different feeding habits remains a mystery, though Little et al. have suggested some possible reasons.[113]

> 'Quite soon after we started working at the lough, we began studying the feeding habits of limpets. Initially we used sensors glued to the limpet shells that could detect the rasping noises made by them as they fed. So with a pair of headphones we could recline on the shore and hear each individual rasp ... Later still, we became more sophisticated in recording how limpets moved around, glued magnets to their shells, and fixed little switches on the rock nearby to tell us when they were "at home" or not. There was a system of wires running up the rock, gathered together on mini-pylons, to a data logger in a waterproof box. John Bohane, rowing past in a boat full of shrimp pots, nicknamed the whole affair the Lough Hyne telephone exchange.'[114]

In addition to their study on limpets, since 1990 Little, Stirling and other scientists who have come with them to Lough Hyne have been making annual recordings of the shore flora and fauna at the lough, monitoring any changes or the presence of invasive species. This provides valuable baseline data and also facilitates the work of other scientists, who, as a result of this work, are able to locate the relevant study species within the lough. Dr Cynthia Trowbridge joined their monitoring team in 2001 and now brings American students to work with her annually using a grant from the US National Science Foundation as part of the IRES programme (International Research Experiences for Students).[115] Trowbridge and the students participate in Little's shore surveys and also carry out 'snorkel surveys' of the entire shoreline of the lough. Trowbridge has also been working on introduced (also known as 'alien') species within the lough since 2001. This is a new challenge to the marine environment and she has identified and catalogued the alien species now present in the lough, including the Japanese seaweed *Sargassum muticum* and *Codium fragile*. Rob McAllen and Little are also part of the IRES project team.

Year	Colin Little	Penny Stirling	Gray Williams	David Morritt	Alison Miles	Linda Teagle	Graham Pilling	Cynthia Trowbridge
1979-85	7	6						
1986	+	+	+	+				
1987	+	+	+	+				
1988	+	+	+					
1989	+	+	+	+		+		
1990	+	+		+				
1991	+	+	+	+	+			
1992	+	+	+	+	+	+	+	
1993	+	+	+		+	+	+	
1994	+	+				+	+	
1995	+	+		+	+	+	+	
1996	+	+	+	+	+	+	+	
1997	+	+	+		+	+	+	
1998	+	+	+	+		+	+	
1999	+	+	+	+	+	+	+	
2000	+	+	+	+	+		+	
2001	+	+			+			+
2002	+	+			+		+	+
2003	+	+			+		+	+
2004	+	+						+
2005	+	+			+			+
2006	+	+					+	+
2007	+	+					+	+
2008	+	+		+			+	+
2009	+	+					+	+
2010	+	+					+	+

Little's team members over the years included researchers who now work for the Environment Agency, University of London, Trinity College Dublin, Secretariat of the South Pacific, University of Essex, University of St Andrews and the University of Hong Kong. Currently, Little and Stirling work with Dr Cynthia Trowbridge of the Oregon Institute of Marine Biology.

Little also supports the scientific studies at Lough Hyne in another practical way. In the 1920s, Renouf divided the lough into different sectors so that work could be referenced to a specific area. In the 1950s, Kitching used yellow paint to mark these defined sectors and set up monitoring sites within them. Little took over the job of maintaining these sector markings from Kitching and has clearly identified the monitoring sites, using steel markers and yellow paint as indicators. He checks the markers annually and renews worn ones as necessary. These markers facilitate the work of other scientists in establishing the locations of study areas and the presence of species. Because they have been in existence for almost a hundred years, areas that are referred to in older scientific papers can still be referenced to an exact location within the lough today. Little's work ensures that this consistency applies on an ongoing basis.[116]

Colin Little has checked and renewed the markers that define the monitoring sites within Lough Hyne on an annual basis for over 30 years. These sectors were originally established by Renouf in the 1920s and Kitching later marked them with yellow paint. Little's work in renewing them with paint and steel markers means that there is consistency in the defined study areas within the lough.

Like the group that first came from Bristol in the 1930s, Colin Little and Penny Stirling have returned to the lough over a long period of time. In the early years, they stayed in the Kitching Laboratory and maintained many of the rituals established by Kitching and others before them. They have a deep affection for the lough and have developed strong friendships in the local area. Their commitment to Lough Hyne has encouraged many others to join their work over the decades and now a new wave of students are coming to the lough, this time from America, to form part of the survey team.

The Biology of Rocky Shores by Little and Kitching was published in 1996, the year Jack Kitching died. A second edition of this book, which includes studies carried out at Lough Hyne, was published in 2009 and was co-authored by Little, Gray Williams and Trowbridge.

UCC and Lough Hyne – 1990s to Today

In 1996 Dr Dave Barnes was appointed as Research Coordinator for Lough Hyne by UCC.[117] A lecturer in zoology, Barnes supervised a number of his students' studies at the lough on a variety of topics, including plankton, sponges and starfish. During his time as Coordinator, access to the Renouf laboratory, then the primary base for UCC work at Lough Hyne, was facilitated by the installation of a new pontoon and dock, and a modern boat, a RIB, was purchased.[118]

In 1999 Máire Mulcahy retired as Professor of Zoology at UCC and was succeeded by John Davenport, a marine biologist who had previously been Director of the Marine Biological Station Millport in Scotland. Davenport had personal access to sustained funding from the Crawford-Hayes Trust and used it for several years to support research at Lough Hyne. He also led a successful bid in 2000 to draw down substantial funding for UCC environmental research from the government's Programme for Research in Third Level Institutions (PRTLI2). This included support for Lough Hyne research by himself, Barnes and a newly appointed researcher, Dr Anne Crook. Barnes conducted much work on sponges, while he and Davenport also studied the dynamics of zooplankton with a PhD student (Kate Rawlinson) in the lough, demonstrating that such plankton avoided the depths of the Western Trough in summer. Crook, a behaviour specialist, demonstrated with her students that 'hatting' behaviour by purple sea urchins (a process by which they place pieces of seaweed on their upper surfaces) was at least partially to avoid damage by UV radiation. Crook also oversaw the updating of the recirculation facilities of the John Bohane Laboratory. Crook took over as UCC's Lough Hyne Coordinator when Barnes moved to the British Antarctic Survey in Cambridge in late 2001.[119]

When Crook left UCC in 2003, a UCC lecturer, Dr Rob McAllen, was appointed as the Lough Hyne Research Coordinator and he still supervises the work of current UCC postgraduate students today.

In 2006, McAllen secured a grant from the Heritage Council to repair erosion to the western wall of the Rapids, the same structure that had first been built as a Famine relief scheme in 1847. (Photo: R. McAllen.)

With further funding from UCC, Cork County Council and the National Parks and Wildlife Service, the project was completed in the autumn of 2006 under the supervision of UCC. (Photo: R. McAllen.)

Since 2005, McAllen and others have also engaged in raising public awareness about the lough by participating in annual Heritage Week events at Lough Hyne, which are organised in conjunction with Skibbereen Heritage Centre. The 'Touch Tanks' event attracts large crowds each year and provide a mechanism for interaction between the marine scientists and the people of the locality.

From 2003 to 2006, a PhD undertaken by Mark Jessopp examined larval exchange of zooplankton between Lough Hyne and the sea outside as part of a cross-border project with Rob McAllen, Mark Johnson of Queen's University and Tasman Crowe of University College Dublin. Jessopp went on to investigate the increasing problem of eutrophication, a term used to describe the enrichment of water by nutrients which results in an accelerated growth of algae and other forms of plant life. This study of this emerging problem in the marine environment was carried out in Lough Hyne under funding provided by the Environmental Protection Agency between 2008 and 2010. This built on an earlier study by Johnson carried out in the early 1990s, which utilised nutrient sampling carried out by Declan O'Donnell.[120]

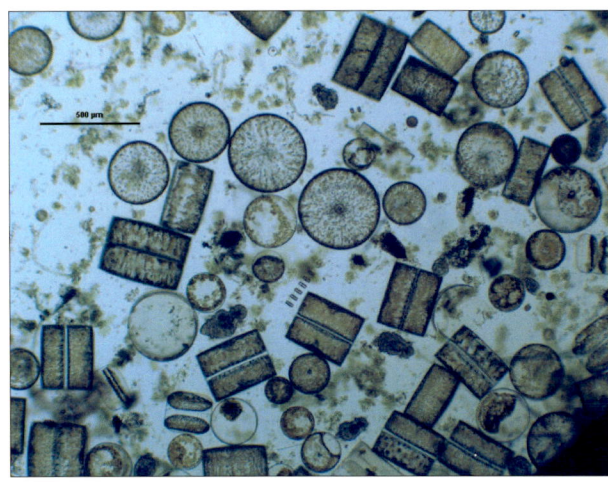

Jessopp's 2008–10 study found a considerable increase in nutrient levels in the lough over the previous decade, resulting in phytoplankton blooms, otherwise known as 'red tides'. This phenomenon is not limited to the confines of Lough Hyne. Increased nutrient levels in the open waters adjacent to the lough suggest that this increase is part of a wider southwestern coastal issue. Lough Hyne, with its limited inflow of freshwater, is an ideal place to monitor these changes, especially as there is accurate baseline data to build upon.[121] (Photo: M. Jessopp.)

In 2009, McAllen, Davenport, Karl Bredenieck of 'Remote Presence' and Declan Dunne of the Coastal Marine Research Centre at UCC published the findings of a two-year study which examined the seasonal dynamics of animals and their movement in and out of the deep Western Trough during thermocline formation and break-up.[122] The thermocline is an annual event in the Trough and occurs when differences in water temperature mean that warmer water 'sits' on the deeper cooler water below. As the water ceases to circulate, oxygen fails to reach below the thermocline level and causes mortality in the sedentary animals beneath. Mobile animals, for example prawns, move to the warmer oxygenated water while making feeding raids below the thermocline level to feed on the dead and dying species. This primary study, which also examined the rapid recolonisation of the Trough after the thermocline break-up, formed the basis for several subsequent in-depth follow-up studies.

Lough Hyne @ 30 was a UCC-led conference held in Skibbereen in 2011 to mark Lough Hyne's 30th anniversary as a marine reserve. McAllen headed up the team that ran the conference in June 2011. This two-day event was the second conference on Lough Hyne, with the first held in UCC in 1990. McAllen compiled a bibliography of publications relating to Lough Hyne, which featured in the *Lough Hyne Marine Reserve @ 30* conference booklet.[123] This covered papers from 1991 to 2011, with some omissions from earlier bibliographies.[124] In addition to Wilson's 1981 compilation, a bibliography of publications featured in the publication of the proceedings of the 1990 conference in Cork, *The Ecology of Lough Hyne*. This was compiled by Mark Costello and Mark Holmes and covered the period 1982 to 1990 as well as some omissions from the 1981 bibliography.[125]

To commemorate Lough Hyne's 30th anniversary as a marine reserve, Skibbereen Heritage Centre, which houses the Lough Hyne Visitor Centre, published a pictorial history of the marine research at the lough entitled *Lough Hyne: The Marine Researchers – in Pictures* by Terri Kearney.

Other Scientists at Lough Hyne

There are many other researchers who have worked at Lough Hyne over the years, who are simply too numerous to mention individually. The researchers who visited in the 1930s covered a wide spectrum, from zoology and biology to botany and meteorology, and included some of the eminent names in science at the time.[126]

Kitching worked with many other scientists at Lough Hyne in the latter years of his time there. Little first came as his guest in 1979 and Kitching also supervised students who subsequently took an interest in the lough, including Vivien Thain, a PhD student who spent several summers at the lough working on snails and urchins.

Simon Thrush first came as a PhD student of Kitching's and worked at the lough with another PhD student, John Turner. Turner later returned to the lough several times with a large research diving team from Bangor University. Another diving team, this one from Bristol University, returned to the lough many times and collaborated with Kitching to produce a paper on Whirlpool Cliff in the 1980s.[127] Julian Partridge, a member of this Bristol diving group, would later act as co-editor with Alan Myers, Colin Little and Mark Costello in the publication *The Ecology of Lough Hyne*. This was the proceedings of the first conference on Lough Hyne, held in UCC in September 1990. Mark Johnson studied, for his PhD, the plankton of Lough Hyne in the early 1990s under the supervision of Mark Costello and this work established that there were differences in productivity and phytoplankton populations between the lough and the open sea.[128]

Lough Hyne has long been a focus of attention from marine biologists around the world, drawing in specialists who have visited, often frequently, to study their speciality and who have provided such a wealth of background information, such as Professor Mike Guiry (algae), Dr Julia Nunn (molluscs) and Dr Bernard Picton (sponges and sea slugs).[129] Dr Ruth Ramsey has been studying barnacles in Lough Hyne for many years, at first with Myers and later with Davenport and McAllen.[130] Dr Mark Holmes from the National Museum of Ireland has been carrying out research on crustaceans at Lough Hyne since the 1970s, often using his underwater light trap to catch the smaller animals, and he still works at the lough today.[131]

There are a number of other scientists who have worked, and continue to work, at Lough Hyne. Professor Tony Hawkins first visited the lough in 1962 as a student from Bristol University. After a career in fisheries research, Hawkins returned to work at Lough Hyne in 2007 with his wife Sue, who had also first visited there as a student from Bristol. They now make several trips to the lough annually with other scientists. Thanks to Lough Hyne's growing international reputation, over the last three years alone, staff and students from institutions in the USA, Italy, Spain, the UK and Norway have worked at the lough as part of their team. After their initial visit, all of these international scientists have returned again to work at the lough, or else expressed a wish to do so. The work of Hawkins et al. involves monitoring the movements, behaviour and sounds made by fish, using underwater television, sonar and underwater listening devices.[132] This work has only been possible because of the unique knowledge base and conditions available at Lough Hyne.[133]

Professor Tony Hawkins and his wife Sue first visited Lough Hyne as students from Bristol University in the 1960s and later married. They now return to the lough several times a year to carry out research, bringing other international scientists with them to study the behaviour and sounds of fish, using TV, sonar and underwater listening devices. Hawkins' interest in sound levels in the lough is motivated by concern over the impact of man-made noise on the marine environment, especially with the increasing development of offshore oil and gas installations and the advent of offshore windfarms and tidal generators. Lough Hyne offers a very quiet environment, isolated from sources of man-made noise, where the only sounds are natural and made by the animals living there, and so is an ideal location for his work.[134] (Sue's painting of the 'Gleann' road at Lough Hyne features on the back cover of this book.)

The marine environment at Lough Hyne is as worthy of investigation today as it was when it was first 'discovered' by scientists in the nineteenth century. There is now comprehensive baseline data, compiled over decades, about the marine flora and fauna of the Lough Hyne Marine Nature Reserve, which is particularly relevant now as invasive species begin to become established and eutrophication levels increase.

Lough Hyne will face these and other future challenges under the management of the National Parks and Wildlife Service (NPWS), which monitors and controls activities within its environs. With the co-operation of the general public, UCC and the scientific community who work there, this unique marine environment will be available as a research station to successive generations of scientists. No doubt, like those before them, many of these future researchers will play a part in the lough's conservation and protection.

Cynthia Trowbridge brings students from the US to Lough Hyne each year under the International Research Experiences for Students programme, which is grant-aided by the US National Science Foundation. Trowbridge and the students participate in Little's shore surveys and also monitor the invasive species now present in the lough.

However, as Lough Hyne is under the ownership of the Irish State, it belongs to us all and it is up to each and every one of us to ensure that it is protected. As we have seen, Lough Hyne has been utilised and enjoyed by man for millennia. We are simply its current caretakers. The marine reserve has been given statutory protection but the greatest safeguard is the effect that this 'magic world of another law' has on practically everyone who encounters it. Lough Hyne is a place that lingers in the heart. This, it might be said, is what grants it the best protection and will, hopefully, ensure its conservation for the enjoyment of generations yet to come. We owe them that pleasure.

A Brief Introduction to the Organisms That Live in Lough Hyne ...

... and what the scientists know about them

by Dr Colin Little & Dr Cynthia Trowbridge

After nearly a century of scientific research in the lough, there is a wealth of information about the animals and plants that are found there. However, it is only in the last sixty years or so that the science of ecology has tried to uncover the ways in which these organisms interact: what eats what, what determines where each species lives and reproduces, why do populations change radically in size, and so on. Here we try to provide a little insight into how these factors determine the variety of communities found in the lough's different habitats.

The Rocky Intertidal Zone

This habitat is perhaps the region most familiar to non-scientists: patches of seaweeds alternate with 'bare' rock on which the commonest animals are limpets, barnacles and mussels. Before the 1940s, it was thought that the distribution of seaweeds was mainly governed directly by physical factors such as wave action, but then field experiments showed that it was the feeding activity of limpets, mostly *Patella vulgata* (Fig. 1), that determined whether or not seaweeds formed their intertidal forests. Limpets are 'lawn-mowers of the sea' and graze on both the microscopic algae that coat rocks and on the juvenile stages of seaweeds. Limpets can move surprising distances when grazing, and the marks of their grazing teeth often stand out as little rows of scrapings; on a quiet night you can hear them scraping! When limpets are in the ascendant, the rock is 'bare', allowing barnacles and mussels to settle.

Fig. 1. The common limpet, *Patella vulgata*, occurs on most rocky shores. Individuals have a home 'scar', to which they return after foraging.

In cycles of many years, limpets may then be reduced in numbers, and the seaweeds take over: perhaps the commonest of these in the lough is the bladderwrack, *Fucus vesiculosus* (Fig. 2).

Fig. 2. The bladderwrack, *Fucus vesiculosus*, is a brown seaweed common on the low shore. The paired bladders help keep the alga upright during high tide; during low tide, the wrack collapses onto the rocky shore.

There are several species of barnacles in the seaweed-free areas – sedentary crustaceans that feed by means of feathery legs combing the water for microscopic plankton. Most of these barnacles are native – some species more tolerant of warm conditions and others preferring cold – but the most prevalent now is an Australasian species, *Austrominius modestus* (Fig. 3), which arrived in the lough in the 1980s and currently dominates most available rock surfaces.

Fig. 3. The introduced acorn barnacle, *Austrominius modestus*, can be identified by four lateral plates encasing each animal rather than the six plates encircling the native barnacles.

Mussels are also filter-feeders, sucking in tremendous volumes of water and straining this through their delicate gills. The mussels have flourished in the lough in recent years and form a dense band on the lower shore, especially where the rocks are steep, as well as covering the floor of the Rapids. There are two species in the lough, the commonest being *Mytilus edulis* (Fig. 4).

Fig. 4. The mussel *Mytilus edulis* gapes its two shells or valves open to feed on microscopic plants in the water column. It pumps water in through one opening and out of the other, using the rhythmic beating of tiny little hair-like structures covering the gills. Thus, the gills are used not only for respiration but also for feeding.

The community on the rocky shore is not, however, self-contained: predators from outside the community take advantage of the rich harvest of animal flesh available. In the winter, hooded crows, *Corvus corone cornix*, forage for mussels and winkles, then drop them at selected sites to smash open the shells. At high tide, crabs such as the common green shore crab, *Carcinus maenas* (Fig. 5), invade the rocks searching for limpets that are not firmly clamped down and prise them off using their pincer-like claws; empty limpet shells lying upside-down can often be seen when the tide has retreated.

Fig. 5. The common green shore crab, *Carcinus maenas*, has been introduced to temperate shores around the world. On European shores, however, this crab species is native to rocky shores, mudflats and shallow subtidal habitats. (Photo: Brittney Dlouhy-Massengale.)

Intertidal Gravel Beaches

These have attracted very little interest from researchers because they have a relatively low species diversity. However, they provide a haven for species such as the edible winkle, *Littorina littorea* (Fig. 6), thus providing a convenient food supply for crabs and hooded crows. In recent years, these gravel beaches have been invaded from outside the lough by another native species of snail, the top shell, *Osilinus lineatus* (Fig. 7), which is now a regular member of the lough's fauna.

Fig. 6. The large, edible winkle *Littorina littorea* is an ecologically important grazer that occurs at high densities in areas of the lough.

Fig. 7. The large top shell *Osilinus lineatus* is a warm-water or 'southern' species; its northward expansion in Europe may indicate climatic warming.

The Shallow Subtidal Rocks

Here there is a much greater diversity of species than on the rock faces that are exposed to the air twice a day. Until recently, the most obvious animal in the shallows was the purple sea urchin, *Paracentrotus lividus* (Fig. 8), but this species, which has in the past shown extraordinary fluctuations in numbers, has declined dramatically since the early 2000s. This urchin is the subtidal equivalent of the limpet, grazing voraciously on the fine seaweeds that settle where they are never exposed to the air.

Fig. 8. The purple sea urchin, *Paracentrotus lividus*, is common in intertidal rockpools on western Irish shores; in Lough Hyne, the species dwells on and under rocks, although it has recently become uncommon. Its presence is often noted by areas on rocky shores that are grazed clear of seaweed.

Now that the urchins are rare, these delicate seaweeds have become dominant in the summer, though they are usually ripped away by autumn gales. Other, larger seaweeds, such as the brown algae *Cystoseira foeniculacea* and strapweed *Himanthalia elongata* (Fig. 9), have also taken advantage of the freedom from grazing, and have spread around the lough more than ever before.

Fig. 9. The bushy feather wrack, *Cystoseira foeniculacea*, and strapweed, *Himanthalia elongata*, are large, native brown seaweeds in the lough.

Some seaweeds, however, have actually decreased in abundance in recent years. *Codium fragile* ssp. *fragile* bloomed amazingly back in the 1920s and covered large areas of the lough. It then fluctuated wildly and is now rare – perhaps fortunately, for it is now known that this species is an alien, originally from Japan. Its native relative, *Codium vermilara* (Fig. 10), is now quite common and spreading.

On the under-sides of rocks there is a dense community of sessile animals: sponges (Fig. 11), sea squirts, bryozoans, hydroids (Fig. 12) and tube-dwelling worms form an almost continuous cover, while some tubeworms such as *Bispira volutacornis* (Fig. 13) are visible from above. Many of these animals consist of numerous small individuals that form colonies and exist by filtering tiny prey from the water. Some, such as the lantern sea squirt *Clavelina lepadiformis* (Fig. 14), are spectacular. In fact, the large *Ascidia mentula* Ascidiella (Fig. 15) is particularly striking, with its vibrant red-coloured body lying under or on the sides of rocks. Other animals, such as the sponges, form masses that are red, orange, grey, blue, yellow, or even black or startling white. Suspension and deposit-feeding brittle stars dwell under the rocks, snaking their five delicate arms (Fig. 16) around and often shedding them when disturbed, much like a lizard dropping its tail.

Fig. 10. The seaweed *Codium vermilara* forms dark-green clumps, particularly along the west shore of the lough. A major consumer of the alga is a sap-sucking sea slug, *Elysia viridis*; the slug ingests the alga's chloroplasts and stores them in its own tissues, where they continue to photosynthesise for weeks to months. The sea slugs derive energetic benefit from the captured chloroplasts and, therefore, have been named 'leaves that crawl'.

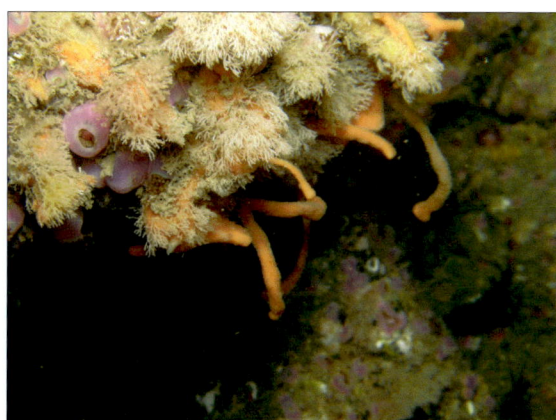

Fig. 11. The high diversity of suspension-feeding sponges, sea squirts and bryozoans is one of the striking aspects of the lough: they form dense carpets under rocks, attached to seaweeds and shells and anchored to all hard surfaces, including ropes, buoys and boat hulls.

Fig 15. The large red sea squirt, *Ascidia mentula*, is abundant in the lough in recent years, particularly on the western shore and the south-western corner of the lough near the Goleen. This large animal is not only brilliantly coloured but also it often has many small, striped mussels living within its body wall, protected from their predators.

Fig. 12. Hydroids are delicate colonies of individuals that share a common gut. These amazing colonies have a life cycle where the colonies typically release small jellyfish (medusae) into the water column. Although related to larger, saucer-like or cannon-ball shaped jellyfish, the hydroid medusae are typically thimble-shaped.

Fig. 13. The lough contains many species of segmented worms, including tubeworms such as *Bispira volutacornis*. The crown-like tentacles are used for feeding; they have eyespots that sense light and dark, so the worms will snap back into their tubes after a shadow passes over them (as a predator defence mechanism).

Fig. 14. (Shown opposite.) The lantern sea squirt, *Clavelina lepadiformis*, forms delicate clumps on the sides of rocks. Of all the invertebrates (i.e. animals lacking a backbone), these small animals are most closely related to vertebrates. (Photo: Brittney Dlouhy-Massengale.)

Fig. 16. There are many species of brittle stars within the lough; they vary in size, colour and behaviour. In fact, at least one species broods its young within specialised pouches in the central disc.

This is an ideal environment for slow-moving predators, and the large, orange nemertean *Paradrepanophorus crassus* (Fig. 17) can be quite common. Here the very mobile animals are abundant too: shrimps and prawns (Fig. 18), gobies, and larger predators such as crabs like squat lobsters *Galathea* sp. (Fig. 19), *Cancer pagurus* (Fig. 20) and *Necora puber* (Fig. 21), the latter often giving a frightening display when disturbed, arms wide and the whole body raised in 'attack' mode or nestling in a paired embrace (while the male waits to mate with the female). Larger predators like the dogfish (catshark), *Scyliorhinus canicula* (Fig. 22), lurk in the shallow subtidal, often hiding in caves during the day and foraging only at night.

Fig. 17. The large orange nemertean, *Paradrepanophorus crassus*, is a warm-water species that is currently increasing in the lough. The worms form delicate membranous tubes under the rocks, including those where the purple sea urchins used to dwell.

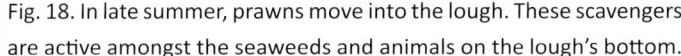

Fig. 18. In late summer, prawns move into the lough. These scavengers are active amongst the seaweeds and animals on the lough's bottom.

Fig. 19. Squat lobsters, *Galathea* sp., are shy but brilliantly coloured denizens of the lough. They occur on and under rocks in the day but can actively swim through the water.

Fig. 20. *Cancer pagurus*, commonly known as the edible crab, is a nocturnal predator of animals dwelling on the sea floor.

Fig. 22. The small-spotted catshark or lesser-spotted dogfish, *Scyliorhinus canicula*, is frequently seen within the lough. Male and female catsharks dwell in separate subtidal caves but individuals are occasionally seen resting in shallow seaweed beds near the shore or swimming through the Rapids. (Photo: Brittney Dlouhy-Massengale.)

Fig. 21. The red-eyed devil crab, velvet swimming crab or lady crab, *Necora puber*, is abundant within the lough. Pairs of crabs are often seen with the male (top animal) holding the female (bottom crab), waiting for her to moult, at which time he copulates with her. (Photo: Brittney Dlouhy-Massengale.)

The Rapids

This area of the lough was the first to be studied by scientists, who tried to carry out ecological experiments in the field – as opposed to experimenting within their laboratories as others had done. Here the dominant physical factor is rapid water flow, and this determines to a great extent what can live in the Rapids. This flow provides an even better supply of food and oxygen than on the subtidal cliffs, and the fauna underneath boulders is extremely rich. Rare sea slugs are here, together with many small snails that are rare elsewhere and dense colonies of bryozoans, hydroids and sponges.

Long fronds of the kelp *Laminaria digitata* rise in the water, and turn over when the tidal current through the Rapids changes direction. Another kelp ally, furbelows *Saccorhiza polyschides*, also forms large forests, with stiffer stipes (stalks) that stand upright at low tide. The blades of both species are covered in a fascinating mosaic of bryozoans (sea mats). Both seaweeds are less common than they were a decade ago, and between the plants now are sheets of large mussels, *Mytilus* sp., together with armies of predatory starfish *Marthasterias glacialis*. (Fig. 23a)

Fig. 23a. The spiny starfish, *Marthasterias glacialis*, comes in a variety of colours and sizes. Although this predator most commonly has five tapering arms, many individuals in the lough have six to seven arms. (Photo: Brittney Dlouhy-Massengale.)

Subtidal Cliffs and the Deeper Rocky Subtidal

This is the realm of more big seaweeds such as the sugar kelp, *Saccharina latissima*, and recently of the immigrant Japanese seaweed *Sargassum muticum*, which has a record of blanketing rock communities and smothering them so that other species die out. The major grazer in this region is the large sea urchin *Echinus esculentus* (Fig. 23b), which has powerful scraping and biting jaws capable of removing sessile invertebrates as well as kelp itself.

The diversity of the sessile invertebrates is extraordinary: conditions for them are ideal, because currents continually bring new food and oxygenated water and sweep away sediment that might otherwise settle and clog their delicate filtering mechanisms. So there are record numbers of sponges and many filter-feeding molluscs such as saddle oysters, bryozoans, sea squirts (Fig. 15) and so on. Perhaps the most colourful examples are the jewel anemones, *Corynactis viridis* (Fig. 24), which can be emerald green, red or orange.

Fig. 23b. The edible sea urchin, *Echinus esculentus*, feeds on kelp, forming a sizeable population near the Rapids. This species is considered 'near threatened' in the IUCN *Red List of Threatened Species*; the internal skeleton, or 'test', is often used as a lampshade. (Photo: Brittney Dlouhy-Massengale.)

Subtidal cliffs are also havens for a variety of mobile species. Fish such as wrasse use holes or caves in the cliffs to hide during the day, and other species use the same holes at night, reminiscent of a time-sharing arrangement. Conger eels, *Conger conger*, (Fig. 25) and lobsters, *Homarus gammarus* (Fig. 26), on the other hand, tend to maintain holes strictly for themselves. Other predators, like the starfish *Henricia sanguinolenta* (Fig. 27), are more likely to remain in the open day and night.

Fig. 25. Conger eels, *Conger conger*, lurk in many caves and amongst piles of rocks. Although generally nocturnal predators, they are occasionally seen near the top of the Rapids or elsewhere in the lough. (Photo: Brittney Dlouhy-Massengale.)

Fig. 26. The European or common lobster, *Homarus gammarus*, dwells in caves within the lough. Although usually nocturnal, the lobsters are occasionally seen in deep water near Whirlpool or the island. (Photo: Brittney Dlouhy-Massengale.)

Fig. 27. The starfish *Henricia sanguinolenta* is native to both North Atlantic and North Pacific Oceans. This species, often brilliantly coloured red to purple, is found in deep water within the lough.

Fig. 24. (Shown opposite.) Jewel anemones, *Corynactis viridis*, form extensive areas of brilliant colour in areas of high water flow in the lough. The tentacle tips end in a ball-like structure filled with stinging cells that help these sit-and-wait predators stun and capture their small prey.

Soft Bottoms

Because of its shelter, Lough Hyne has large areas of subtidal soft bottom – mud, muddy gravel, and empty shells. Here there are innumerable burrowing invertebrates such as the polychaete worms, bivalves and burrowing sea anemones. Resting on the mud surface there are often scallops, *Pecten maximus*, their eyes peering out around the rim of the shell valves (Fig. 28).

Fig. 28. Many scallop species occur within the lough; the great scallop, *Pecten maximus*, is often camouflaged by sediment and/or sponges. When the two shells gape open, the delicate sensory 'feelers' extend out and highly developed eyes are visible.

With such a rich food source, it is not surprising that it is here that lurk some of the largest invertebrate predators. Perhaps the commonest is the spiny starfish, *Marthasterias glacialis* (Fig. 23), which reaches diameters of over 30 cm in the lough. This species specialises in consuming bivalves, although it will take snails, polychaetes and even sea squirts. It is not restricted to soft bottoms, and juveniles are found under shallow subtidal rocks. More colourful, and usually only found at depth, is the starfish, *Luidia ciliaris* (Fig. 29), brick orange and a predator, mainly of other echinoderms such as starfish and brittlestars.

Fig. 29. The seven-armed starfish *Luidia ciliaris* is found in shallow to deep water. It is most common on soft sediments, but juvenile specimens are frequently seen on subtidal rocky shores in the lough. (Photo: Brittney Dlouhy-Massengale.)

Saltmarshes and Shallow Mud

Saltmarshes are restricted to the Goleen, and parts of the Island. They have little 'marine' fauna or flora but do provide a habitat for the glasswort, *Salicornia* sp., and a small amphibious sea slug, *Alderia modesta*.

Shallow mud, also common in the Goleen but patchy elsewhere, is visited regularly by grey mullet, *Chelon labrosus* (Fig. 30). This fish feeds on the microscopic algae that form a green/brown coating on shallow mudflats, and its feeding marks – pairs of oval-shaped scoops – can be seen regularly.

Fig. 30. Grey mullet, *Chelon labrosus*, feed by scraping micro-algae off the mud surface. They can frequently be seen in shallow water, cruising in groups or basking in the sun. (Photo: Brittney Dlouhy-Massengale.)

The Open Water

At the bottom of the food chain in open water are microscopic algae, the phytoplankton, which have recently become more abundant because their nutrient supplies have been enhanced by fertilisers in the run-off from the land and from sewage outfalls around the coast of Ireland. Usually these algae are invisible to the naked eye, but occasionally they form a 'bloom' of one particular species and colour the water. *Noctiluca* (Fig. 31) is the most spectacular, forming what are called 'red tides' when the bloom is blown in to the shore. The small animals that feed on the phytoplankton are the zooplankton, with a fascinating diversity, from the larvae of bottom-living invertebrates to those that live their whole life in the water column.

The zooplankton provide food for small fish such as the gobies, which live around the edge of the lough, and the sprat, *Sprattus sprattus* (Fig. 32), which form enormous shoals offshore. Attacking the sprat shoals are predatory mackerel, *Scomber scombrus*, (Fig. 33), which sometimes cause the sprat to leap from the water, attracting gulls that dive in as opportunist predators.

Fig. 31. Red tides are formed by high-density populations of the micro-algae called dinoflagellates, which contain reddish pigments. *Noctiluca* is one common dinoflagellate taxon in the lough and, when abundant, produces spectacular bioluminescent displays, particularly when disturbed by the oars or paddles of boaters.

Fig. 32. Sprat, *Sprattus sprattus*, form dense shoals and these can often be seen by looking down through the water as they head around the edge of the lough. Herons and seals hunt these fish in the summer. (Photo: Brittney Dlouhy-Massengale.)

At the top of the food chain are fish-eating birds and mammals. There is a great variety of birds that depend upon the fish, shrimps and other invertebrates in the lough. Cormorants are always present, and herons stand on duty around the lough waiting to pounce on fish in the shallows. Gulls are often seen in a feeding frenzy when the mackerel drive the sprats to the surface, but can also be seen on the shore, attacking and dismembering crabs or pulling off the arms of starfish.

Seals are common and sometimes haul out on the Pobbles. Dolphins had never been seen before 2012, but then the appearance of Kris and her mother showed that the Rapids is no bar to their entry. Otters are very shy but are occasionally seen.

Fig. 33. Predatory mackerel, *Scomber scombrus*, frequently chase the shoals of sprat, which may leap into the air to avoid escape but in so doing often attract crowds of gulls that feed on them.

Miscellany of Lough Hyne

Formation of Lough Hyne

How this landlocked lake with a *c.* 50m-deep trough, encircled by hills including Knockomagh at just under 200m high, came to be formed is 'puzzling', according to the Irish naturalist Robert Lloyd Praeger.[1] Several geologists and geographers have presented different hypotheses about its creation.

What is agreed upon is that it cannot have been formed by marine erosion, as no rivers flow into it or through it.[2] Formation by rock solution is also not a possibility, as the local rocks are durable Old Red Sandstone and not soft porous limestone.[3]

One theory is that it came about as a result of tectonic activity and the movement of the earth's crust. Mitchell and Whittow both support this view, which says that the lake was formed by subsidence and erosion along a faultline.[4] However, this suggestion has been rejected by many hard-rock geologists who say that they cannot see any evidence of a fault movement on the surrounding rocks.[5]

The other hypothesis as to its formation says that it was formed by glacial erosion.[6] This suggests that, when the sea level was up to 100m lower than at present, ice entered the basin from the north-north-east (where the Highfield road now runs) and met a stream of ice of east-north-easterly origin (emerging where Lough Hyne House now stands), forming the northern basin.[7] The effect of the two streams of ice converging produced a 'corkscrew' of ice which gouged out the Western Trough.[8]

That Mitchell and Holland, two of Ireland's foremost geologists, cannot agree on its origin and disagree about the issue in more than one paper suggests that we may never definitely know how it was formed.[9] As Mitchell expressed it, 'the mystery remains unsolved', regardless of the expert attention focused on it.[10]

What we do know from Buzer's pollen analyses study is that it was originally a fresh-water lake until around 4,000 years ago.[11] Rising sea levels after the last Ice Age caused salt water from Barlogue Creek to find its way into the lake via the Rapids. Buzer also found evidence of forest clearances at the lake around the same time as the marine transgression, indicating the presence of Neolithic man.[12]

Holland offers a controversial suggestion as to how the Rapids might have been formed when he poses the question 'is it too imaginative to suggest that Neolithic man might have had a hand in trying to introduce the sea and all its richness into this sheltered basin?'[13] This hypothesis has not been supported by any of the other scientists who have examined the lake, but it is, nevertheless, an interesting concept to consider. The western wall at the Rapids was constructed in 1847 to aid the passage of boats in and out of the lough, and was rebuilt in 2006. Perhaps early man might have had the same idea and, at the very least, could have cleared the Rapids as much as was possible to enable the free flow of water?

Local folklore offers yet another alternative as to how the lough was formed. It seems that two giants had a fight. One grabbed a handful of earth to throw at the other, forming the lough as he did so. His middle finger gouged out the Rapids and the island was left by his palm. He threw the earth at the other giant and this, in turn, formed Knockomagh Hill.[14]

Perhaps we will never definitely know how Lough Hyne was formed, but the theories and stories about it are interesting in any case.

Lough Hyne House

The structures shown here on the Carbery Estate map of 1788 may have been a hunting lodge of Lord Carbery. This is the first map to show a building on the site where Lough Hyne House now stands today. [15] (Image courtesy of the Dean and Chapter of St Fachtna's Cathedral, Rosscarbery, Co. Cork.)

Lord Carbery leased land in Ballyisland townland to Daniel McCarthy in 1834. McCarthy is said to have built the original 'graceful-looking villa' there, which was then known as Lough Ine Cottage.[16] McCarthy was a wealthy man, described as 'the largest ratepayer in the Union' and the owner of a porter brewery in North Street, Skibbereen which was 'far and away the most valuable property in the whole Skibbereen district'.[17] McCarthy lived for some years at Lough Hyne and his twin sons were born there in 1847. He was very active in helping the people of the locality during the Great Famine. He moved to Skibbereen and built a replica of Lough Ine Cottage in Skibbereen, Glencurragh House, which was burnt down in 1922.[18]

In 1851, the lease transferred to Jane Matthews who subsequently married George Pinchion, a Sub-Inspector of the Constabulary, in 1854.[19] Ellen Jervois Becher was the next occupant. She was the widow of Henry Becher of Aughadown House and she came to Lough Ine Cottage in 1861. She died at Lough Hyne in March 1865, and the house passed to her son, John Richard Hedges Becher. After he died in April 1901, his estate was administered by his son, Rev. Henry Becher, who would later become Dean of Rosscarbery.[20]

The person most strongly associated with Lough Hyne house is probably the inventor Gerald Macaura, who owned the house from 1913, having rented it from the Bechers for several years prior to the purchase. Gerald Joseph Macaura (McCarthy) was born in Skibbereen in 1871 and emigrated to America as a young man. He worked in the Edison Laboratories of Industrial Research in New Jersey in the 1890s where he met Edison, Marconi and Henry Ford. Macaura visited Lough Hyne with Marconi in 1904 and fell in love with Lough Ine Cottage (as it was then known).[21] He subsequently carried out an extensive refurbishment of the property, installing central heating and a new wing to the house and, in the garden, a fountain and glasshouse in the garden to grow roses to supply the house.[22]

Macaura's most famous invention, 'the pulsoconn', was a 'vibrating massage machine' which was said to cure rheumatism, arthritis and other pains. It was sold from his clinics in Wimpole Street, London; Boulevard Hausmann, Paris; Berlin, Belgium, Italy and Russia.[23]

Macaura decided to revive the band in Skibbereen and commissioned a set of 40 silver 'Bessons' No. 1 Best Quality Procurable Instruments'. He hired Mr Chipchase, a former bandmaster of the First Life Guards Household Cavalry, to teach the members of the band how to play. These instruments were used by St Fachtna's Silver Band in Skibbereen until the late 1970s.[24]

Lough Hyne House was owned by the Macaura family into the 1940s and it was sold several times in the intervening years before being bought by the current owners, the Beard family.

Set Dancing

The 1939 diary of the Bristol University Zoological Society records that they visited the platform dancing where 'various members of the party waltzed, much to the delight of the onlookers. An Irish set was even attempted and left two parties feeling somewhat worse for the effort'. As in many other areas in West Cork, the Sunday afternoon 'platform dance' was a popular meeting place at Lough Hyne, especially for young people.

There is a long tradition of dancing at Lough Hyne. A rock called *Carraig na Piobáire* (Piper's Rock) on the 'Gleann Road' (pronounced Gloun) is named in honour of 'Donalín the Piper', a musician who played for dancers at this spot in the late nineteenth century.[25] A timber platform as later used in the 1920s at the Gleann Quay (now known as Kellys' Quay) for set dancing on Sunday afternoons. The platform was in three sections and was stored against the wall when not in use. A concrete platform was erected in the 1930s behind the *Slátín* (now known as the North Quay) which was used into the 1950s for Sunday afternoon set dancing sessions.[26] There is a picnic bench located on this site today.

Ellie O'Driscoll's Shop

Ellie O'Driscoll, a native of Pookeen in Lough Hyne, opened a shop in Townshend Street, Skibbereen in the mid-1920s. She drove a van, loaded with provisions, to Lough Hyne each Sunday afternoon to cater for the set dancing sessions. In the early 1930s, she bought land in Pookeen from the Jennings family and built a shop there, which overlooked the Gleann Quay (now known as Kellys' Quay).[27] Built of corrugated iron, this structure is still in place today. She later build a bungalow, called 'Lakeview', on the site above the shop which she rented out to visitors to the area. This is where the first party of scientists from Bristol University stayed in 1937. This photo, taken by them in 1937, shows Ellie's corrugated iron shop above the Gleann Quay (on the right) and her house 'Lakeview' (bungalow above shop). Both houses now belong to the Kelly family and the Gleann Quay, now owned by the NPWS, is known as 'Kellys' Quay' in their honour.

Lough Hyne Schools

The first known National School at Lough Hyne was located in Pookeen townland and, in 1884, a new school opened further up the hill in the same townland, in the building shown here, which is now the property of the Crockett family. (Photo: R. O'Regan, with kind permission of the Crockett family.)

In 1900, a second school was built and, while it was just across the road, it fell into Barnabah townland. In the 1920s, these two schools catered for over two hundred pupils.[28] As the number of schoolchildren dropped, the two schools were again amalgamated into a single National School which was housed in the newer building in Barnabah. This finally closed in November 1977 when there were just 15 pupils attending the school.[29] This photo shows Miss O'Sullivan receiving a presentation from the pupils on the final day of school. It shows (back row, left to right): Pierce O Donovan, Fr Tim O Donovan (PP Rath), Miss Sheila O Sullivan (Principal), Cathy Cahalane. (Next row): Gerard McCarthy, Martin Jennings, Karen Hurley, Ann Whooley, Pat Whooley, Sean O Donoghue, John O Sullivan, Noel McCarthy. (On front left): Stephen Hurley, Mary Rose Jennings, Sheryl O Driscoll, Karen O Sullivan. (On front right): Michael Whooley, Michael Hurley, Carmen O Driscoll. (Photo: C. Lynch née Cahalane with thanks to Sharron Franks.)

Creamery

There were many 'mobile creameries' around West Cork which were run by small creamery companies, like the one shown here in Ballymacrown. Lough Hyne had its own creamery which was owned by the Bradfield family. A tin hut, it was situated on a corner on the right hand side on the road to Skibbereen from the lough. Managed by Paddy Casey, it closed in the late 1920s and nothing remains on the site today.[30] In this photo from the 1940s, Michael Burke of Ballyoughtera is taking his milk to the Ballymacrown mobile creamery.

Coffin Stone

In an era when coffins had to be shouldered and carried on foot to places that were not serviced by roads, 'coffin stones' were placed where the heavy load could be rested at key locations. These were also found on the quays of islands, where the coffin would be placed while awaiting transportation to the mainland, and also outside some old graveyards.

The coffin stone at Knockeencon was situated on top of a steep hill leading from a once densely populated area of Glannafeen. At the time, the road that now skirts the lake to the west, known locally as the Gleann road, did not exist and so this steep road over Knockeencon was the one used as the main route to Baltimore.[31] The coffin-bearers would have had to carry the remains up a steep hill to this spot where it could be rested before continuing its journey onwards. (Photo: R. O'Regan. With thanks to Adomas Glodenis.)

McCarthy's Cottage Knockomagh Hill

Michael McCarthy was the woodranger at Lough Hyne on the Wrixon-Becher estate in the early nineteenth century. The remains of his house can still be seen on Knockomagh Hill today. McCarthy was paid 18 shillings and 6 pence a month in 1827.[32] Because of the absence of records of wage rates in country towns in the nineteenth century, we can only compare this wage rate with similar jobs in Cork city for which records exist. The top wage for a cabinet-maker, for example, was 3 shillings and 6 pence per day, which would be over five and a half times the rate that McCarthy was paid.[33] Even allowing for the provision of a house and city versus country wage rate differences, this suggests that those working on the Wrixon-Becher estate were not highly paid.

O'Sullivan's Gate at Coomavarrodig

O'Sullivans' gate in Coomavarrodig townland, just opposite the ringfort, was made in the forge in Rath Bridge by Jeremiah O'Sullivan. Using recycled metal, the gate was made by re-using old wheelbands (the strip of iron that ran around the rim to protect the wooden cartwheel) and the heavy gate is held together by solid bolts. Jeremiah was born on this farm and was the person who found the bronze axe-head in a bog in Rath Hill in June 1940, which is now held by the National Museum of Ireland (see pages 12-13). (Photo: R. O'Regan.)

Sandboats and the Coosh Stone

Before the advent of artificial fertilisers, sand and seaweed were used to promote crop growth. Because of this, in nineteenth century Ireland, properties which had access to good weed or shoreline sand had their valuations increased.[34] Sand was also collected and transported to inland locations for the same purpose. There is a sandy area on the eastern side of Bullock Island just outside Lough Hyne and many boats travelled there – and to other beaches in the area – to collect sand. The sand was dredged and loaded into the boat, then brought into the lough and shovelled from the boat onto the quay where it was collected by horse and cart and transported to inland areas. Heaps of sand await collection in this late nineteenth century photo of the Gleann Quay (Kellys' Quay). (Lawrence Collection, National Library of Ireland.)

The sand was collected at low tide from off-shore beaches. The heavily laden sandboats would have to enter the lough via the Rapids, which was only possible on a higher tide. The boats would therefore have to wait for the tide and would standby on the eastern side of the sandbank called the Coosh, which connects Bullock Island to the mainland, while the water level rose. (Photo: R. O'Regan.)

The boatmen had to judge when the water level was sufficiently high for the sand-laden boats to clear both the Coosh, and the Rapids themselves. A small stone on the eastern side of the Coosh, 'the Coosh Stone' shown here, let the boatmen know when the water level was high enough. This Coosh Stone has a small indentation, shaped like a human footmark, which filled with water as the tide got higher. When the stone filled with water, the sandboatmen knew that the water level was high enough for the laden boats to safely enter the lough.

References by Chapter

1 - Archaeology

1. Terri Kearney, 'The Lough Hyne Area Through History' (unpublished MA Thesis, UCC School of History, 2012), Appendix 1: Total of 51 archaeological sites in the townlands of Glannafeen, Dromadoon, Ballyisland, Ballyoughtera, Pookeen, Ballinard, Barnabah, Coomavarrodig, Knockeencon, Highfield in a total survey area of 1636 acres plus related sites in nearby areas, Lick Hill Mine and Drishanemore Wedge Tomb and two Fish Pallices. Three archaeological objects found in the survey area, a stone axe-head, a flint and a Viking stick-pin, also form part of the survey, with a bronze axe-head found in nearby Rath.
2. Michael J. O'Kelly, *Early Ireland: An Introduction to Pre-History* (Cambridge University Press, Cambridge, 1997), p. 10.
3. Jenny Buzer, 'Analyses of Sediments from Lough Ine, Co. Cork, Southwest Ireland', in *New Phytologist* [online], Vol. 86, No. 1 (Sep., 1980), pp. 99–100 (accessed 01/10/09). Available at: http://www.jstor.org/stable/2434418.
4. Ibid., p. 93.
5. Michael Connolly, 'Prehistory: Settlement and Ritual in Iveragh', in John Crowley & John Sheehan (eds.), *The Iveragh Peninsula: A Cultural Atlas of the Ring of Kerry* (Cork University Press, Cork, 2009), p. 98.
6. Peter C. Woodman, 'The Mesolithic Period', in Michael Ryan (ed.), *Irish Archaeology – Illustrated* (Town and Country House, Dublin, 1997), p. 38.
7. Anna Brindley, *Irish Pre-History: An Introduction* (Town and Country House, Dublin, 1994), p. 9.
8. John Waddell, *The Prehistoric Archaeology of Ireland* (Galway University Press, Galway, 2006), p. 23.
9. Frank Mitchell & Michael Ryan, *Reading the Irish Landscape* (Town and Country House, Dublin, 1997), p. 161.
10. Alison Sheridan, 'The First Farmers', in Ryan, *Irish Archaeology*, p. 47.
11. Brindley, *Irish Pre-History*, p. 9.
12. Ibid.
13. William O'Brien, *Sacred Ground: Megalithic Tombs in Coastal South West Ireland* (National University of Ireland, Galway, 1999), p. 31: 'Radiocarbon dates suggest that these [Cape Clear and Ringarogy passage tombs] ... monuments broadly date to the fourth millennium BC'. Cape Clear Reference: Archaeological Survey of Ireland. *Archaeological Inventory of County Cork*, Vol. 1: West Cork (OPW, Dublin, 1992), p. 17. Ringarogy Reference: Archaeological Survey of Ireland. *Archaeological Inventory of County Cork,* Vol. 5 (Government Stationery Office, Dublin, 2010), p. 7.
14. Elizabeth Shee Twohig, 'An Inter-Tidal Passage Tomb at "The Lag", Ringarogy Island. Co. Cork', *Archaeology Ireland*, Vol. 9 (1995), pp. 7-10.
15. William O'Brien, *Iverni: A Prehistory of Cork* (Collins Press, Cork, 2012), p. 49.
16. William O'Brien, *Local Worlds: Early Settlement Landscapes and Upland Farming in South-West Ireland* (Collins Press, Cork, 2009), p. 22.
17. Buzer, 'Analyses of Sediments from Lough Ine', pp. 93–108.
18. Ibid.
19. *Southern Star,* 5 November 1954, 'New Stone Age Axe at Lough Ine'.
20. O'Kelly, *Early Ireland,* p. 45.
21. Ibid., pp. 40–41.
22. O'Brien, *Iverni,* p. 55.
23. Sheridan, 'The First Farmers', p. 48.
24. Gabriel Cooney, *Landscapes of Neolithic Ireland* (Routledge, London & New York, 2000), p. 5.
25. O'Kelly, *Early Ireland,* p. 115.
26. Ibid.
27. George Eogan, 'Daily Life in the Later Bronze Age', in Ryan, *Irish Archaeology,* p. 100.
28. Brindley, *Irish Pre-History*, p. 20.
29. National Museum of Ireland (1941:1150). George Eogan, *The Socketed Bronze Axes in Ireland* (Franz Steiner Verlag, Stuttgart, 2000), p. 90.
30. George Eogan, 'Daily Life in the Later Bronze Age', in Ryan, *Irish Archaeology,* p. 98.
31. Ibid., p. 100.
32. O'Brien, *Iverni,* p. 198.
33. Laurence Flanagan, 'Metal Production', in Ryan, *Irish Archaeology,* pp. 78–79.
34. Mitchell & Ryan, *Reading the Irish Landscape*, p. 212.
35. Ryan, *Irish Archaeology,* p. 65.
36. D. Cowman and T.A. Reilly, *The Abandoned Mines of West Carbery: Promoters, Adventurers and Miners* (Geological Survey of Ireland, Dublin, 1988), p. 12.
37. Brian Marten, 'Previously Unrecorded Bronze Age (?) Copper Working, West Cork, Ireland' (unpublished), December 1998, pp. 1–3.
38. William O'Brien, 'Copper Mining in South-West Ireland', in Ryan, *Irish Archaeology,* pp. 76–77.
39. Séan Ó Nualláin, 'The Megalithic Tomb Builders', in Ryan, *Irish Archaeology*, p. 59.
40. William O'Brien, 'Copper Mining in South-West Ireland', pp. 76–77.
41. O'Brien, *Iverni,* p. 84.
42. Michelle Comber & Connie Murphy, 'The Archaeology of Prehistoric and Early Medieval Beara', in O'Brien, *Local Worlds: Early Settlement Landscapes*, p. 29.
43. Mitchell & Ryan, *Reading the Irish Landscape*, p. 97.
44. O'Brien, *Sacred Ground*, pp. 276–278.
45. O'Brien, *Iverni,* p. 73.
46. M. Morris, '1974 Megalithic Exegesis. Megalithic Monuments as Sources of Socio-cultural Meanings: The Irish Case', *Irish Research Forum 1,2, 10–25,* p. 12 (quoted in O'Brien, *Sacred Ground*, p. 278.)
47. O'Brien, *Iverni,* p. 73.
48. O'Kelly, *Early Ireland*, p. 124.
49. O'Brien, *Iverni,* p. 73.
50. O'Brien, *Sacred Ground*, pp. 7–8.
51. C.J.F. McCarthy wrote several articles in the *Journal of the Cork Archaeological and Historical Society* (*JCHAS*) and the local history room in Cork City Library is named in his honour. File number C0150-079002 in DOELG in Dublin contains the following note: 'info from Ellen Macaura (75 years of age) who lived in Lough Hyne house in the 1940s. Remembers going out with group to dig pre-historic grave. Shell midden nearby near water's edge as tide began to come in. Stones put back as they were found. EB July 1993.' Ellen Macaura is now suffering from dementia but her sister Moyra confirmed that McCarthy said that he told them that it was a 'very old grave' after he had excavated and replaced its contents of 'bones and shells' (phone interview, 17 November 2009).
52. O'Brien, *Iverni,* p. 189.
53. One cupmarked stone in Ballyisland, three in Glannafeen, one on Castleisland, three in Barnabah and one in Knockeencon.
54. Frank Coyne, 'Rock Art', in Crowley & Sheehan, *The Iveragh Peninsula*, p. 107.
55. Waddell, *The Prehistoric Archaeology of Ireland,* p. 168.
56. Frank Coyne, 'Rock Art', p. 107.
57. Waddell, *The Prehistoric Archaeology of Ireland,* p. 174.
58. Cooney, *Landscapes of Neolithic Ireland,* pp. 134–135.
59. Martin Doody, 'Bronze Age Houses in Ireland', in E. Shee Twohig & M. Roynayne (eds.), *Past Perceptions: The Prehistoric Archaeology of South-West Cork* (Cork University Press, Cork, 1993), p. 149.
60. Waddell, *Prehistoric Archaeology of Ireland*, p. 174.
61. Ibid., p. 177.
62. Mitchell & Ryan, *Reading the Irish Landscape*, p. 200.
63. O'Brien, *Iverni,* p. 181.
64. Ibid.
65. Mike Wilson: 'Having done the appropriate survey I can say that this almost certainly was a bronze age cairn', transcribed from an undated letter in file number C0150- 0073, DOELG offices, Dublin, on 17 July 2009.
66. O'Brien, *Early Settlement Landscapes,* p. 23.
67. Brindley, *Irish Pre-History*, p. 38.
68. Connie Murphy, 'The Prehistoric Archaeology of Beara', in O'Brien, *Early Settlement Landscapes,* p. 36.
69. O'Brien, *Iverni,* p. 233.
70. O'Kelly, *Early Ireland*, p. 261.
71. Conchubhar Ó Cuilleanáin, 'Excavation of a Circular Stone House at Glannafeen (Lough Hyne) Co. Cork by Conchubhar Ó Cuilleanáin', *Journal of the Royal Society of Antiquities of Ireland*, Vol. 85 (1955), pp. 98–99. Interview with Denis O'Donovan, 20 January 2010: 'It was always known as the Druids' Altar.'
72. Edwards, Nancy, *The Archaeology of Early Medieval Ireland* (Batsford, London, 1990), p. 263.
73. O'Kelly, *Early Ireland,* pp. 262–263.
74. Barry Raftery, *Pagan Ireland* (Thames and Hudson, London, 1997), p. 184.
75. *Cashel/caher* are usually used for the stone-built version of this structure.
76. Dáibhí Ó Cróinín, *Early Medieval Ireland: 400–1200* (Longman, London and New York, 1995), p. 50.
77. Matthew Stout, *The Irish Ringfort* (Four Courts Press, Dublin, 1991), pp. 24–28. Ringforts continued to be constructed down to the seventeenth century, but the majority are structures of the Early Christian period, see O'Kelly, *Early Ireland*, p. 307.
78. Donncha Ó Corráin, *Ireland before the Normans* (Gill & MacMillian, Dublin, 1972), p. 48.
79. Ó Cróinín, *Early Medieval Ireland,* pp. 102–106.
80. Ibid., p. 86.
81. Ibid., p. 121.
82. Ibid., p. 109.
83. Edward MacLysaght, *Irish Life in the Seventeenth Century* (Dublin Academic Press, Dublin, 1979), p. 138. The last wolf in West Cork was said to have been killed in 1710 by Brian Townsend.
84. Stout, *The Irish Ringfort*, p. 124.
85. Ibid., p. 48.
86. Ibid., pp. 112–126. A *bóaire* or freeman/independent farmer would have held such a farmstead.
87. Ibid., pp. 110–118.
88. Ó Corráin, *Ireland before the Normans*, p. 46. *Cumal* was a legal unit of exchange in Ireland as in Europe at this time.
89. Ibid., p. 113.
90. Sheehan, 'Early Medieval Iveragh, AD 400–1200', p. 116.
91. V. Hurley, 'The Distribution, Origins and Development of Temple as a Church Name in the South-West of Cork', *JCHAS,* Vol. 84 (1979), p. 74.
92. Breandán Ó Cíobháin, 'The Early Ecclesiastical Toponymy of Uíbh Ráthach', in Crowley & Sheehan, *The Iveragh Peninsula,* p. 93.
93. Mitchell & Ryan, *Reading the Irish Landscape*, p. 289.
94. D. Leo Swan, 'Early Monastic Sites', in Ryan, *Irish Archaeology,* p. 138.
95. Mark Clinton, *The Souterrains of Ireland* (Wordwell, Bray, 2001), p. 17.
96. Ibid., p. 63.
97. Richard Warner, 'The Irish Souterrains and their Background', in H. Crawford (ed.), *Subterranean Britain: Aspects of Underground Archaeology* (Black, London, 1979), p. 142.
98. Clinton, *The Souterrains of Ireland*, p. 7.
99. Warner, 'The Irish Souterrains', p. 103.
100. Ibid
101. This chamber has now collapsed but its existence was confirmed by Denis and Michael O'Donovan.
102. Eileen M. Murphy, 'Children's Burial Grounds in Ireland (Cillíní) and Parental Emotions Towards Infant Death', *International Journal Historical Archaeology,* Vol. 15 (2011), p. 409.
103. Ibid
104. Ibid., p. 411.
105. The *cillín* at Dromadoon was destroyed in recent years as a result of a drainage programme and the burial ground at Ballyoughtera, which was shown on the 25" map of *c.* 1903, was likewise removed. Its circular shape is still evident in aerial views of the area. Interview with Neily Bohane, 11 October 2009 (referring to the Dromadoon site): 'the *cillín* was in the field below and it was called *garraí na cille* (field of the cill). Mr and Mrs Hall also call the burial ground near Tobarbreedy a site for 'the interment of children', see S.C. Hall, *Mr & Mrs Hall's Tour of 1840* (Hall Virtue & Co., London, 1984), p. 136.
106. Stout, *The Irish Ringfort*, p. 131.
107. Ibid., p. 124.
108. James Lydon, *The Making of Ireland: From Ancient Times to the Present* (Routledge, New York, 1998), p. 16.
109. Charles Webster, 'The Diocese of Ross and Its Ancient Churches', *Proceedings of the Royal Irish Academy,* Vol. 40 (1932), p. 283.
110. Hurley, 'The Distribution, Origins and Development of Temple', p. 83.
111. Tadhg O'Keeffe, 'Architectural Traditions of the Early Medieval Church in Munster', in Michael A. Monk and John Sheehan (eds.), *Early Medieval Munster: Archaeology, History and Society* (Cork University Press, Cork, 1998) p. 119.
112. This is also the Celtic festival of *Imbolg.* Denis and Michael O'Donovan confirmed the date that it was visited.
113. Robert Day, 'St. Bridget's Church, Lough Hyne', *JCHAS*, Vol. X (1904), pp. 18–24.
114. Swan, 'Early Monastic Sites', in Ryan, *Irish Archaeology: Illustrated,* p. 138.
115. Hall, *Hall's Ireland*, p. 136.
116. Daniel Donovan, *Sketches in Carbery* (McGlashan & Gill, Dublin, 1876), p. 128.
117. Interview with Paddy and Mary Burke, 23 October 2009: 'There was a story where a Protestant man who lived where Mrs Kelleher lives now [coastguard station] saw the stone with the cross on it and he threw it into the Rapids and it reappeared the following day. He threw it in again and again it reappeared. On the third time he took a sledge to it to crack it in frustration and that's how the stone is broken. But he couldn't break where the cross is y'see, no matter how he tried!'
118. Donovan, *Sketches in Carbery,* p. 128.
119. Tony Daly, *Coastguard Cutter,* Vol. 6 (1996), p. 21.
120. John Keats to Benjamin Bailey, November 1817.
121. Hall, *Mr & Mrs Hall's Tour of 1840*, p. 136.
122. Interviews with Neily Bohane, 12 December 2009, and Paddy Burke, 23 October 2009.
123. Ó Maidín, 'Pococke's Tour of South and South West Ireland in 1758', p. 135.

124. In NW section of the field of SMR C0150-028002 but now not visible due to land reclamation. The presence of the site was confirmed by the owner of the field, Mary O'Driscoll, who heard about it from her parents.
125. Interview with Neily Bohane, 17 September 2009: 'And there's a place up there where there was a monastery. There's nothing there now only a big bank of briars. There's some bit of the walls there but I'd say that the stone was taken and drawn for building. I don't know but there was a well there too called *Tobar na mainistreach*. We used to go there for the water in the summer time if the well here went dry, there was still water in that. But It's covered in briars. Whatever was there anyway, there was a little garden there and it's left into a bigger field now and it was called *Gairdín na mainistreach*, the monastery garden, and there was very good earth there.'
126. Interview with Neily Bohane, 12 December 2009: 'That is St Ina's well then you see and that's why they think Lough Ine was called after St Ina then you see.'
127. Ibid: 'There used be no mass in Skour until Fr Tim came there. I remember him saying the first mass there. But there used to be a pilgrimage there all the time, from before my father's time, every May Eve.'
128. Paddy Doyle, 'Reassessing the Irish Holy Well Tradition' (unpublished thesis, UCC Archaeology Department, 2006), p. 35.
129. Interview with Paddy Burke, 23 October 2009: 'Skour Well's water does not boil and there was always a pilgrimage to it on May Eve and people would pray and bring water away from it to cure ills [before Fr O'Donovan started having mass there] my grandfather used to go there.'
130. Interview with Neily Bohane, 17 September 2009: 'They used go to the mass in Skour alright ... there was supposed to be some fella there, he used to live somewhere around here and he used hardly go to mass at all only very seldom, once in a blue moon. But anyway, one Sunday he went to Skour mass, they said. And they used to wear white báneens then, they used to call them wrappers, flannel jackets, coats they had. And anyway, he went off to walk over to Skour to the mass and he was covered in sweat when he arrived in anyway. And there was no windows in them churches you know, only slits in the wall, and the sun was shining in through it you see, the rays of the sun. So he threw off the auld wrapper and pegged it away from him onto the floor. And it hung up on a sunbeam! And it stayed hanging on the sunbeam and all that were inside stayed looking at it. And they couldn't believe it, you see, that the wrapper stayed hanging up, and he used hardly ever go to mass. But he was kinda ashamed then about the wrapper man and he had a coat too and he brought that the next Sunday and he threw it again but if he did, Jesus, they said that it fell to the floor. D'ya see he was suffering pride then, do you see?'
131. Information provided by Neily Bohane and Patrick Burke.
132. John Sheehan, 'Ireland's Viking Age Hoards', in Anne-Christine Larsen (ed.), *The Vikings in Ireland* (Roskilde, Denmark, 2001), p. 51.
133. Ibid.
134. Ó Corráin, *Ireland Before the Normans*, p. 96.
135. Henry A. Jeffries, 'The History and Topography of Viking Cork', *JCHAS*, Vol. 90 (1985), p. 14.
136. Ibid., p. 15.
137. Ibid., p. 16.
138. Ibid., pp. 16–17.
139. Ibid., p. 21.
140. Ibid.
141. John Sheehan, 'The Viking Age Hoard at Castlefreke', *Ardfield Rathbarry Journal*, Vol. 5 (2006), p. 43.
142. Ibid., p. 42.
143. Dr Andy Halpin of the National Museum of Ireland dates this object between 1050 and 1250.
144. Kearney, 'The Lough Hyne Area Through History', Appendix Three, compares the area around Lough Hyne with that of two other local lakes. Lake Abisdealy, survey area 1532 acres, number of sites of a ritualistic or religious nature = 1. Lough Cluhier, survey area 1454 acres, ritualistic/religious sites = 7. Lough Hyne, survey area 1635 acres, ritualistic/religious sites = 33.
145. Cooney, *Landscapes of Neolithic Ireland*, p. 89.
146. Patrick Kavanagh, *Collected Poems* (Penguin Books, London, 2004), p. 47.

2 - O'Driscoll

1. James Coleman, 'The Old Castles of South-West Cork', *JCHAS*, Vol. 30 (1925), p. 31. 'Collymore' covered an area running from a point on the Ilen River a little below the town of Skibbereen, and south-east to the sea near Toe Head, bounded on all other sides by water. It covered the parishes of Tullagh, Creagh and part of Castlehaven as well as the islands of Cape Clear, Sherkin and Heir. Éamon Lankford, *The O Driscolls, Past and Present* (Cape Clear Museum, Cork, 2005), p. 12.
2. Ibid., p. 1.
3. Kenneth Nicholls, 'The Development of Lordship in County Cork, 1300–1600', in Patrick Flanagan & Cornelius Buttimer (eds.), *Cork History and Society* (Geography Publications, Dublin, 1993), p. 191.
4. Edward O'Mahony, 'Baltimore, the O'Driscolls, and the End of Gaelic Civilisation, 1538–1615', *Mizen Journal*, Vol. 8 (2000), p. 110.
5. Walter Arthur Copinger, *History of the Copingers or Coppingers of the County of Cork and of the counties of Suffolk and Kent, England* (Southern, London, 1884), p. 47.
6. Rev. W. Holland, *History of West Cork and the Diocese of Ross* (Southern Star, Skibbereen, 1949), p. 247.
7. Terence Barry, *The Archaeology of Medieval Ireland* (Routledge, London, 1988), p. 15.
8. K.W. Nicholls, *Gaelic and Gaelicized Ireland in the Middle Ages* (Lilliput Press, Dublin, 2003), p. 9.
9. Ibid., p. 25. A *tuath* is described as a 'territory, local lordship, local community', Donnchadh Ó Corráin, 'Corcu Loígde: Land and Families', in O'Flanagan & Buttimer (eds.), *Cork History and Society*, p. 64, & Nicholls, *Gaelic and Gaelicized Ireland*, p. 25.
10. Nicholls, *Gaelic and Gaelicized Ireland*, p. 25.
11. John O'Donovan, *Miscellany of Celtic Society* (The Celtic Society, Dublin, 1849), p. 145.
12. Lankford, *The O Driscolls*, p. 1.
13. Ibid.
14. Seán Duffy, *Ireland in the Middle Ages* (Gill & Macmillan, Dublin, 1997), p. 18.
15. O'Donovan, *Miscellany of Celtic Society*, pp. 141–142.
16. Connie Kelleher, 'The Gaelic O'Driscoll Lords of County Cork', in Linda Doran & James Littleton (eds.), *Lordship in Medieval Ireland: Image and Reality* (Four Courts Press, Dublin, 2007, p. 133).
17. Bernie McCarthy, *Baltimore Castle: An 800-Year History* (Baltimore Castle Publications, Baltimore, 2012), pp. 13–15.
18. Bernie McCarthy, *Dún na Séad Castle* (Bernie McCarthy, Baltimore, 2006), p. 3.
19. Kelleher, 'The Gaelic O'Driscoll Lords', p. 135.
20. A.F. O'Brien, 'Politics, Economy and Society: The Development of Cork and the Irish South-Coast Region c. 1170 to c. 1583', in O'Flanagan & Buttimer (eds.), *Cork History and Society*, p. 107.
21. Nicholls, 'The Development of Lordship', p. 191.
22. A.T.Q. Stewart, *The Shape of Irish History* (Blackstaff Press, Belfast, 2001), p. 63.
23. Ibid., p. 65.
24. Duffy, *Ireland in the Middle Ages*, p. 151.
25. O'Brien, 'Politics, Economy and Society', pp. 116–117.
26. Kelleher, 'The Gaelic O'Driscoll Lords', p. 137.
27. O'Brien, 'Politics, Economy and Society', p. 117.
28. Nicholls, 'The Development of Lordship', pp. 165–191.
29. Holland, *History of West Cork and the Diocese of Ross*, p. 24.
30. Nicholls, 'The Development of Lordship', p. 191.
31. Duffy, *Ireland in the Middle Ages*, p. 165.
32. Kelleher, 'The Gaelic O'Driscoll Lords', p. 137.
33. O'Donovan, *Miscellany of Celtic Society*, p. 143. This is a direct quote, but O'Donovan is incorrect in including the parish of Kilcoe, and only part of the parish of Myross was part of the O'Driscoll territory.
34. Kelleher, 'The Gaelic O'Driscoll Lords', p. 151.
35. McCarthy, *Dún na Séad Castle*, p. 5.
36. Nicholls, 'The Development of Lordship', pp. 157–158.
37. Nicholls, *Gaelic and Gaelicized Ireland*, p. 54.
38. Ibid., p. 52.
39. Nicholls, 'The Development of Lordship', p. 158.
40. Ibid., p. 157.
41. Ibid., p. 158.
42. Lankford, *The O Driscolls*, p. 18.
43. Edward O'Mahony, 'The O'Driscolls and their Revenues from Fishing – the 1609 Inquisition', *Mizen Journal: Selections from the Mizen Journals 1993–2004*, Part 2 (Inspire Design and Print, Skibbereen, 2010), p. 190.
44. Lankford, *The O Driscolls*, p. 18.
45. O'Mahony, 'The O'Driscolls and their Revenues from Fishing', p. 190.
46. Kelleher, 'The Gaelic O'Driscoll', p. 139.
47. Ibid.
48. O'Mahony, 'The O'Driscolls and their Revenues from Fishing', p. 190.
49. Ibid., p. 192.
50. Rev. J. Coombes, 'The Pilchard Fisheries of South-West Cork', *JCHAS*, Vol. 73 (1968), p. 117.
51. Ibid. Coombes refers to just one of these sites, which is also shown on the Petty Parish Map (see fig. 45), but the author has additionally recorded a second such site nearby. Kearney, 'The Lough Hyne Area Through History', Appendix 1, p. 161.
52. J. Coombes, 'The Pilchard Fisheries of South-West Cork', p. 118.
53. Michael McCarthy Morough, *The Munster Plantation: English Migration to Southern Ireland 1583–1641* (Clarenden Press, Oxford, 1986), p. 224.
54. MSS 714, 'Parish of Creagh', Drishanemore, plot number 361. The Books of Survey and Distribution record that ownership of this plot was transferred to Col. Richard Townsend.
55. Kearney, 'The Lough Hyne Area Through History', Appendix 1, p. 161.
56. Arthur E.J. Went, 'Pilchard in the South of Ireland', *JCHAS*, Vol. 51 (1946), p. 137.
57. McCarthy Morrogh, *The Munster Plantation*, p. 224.
58. Ibid.
59. Went, 'Pilchard in the South of Ireland', p. 137.
60. Ibid.
61. Ibid., p. 151.
62. Coombes, 'The Pilchard Fisheries of South-West Cork', p. 117.
63. Colin Breen, 'The Maritime Cultural Landscape in Medieval Gaelic Ireland', in Patrick J. Duffy, David Edwards & Elizabeth Fitzpatrick (eds.), *Gaelic Ireland: c.1250–1650, Land, Lordship and Settlement* (Four Courts, Dublin, 2001), p. 425.
64. Ibid.
65. Eugene Daly, 'Heir Island', in *Mizen Journal: Selections from the Mizen Journals 1993–2004*, pp. 144–145.
66. Went, 'Pilchard in the South of Ireland', p. 144.
67. Ibid., p. 146.
68. Ibid., pp. 140–151.
69. Ibid., p. 155.
70. Kelleher, 'The Gaelic O'Driscoll', p. 140.
71. Charles Smith, *The Ancient and Present State of the County of Kerry* (Mercier Press, Cork, 1979), p. 311.
72. Went, 'Pilchard in the South of Ireland', p. 153.
73. O'Mahony, 'The O'Driscolls and their Revenues from Fishing', p. 191.
74. Ibid.
75. Kelleher, 'The Gaelic O'Driscoll Lords', p. 142.
76. George Bennett, *The History of Bandon* (Frances Guy, Cork, 1869), p. 83.
77. Bernie McCarthy, *The Pirates of Baltimore* (Baltimore Castle Publications, Baltimore, 2012), p. 3.
78. O'Donovan, *Miscellany of Celtic Society*, pp. 94–95.
79. http://chancery.tcd.ie/document/patent/5-richard-ii (Trinity College Dublin, Chancery Papers), quoting: Herbert Wood (ed.), 'The Public Records of Ireland before and after 1922', *Transactions of the Royal Historical Society*, 4th series, Vol. 13 (1930), p. 40.
80. O'Donovan, *Miscellany of Celtic Society*, p. 94.
81. Kelleher, 'The Gaelic O'Driscoll Lords', p. 142.
82. McCarthy Morrogh, *The Munster Plantation*, pp. 216–218.
83. George Bennett, *The History of Bandon* (Frances Guy, Cork, 1869), p. 85.
84. O'Donovan, *Miscellany of Celtic Society*, p. 94.
85. Colin Breen & Wes Forsythe, *Boats and Shipwrecks of Ireland* (Tempus Publishing, Gloucestershire, 2004), p. 92.
86. Kelleher, 'The Gaelic O'Driscoll Lords', p. 148.
87. O'Donovan, *Miscellany of Celtic Society*, p. 95. 'Pinnaces were medium-sized single or two-masted wooden vessels that were in common use throughout the medieval and the early modern period ... and ... the O'Driscolls had a number of such vessels among their fleet'; see Kelleher, 'The Gaelic O'Driscoll Lords', pp. 148–149.
88. Lankford, *The O Driscolls*, p. 19.
89. Nicholls, *Gaelic and Gaelicized Ireland*, p. 29.
90. Ibid., p. 30. After the Norman arrival, the term *tuath* became obsolete and was replaced by the term 'country', as used here; ibid., p. 25.
91. As long as he was 'of age'; i.e. an adult.
92. O'Mahony, 'Baltimore, the O'Driscolls', p. 113.
93. Colm Lennon, *Sixteenth-Century Ireland: The Incomplete Conquest* (Gill & MacMillan, Dublin, 1994), pp. 209–210.
94. Ibid., pp. 214–215.
95. O'Mahony, 'Baltimore, the O'Driscolls', p. 113.
96. James M. Burke, 'Sir Fineen O'Driscoll', *JCHAS*, Vol. 25 (1919), p. 52.
97. Lennon, *Sixteenth-Century Ireland*, pp. 159–220.
98. O'Mahony, 'Baltimore, the O'Driscolls', p. 114.
99. Nicholls, *Gaelic and Gaelicized Ireland*, p. 32.
100. Ó Corráin, *Ireland before the Normans*, p. 35.
101. Ibid., p. 36.
102. Stewart, *The Shape of Irish History*, p. 63.
103. Nicholls, 'The Development of Lordship', p. 196. This early campaign, led by St Ledger as Lord Deputy, was considered a success. When England was engaged in a two-front war in France and the Scottish borders shortly afterwards, there were none of the usual diplomatic overtures from Irish magnates to English enemy rulers; see Lennon, *Sixteenth-Century Ireland*, p. 159.
104. Nicholls, 'The Development of Lordship', p. 196.
105. O'Mahony, 'Baltimore, the O'Driscolls', p. 113.
106. Ibid., p. 114.
107. Nicholls, *Gaelic and Gaelicized Ireland*, p. 67.
108. O'Donovan, *Miscellany of Celtic Society*, pp. 100–101.
109. O'Mahony, 'Baltimore, the O'Driscolls', p. 114.
110. Ibid., p. 117.
111. Ibid.
112. Ibid.
113. Burke, 'Sir Fineen O'Driscoll', p. 51.
114. Duffy, *Ireland in the Middle Ages*, p. 97.
115. Ibid.
116. Burke, 'Sir Fineen O'Driscoll', p. 51.
117. Ibid.
118. *Irlandiae Accurata Descriptio, Auctore Baptista Boazio*, 1612.
119. Lankford, *The O Driscolls*, pp. 24–25.
120. O'Mahony, 'Baltimore, the O'Driscolls', p. 122.
121. Kelleher, 'The Gaelic O'Driscoll Lords', p. 138.
122. O'Mahony, 'Baltimore, the O'Driscolls', p. 122.
123. Lankford, *The O Driscolls*, pp. 24–25.

124. Rev. W. O'Halloran, *Early Irish History and Antiquities and the History of West Cork* (Sealy, Bryers & Walker, Dublin, 1916), pp. 89–90.
125. William Kingston, *The Story of West Carbery* (The Friendly Press, Waterford, 1985), p. 43.
126. Ibid., p. 26.
127. Ibid.
128. O'Donovan, *Miscellany of Celtic Society*, pp. 352–357.
129. John Hawkes, 'Kilcoe Castle and Clan Dermot MacCarthy', in Mackey (ed.), *Selections from the Mizen Journals 1993–2004*, p. 119.
130. Coleman, 'Old Castles of South West Cork', p. 97.
131. Hawkes, 'Kilcoe Castle and Clan Dermot MacCarthy', p. 119.
132. Ibid.
133. Ibid.
134. O'Donovan, *Miscellany of Celtic Society*, p. 390.
135. O'Mahony, 'Baltimore, the O'Driscolls', p. 123.
136. Ibid., p. 124.
137. O'Donovan, *Miscellany of Celtic Society*, p. 99.
138. O'Mahony, 'Baltimore, the O'Driscolls', p. 124.
139. O'Donovan, *Miscellany of Celtic Society*, p. 99.
140. Ibid.
141. McCarthy Morrogh, *The Munster Plantation,* p. 152.
142. Ibid.
143. Ibid.
144. Ibid.
145. Copinger, *History of the Copingers or Coppingers*, p. 47.
146. Kelleher, 'The Gaelic O'Driscoll Lords', p. 139. Folklore has it that Fineen's last resting place is marked by the cross-slab; ibid., p. 156.
147. O'Donovan, *Miscellany of Celtic Society*, pp. 340–343. The O'Dalys (O'Dalaigh) were a sept especially privileged because of their poetic gifts and chieftains would grant them land in recognition of their importance. They had a number of bardic schools, including one on Sheep's Head; see Peter Somerville-Large, *The Coast of West Cork* (Appletree Press, Belfast, 1985), p. 149.
148. Micheál Ó Siochrú, *God's Executioner: Oliver Cromwell and the Conquest of Ireland* (Faber & Faber, London, 2008), pp. 63–65.
149. Breen, *An Archaeology of Southwest Ireland*, p. 36.
150. Ó Siochrú, *God's Executioner*, p. 21. The intervening years were a period when religious conflict raged across Europe and distracted attention from Ireland; see William J. Smyth, 'Ireland a Colony', in Terry Barry (ed.), *A History of Settlement in Ireland* (Routledge, London & New York, 2000), pp. 163–164.
151. McCarthy Morrogh, *The Munster Plantation*, p. 155.
152. Holland, *History of West Cork*, pp. 248–249.
153. Trinity College Dublin, MSS 809–841.
154. Nicholas Canny, 'The 1641 Depositions as a Source for the Writing of Social History: County Cork as a Case Study', in Flanagan & Buttimer (eds.), *Cork History and Society*, p. 198.
155. Ibid., p. 196.
156. Ó Siochrú, *God's Executioner*, p. 30.
157. TCD MS 465, fol. 16r, 1641 Depositions Project, at http://1641.tcd.ie/deposition.php?depID<?php echo 825015r014? (accessed 11 March 2012).
158. Ibid.
159. TCD MS 466, fol. 16v, 1641 Depositions Project, at http://1641.tcd.ie/deposition.php?depID<?php echo 825015r014? (accessed 11 March 2012).
160. Ó Siochrú, *God's Executioner*, p. 26.
161. Ibid.
162. Ibid, p. 30.
163. Holland, *History of West Cork*, p. 100.
164. Lankford, *The O Driscolls*, pp. 32–34.
165. Breen, *An Archaeology of Southwest Ireland*, pp. 44–45.
166. Ó Siochrú, *God's Executioner*, p. 26.
167. Breen, *An Archaeology of Southwest Ireland*, p. 45.
168. Ibid.
169. Bennett, *History of Bandon,* pp. 176–177.
170. Breen, *An Archaeology of Southwest Ireland*, pp. 46–47.
171. Ibid., p. 45.
172. David Attis, 'Sir William Petty and the Mathematical Conquest of Ireland', in David Attis & R.C. Mollen (eds.), *Science and Irish Culture*, Vol. One (Royal Dublin Society, Dublin, 2004), p. 62.
173. MSS 714.
174. Book of Survey and Distribution, County Cork, Barony of Carbery West, parish of Tullagh & Creagh.
175. R.F. Foster, *Modern Ireland, 1600–1972* (Penguin Books, New York, 1988), pp. 115–116.
176. T.W. Moody, 'Early Modern Ireland', in T.W. Moody (ed.), *A New History of Ireland, Vol. 3: Early Modern Ireland, 1534–1691* (Clarendon Press, Oxford, 1993), p. xliv.
177. Holland, *History of Cork,* p. 249.
178. McCarthy, *Baltimore Castle,* p. 180. Townsend was given the task of securing garrisons in the south for the Parliamentarians.
179. *A Census of Ireland, Circa 1659, with Essential Materials from the Poll Money Ordinances 1660–61* (Irish Manuscripts Commission, Dublin, 2002), p. 228.
180. Coleman, 'Old Castles of Southwest Cork', p. 33.
181. Lankford, *The O Driscolls,* p. 33.
182. Kelleher, 'The Gaelic O'Driscoll Lords, p. 150.
183. Mark Samuel, 'A Tentative Chronology for Tower Houses in West Cork', *JCHAS*, Vol. 103 (1998), p. 108.
184. Nicholls, *Gaelic and Gaelicized Ireland.* p. 9. This changed for the O'Driscolls after Sir Fineen took his title under 'surrender and regrant', as this system brought it into his personal ownership.
185. Kelleher, 'The Gaelic O'Driscoll Lords', pp. 156–158.
186. Ibid., p. 151.
187. Samuel, 'A Tentative Chronology', pp. 108–114. The lower walls of tower houses were thicker in size because of structural requirements, so, as the levels were superimposed one upon another, the walls got thinner. Therefore the interior room size of the upper floors was larger than those below.
188. Ibid., p. 108. Windows were bigger for the same reason as the previous reference.
189. Tom McNeill, *Castles in Ireland: Feudal Power in a Gaelic World* (Routledge, London, 1997), p. 218.
190. D. Newman Johnson, 'Irish Castles', in *Irish Environmental Library Series,* Vol. 61, Folens, p. 22.
191. MSS 714, 'and on Ballyisland a small house, a ffishinge palllace on Drishanemore likewise another castle'.
192. Charles Smith, *The Ancient and Present State of the City and County of Cork,* Vol. 1 (Connor, Cork, 1815)), pp. 269–270.
193. T. Sherrard, 'Manuscript Survey of the Estate of Sir John Freke, 1787–88' (Church of Ireland, Rosscarbery, County Cork [undated]), p. 26.
194. Donovan, *Sketches in Carbery*, p. 120. 'A small island ... on which, until recently, the ruins of an old castle stood. It is about six years ago since the walls fell down and at present, only the foundation of this old castle is to be seen.'
195. One version says that the barber told his secret to a reed and the reed was cut to make a flute and another version says that he told it to a tree, which was cut to make a harp. Interviews with Neily Bohane, Paddy Burke and Denis O'Donovan.
196. Poem from Neily Bohane, origin unknown.
197. Donovan, *Sketches in Carbery,* p. 124.
198. Ibid., pp. 124–125.
199. 'Petrus Kaerius, verlegt bei Janssonius, 1651' & 'Fredericum de Wit, Amsterdam, 1650'.

3 - Pre-Famine

1. 'Introduction', in John Crowley, William J. Smyth and Mike Murphy (eds.), *The Atlas of the Great Famine* (Cork University Press, Cork, 2012), p. xiv.
2. William Smyth, 'The *Longue Durée* – Imperial Britain and Colonial Ireland', in Crowley, Smyth & Murphy (eds.), *The Atlas of the Great Famine*, p. 59.
3. James S. Donnelly Jr, *The Great Irish Potato Famine* (Sutton Publishing, Gloucestershire, 2002), p. 7.
4. *Report of the Commissioners Appointed to take the Census of Ireland, for the Year 1841,* pp. 285–288; 1843[504] XXIV.1.
5. Holland, *History of West Cork*, p. 249: 'Carbery's ancestor, Sir Percy Freke, bought a large estate, which included the land to the east of Lough Hyne, in 1703, for £1,809'. Rev. M. Power, *Poor Inquiry (Ireland)*, p. 181; House of Commons 1836 [36], XXXI, Appendix (C): 'Sir William Wrixon-Beecher [*sic*], who primarily lived on his estate near Mallow, owned the parish of Creagh.' (The spellings 'Becher' and 'Beecher' are used for this family.)
6. Peter Foynes, *The Great Famine in Skibbereen* (Irish Famine Commemoration Skibbereen Ltd, Skibbereen, 2004), p. 3.
7. *A Return of the Valuation of Each Electoral Division in Ireland With Its Population in 1841,* p. 17; House of Commons, 1847 (159) LVI, 379.
8. J.F. Collins, 'Influence on Local Circumstances on Land Valuation in South-West Cork in the Mid-Nineteenth Century', in Flanagan & Buttimer, *Cork History and Society*, p. 149.
9. Patrick Hickey, *Famine in West Cork: The Mizen Peninsula, Land and People, 1800–1852* (Mercier Press, Cork, 2002), p. 123.
10. Ibid., pp. 124–125.
11. Ibid., pp. 125–126.
12. Smith, *The Ancient and Present State of the City and County of Cork,* pp. 269–270: 'Here are excellent lobsters, crabs, escalops [*sic*], and small deep oysters'. Páidraig Ó Maidín, 'Pococke's Tour of South and South-West Ireland in 1758', *JCHAS*, Vol. 65 (1960), p. 135: 'Here is a great plenty of fish at all times and oysters always in season'. Isaac Weld, *Illustrations of the Scenery of Killarney and the Surrounding Country* (Longman, Hurst, Rees & Orme, London, 1807), pp. 200–201: 'abounds with every sort of fish that is found on the coast, in particular with oysters of an excellent kind'.
13. Excerpt from 'Report and Estimate by Robert Adams of Proposed Work at the Harbour', dated 15 July 1848, National Archives of Ireland (NAI), OPW/8/Item381/1848/Location: Lough Hyne.
14. Hickey, *Famine in West Cork*, p. 125.
15. Mary E. Daly, *The Social and Economic History of Ireland* (Dublin Educational Company, Dublin, 1981), p. 65.
16. Power, *Poor Inquiry* 1836, p. 181; 'Tullagh, Cree and Part of Abbeystrowry'.
17. Creagh Estate Records, 1826–28, Skibbereen Heritage Centre Archive (uncatalogued).
18. Deeds of Lough Hyne House/Lough Ine Cottage, Wolfe & Co. Solicitors, Skibbereen, consulted with the kind permission of the owners, the Beard family.
19. Donovan, *Sketches in Carbery*, pp. 121–122.
20. William Smyth, 'Landscape Transformations', in Flanagan & Buttimer, *Cork History and Society*, p. 664.
21. Tony Daly, *Coastguard Cutter,* Vol. 6 (1996), p. 21.
22. *Return Relating to Coastguard Establishment of Ireland, 1834,* p. 1; 1834 (117) XLXX, 381.
23. William Webb, *Coastguard: An Official History of HM Coastguard* (HMSO, London, 1976), p. 81.
24. Ibid.
25. NAI, OS 58 B/638.
26. Donnelly, *The Great Irish Potato Famine*, p. 4.
27. Ibid.
28. Smyth, 'Landscape Transformations', p. 685.
29. James S. Donnelly, *The Land and the People of Nineteenth-Century Cork* (Routledge & Kegan Paul, London, 1975), p. 123.
30. See Table One. (At a standard rate of 640 acres per square mile.)
31. Christine Kinealy, *This Great Calamity* (Gill & Macmillan, Dublin, 2006), p. 4.
32. Donnelly,*The Great Irish Potato Famine,* p. 43. The population of Ireland in mid-1846 is likely to have been *c.* 8.75 million and possibly higher: William Smyth, 'Mapping the People: The Growth and Distribution of the People', in Crowley, Smyth & Murphy (eds.), *Atlas of the Great Irish Famine,* p. 13.
33. Leslie J. Dowley, 'The Potato and Late Blight in Ireland', in Cormac Ó Gráda (ed.), *Famine 150: Commemorative Lecture Series* (Teagasc, Dublin, 1997), p. 56.
34. Smyth, 'Mapping the People', p. 17.
35. E. Margaret Crawford, 'Subsistence Crises and Famines in Ireland: A Nutritionist's View', in E. Margaret Crawford (ed.), *Famine, The Irish Experience, 900–1900* (Donald, Edinburgh, 1989), pp. 207–209.
36. Pat Cleary & Philip O'Regan, *Dear Old Skibbereen* (Skibbereen Printers, Skibbereen, 1995), p. 11.
37. Smyth, 'Mapping the People', p. 13.
38. Dowley, 'The Potato and Late Blight in Ireland', p. 57.
39. Cecil Woodham-Smith, *The Great Hunger, Ireland 1845–1849* (Penguin Books, London, 1962), p. 38.
40. Donnelly, *The Great Irish Potato Famine,* p. 41.
41. Donnelly, *The Land and the People of Nineteenth-Century Cork,* p. 18.
42. Townsend, *Statistical Survey of the County of Cork*, p. 336.
43. Woodham-Smith, *The Great Hunger,* p. 33.
44. Smyth, 'Mapping the People', p. 17: 'The exceptions being Denmark and England where life expectancy was greater than in Ireland.'
45. Smyth, 'Landscape Transformations', p. 685.
46. Donnelly, *The Land and the People of Nineteenth-Century Cork,* pp. 16–17.
47. David Nally, 'The Colonial Dimensions of the Great Irish Famine', in Crowley, Smyth & Murphy (eds.), *Atlas of the Great Irish Famine,* p. 66.
48. Rev. W.B. McCartney, *Poor Inquiry* 1836, p. 181: 'Creagh, including Skibbereen'.
49. Ibid.
50. Welt, *Illustrations of the Scenery*, p. 199.
51. Power, *Poor Inquiry* 1836, p. 181: 'Tullagh, Cree and Part of Abbeystrowry'.
52. Ibid.
53. Ibid.
54. Ibid.
55. Daniel McCarthy (Lough Ine Cottage), *Poor Inquiry,* 1836, p. 266.
56. Welt, *Illustrations of the Scenery,* pp. 199–200.
57. *Illustrated London News,* 20 February 1847, p. 2.
58. Census of Ireland, 1911: Area, houses, and population; also the ages, civil or conjugal condition, occupations, birthplaces, religions, and education of the people. Province of Munster BPP 1912–13 CXV [Cd.6050] 152.
59. Donnelly, *The Land and the People of Nineteenth-Century Cork,* p. 59.
60. Ibid., p. 60.
61. Kinealy, *This Great Calamity*, p. 104.
62. Joel Mokyr, *Why Ireland Starved: A Quantitative and Analytical History of the Irish Economy, 1800–1850* (Allen & Unwin, London, 1983), p. 29.
63. Nally, 'The Colonial Dimensions of the Great Irish Famine', pp. 65–68.
64. Kinealy, *This Great Calamity*, p. 19.
65. Christine Kinealy, 'The Role of the Poor Law During the Famine', in Cathal Póirtéir (ed.), *The Great Irish Famine: The Thomas Davis Lecture Series* (Mercier Press, Cork, 1995), p. 105.
66. Kinealy, *This Great Calamity*, p. 19.
67. Peter Gray, 'Idealogy and the Famine', in Cathal Póirtéir (ed.), *The Great Irish Famine* (Mercier Press, Cork, 1995), pp. 88–90.
68. Kinealy, *This Great Calamity*, p. 18.
69. Kinealy, 'The Role of the Poor Law During the Famine', p. 106.
70. Kinealy, *This Great Calamity*, p. 23.
71. Ibid.

72. Ibid., p. 25.
73. Kinealy, 'The Role of the Poor Law During the Famine', p. 106.
74. Cleary & O'Regan, *Dear Old Skibbereen*, p. 14.
75. Ibid.
76. Kinealy, *This Great Calamity*, p. 25.
77. Cleary & O'Regan, *Dear Old Skibbereen*, p. 13.
78. Ibid.

4 - Great Famine

1. The population could have been as high as c. 8.75 million in 1845: Smyth, 'Mapping the People', p. 13.
2. Donnelly, *The Great Irish Potato Famine*, p. 171.
3. Ibid., p. 178.
4. David Fitzpatrick, 'Flight from Famine', in Póirtéir, *The Great Irish Famine*, p. 175.
5. Kirby A. Miller, *Emigrants and Exiles: Ireland and the Irish Exodus to North America* (Oxford UP, New York, 1985), p. 291.
6. L.M. Cullen, *An Economic History of Ireland Since 1660* (Batsford, London, 1972), p. 132.
7. Donnelly, *The Great Irish Potato Famine*, p. 176.
8. Donnelly, *The Land and the People of Nineteenth-Century Cork*, p. 129.
9. Donnelly, *The Great Irish Potato Famine*, p. 178.
10. Kinealy, *This Great Calamity*, p. 4.
11. Dowley, 'The Potato and Late Blight in Ireland', p. 62.
12. Donnelly, *The Land and the People of Nineteenth-Century Cork*, p. 73.
13. John Feehan, 'The Potato: Root of the Famine', in *Atlas of the Great Irish Famine*, p. 35.
14. Melissa Fegan, *Literature and the Irish Famine 1845–1919*, p. 35: 'A series of reports by Campbell Foster entitled "The Conditions of the People of Ireland" ran from 1845–46. He was touring in Ireland when news of the first failure of the potato crop broke.'
15. *Irish Times*, 28 November 1845.
16. *Cork Constitution*, 1 November 1845.
17. *Cork Examiner*, 10 December 1845.
18. Ibid.
19. Peter Gray, 'British Relief Measures', in *Atlas of the Great Irish Famine*, p. 77.
20. Ibid.
21. Richard Griffith, 'Report on the Roads Made at the Public Expense, in the Southern District of Ireland', House of Commons 1831 [119], p. 5.
22. Donnelly, *The Great Irish Potato Famine*, p. 47.
23. Ibid., p. 49.
24. Donnelly, *The Land and the People of Nineteenth-Century Cork*, p. 47.
25. Ibid., p. 49.
26. Woodham-Smith, *The Great Hunger*, p. 55.
27. Donnelly, *The Great Irish Potato Famine*, p. 47.
28. Mary E. Daly, 'The Operation of Famine Relief, 1845–47', in Póirtéir, *The Great Irish Famine*, p. 127.
29. Foynes, *The Great Famine in Skibbereen*, p. 27.
30. Ibid., p. 28.
31. Liam O'Regan, 'Two Catholic Gentlemen of the 1860s', *Mizen Journal*, Vol. 4 (1996), pp. 28–29.
32. Foynes, *The Great Famine in Skibbereen*, p. 31.
33. *The Irish University Press Series of the British Parliamentary Papers: Subject Set on Famine (Ireland)*: Vol. 5 (Irish University Press, Shannon, 1970), p. 233. (Hereafter referenced as *British Parliamentary Papers*.)
34. Donnelly, *The Land and the People of Nineteenth-Century Cork*, p. 84.
35. Woodham-Smith, *The Great Hunger*, p. 107.
36. Donnelly, *The Great Irish Potato Famine*, p. 16.
37. Ibid.
38. Peter Gray 'Idealogy and the Famine', in Póirtéir, *The Great Famine*, pp. 91–93.
39. Sir Charles Trevelyan, *The Irish Crisis* (Macmillan & Co., London, 1880), pp. 78–79.
40. Smyth, 'The *Longue Dureé*', p. 48.
41. Donnelly, *The Great Irish Potato Famine*, p. 16.
42. Ibid., p. 65.
43. Trevelyan, *The Irish Crisis*, pp. 78–79.
44. Donnelly, *The Great Irish Potato Famine*, p. 65.
45. Smyth, 'The *Longue Dureé*', p. 50.
46. Donnelly, *The Great Irish Potato Famine*, p. 65.
47. Ibid., p. 69
48. 'Death by Starvation (from a Skibbereen Correspondent)', *Cork Examiner*, 16 November 1846; Jeremiah O'Callaghan, 'More Deaths From Starvation!!!', *Cork Examiner*, 28 October 1846; 'Another Death by Starvation', *Cork Examiner*, 6 November 1846; 'More Deaths from Starvation – letter to the editor from J. Mulcahy, *Cork Examiner*, 20 November 1846; 'Deaths from Starvation (from our reporter)', *Cork Examiner*, 27 November 1846; 'The Deaths from Starvation at Skibbereen – The Inquests', *Cork Examiner*, 30 November 1846; 'Horrible Distress in the West – Another Death from Starvation (from our correspondent)', *Cork Examiner*, 11 November 1846; 'Awful State of Skibbereen District – Destruction of the People – Famine, Disease and Death', *Cork Examiner*, 16 December 1846.
49. *British Parliamentary Papers*, Vol. 5, p. 508: letter from Mr Hughes to Sir R. Routh, Skibbereen Reserve Depot, 20 September 1846.
50. Donnelly, *The Land and the People of Nineteenth-Century Cork*, p. 84.
51. Ibid., pp. 84–85.
52. Ibid., p. 85.
53. Foynes, *The Great Famine in Skibbereen*, pp. 50–51.
54. Kinealy, *This Great Calamity*, p. 79.
55. Ibid.
56. *Fourth annual report of the commissioners of the Loan Fund Board*, H.C. 1842 [392], pp. 63–64.
57. *British Parliamentary Papers*, Vol. 5, pp. 459–460: Mr Caulfeild to Sir G. Grey, Creagh Rectory, 4 January 1846.
58. Ibid., pp. 503–504: Assistant Commissary-General Bishop to Sir R. Routh, Skibbereen, 15 January 1847.
59. Foynes, *The Great Famine in Skibbereen*, p. 57.
60. Donnelly, *The Great Irish Potato Famine*, p. 65.
61. Daly, 'The Operation of Famine Relief', pp. 123–124.
62. Donnelly, *The Great Irish Potato Famine*, p. 71.
63. Kinealy, *This Great Calamity*, p. 95.
64. Donnelly, *The Great Irish Potato Famine*, p. 72.
65. Ibid., p. 70.
66. Ibid. The inquest into the death on 13 October of Denis McKennedy, a labourer working on a relief scheme at Caheragh near Skibbereen, found that he had 'died of starvation due to the gross negligence of the Board of Works' and Jeremiah O'Callaghan, 'Another Death by Starvation', *Cork Examiner*, 6 November 1845, reported that 'He was owed three weeks' wages when he died on the side of the road'.
67. Donnelly, *The Great Irish Potato Famine*, pp. 70–72.
68. Nally, 'The Colonial Dimensions of the Great Famine', p. 71.
69. Donnelly, *The Great Irish Potato Famine*, p. 65.
70. Ibid., p. 71.
71. Kinealy, *This Great Calamity*, p. 95.
72. Laurence M. Geary, 'What People Died of During the Famine', in Ó Gráda, *Famine 150*, p. 95.
73. Hilary O'Kelly, 'Famine and Workhouse Clothing', in *Atlas of the Great Irish Famine*, pp. 146–147.
74. Elihu Burritt, *A Journal of a Visit of Three Days to Skibbereen and Its Neighbourhood*, pp. 7–15, available at: http://www.gutenberg.org/ebooks/25115 (accessed 25 October 2010).
75. NAI, excerpt from 'Report and Estimate by Robert Adams of Proposed Work at the Harbour'. William A.Treacy was County Surveyor for Cork (West Riding) from April 1846 to March 1855.
76. Donnelly, *The Great Irish Potato Famine*, p. 83.
77. Interview with Dr Rob McAllen, 20 February 2011.
78. Cleary & O'Regan, *Dear Old Skibbereen*, p. 22. On 6 February 1847, the Committee wrote to Routh giving estimates of its expenditure over the following months. These show that the Committee was planning to feed approximately 8,600 people per day.
79. Burritt, *A Journal of a Visit of Three Days to Skibbereen*, p. 2.
80. Cleary & O'Regan, *Dear Old Skibbereen*, p. 42.
81. Ibid., p. 22.
82. O'Regan, 'Two Catholic Gentlemen of the 1860s', p. 28.
83. *British Parliamentary Papers*, Vol. 7, pp. 397–398, Assistant Commissary-General Bishop to Sir R. Routh, Skibbereen, 27 January 1847.
84. *British Parliamentary Papers*, Vol. 5, p. 327, Trevelyan to Sir R. Routh, 3 December 1846.
85. *Cork Examiner*, 'Death by Starvation (from a Skibbereen Correspondent)', 16 October 1846; Jeremiah O'Callaghan, *Cork Examiner*, 'More Deaths From Starvation!!!', 28 October 1846; *Cork Examiner*, 'Another Death by Starvation', 6 November 1846; *Cork Examiner*, 'More Deaths from Starvation – letter to the editor from J. Mulcahy, P.P. Castlehaven and Myross', 20 November 1846; *Cork Examiner*, 'Deaths from Starvation (from our reporter)', 27 November 1846; *Cork Examiner*, 'The Deaths from Starvation at Skibbereen – The Inquests', 30 November 1846; *Cork Examiner*, 'Horrible Distress in the West – Another Death from Starvation (from our correspondent)', 11 December 1846; *Cork Examiner*, 'Awful State of Skibbereen District – Destruction of the People – Famine, Disease and Death', 16 December 1846.
86. Melissa Fegan, *Literature and the Irish Famine 1845–1919*, p. 48.
87. Philip O'Regan, 'Skibbereen and the Great Hunger', *Southern Star*, 9 May 2009.
88. Donnelly, *The Great Irish Potato Famine*, p. 81.
89. Ibid., p. 82.
90. Ibid., pp. 82–87.
91. Ibid., p. 85.
92. Donnelly, *The Great Irish Potato Famine*, p. 92.
93. Ibid., p. 94, quoting from *The Times*, 18 April 1847.
94. Figures of 74% in Creagh and 74% in Tullagh, based on 1841 population figures. *British Parliamentary Papers*, Vol. 8, pp. 350–351, Supplementary Appendix of the Seventh Report of the Relief Commissioners.
95. Ibid.
96. Ibid., p. 277.
97. Donnelly, *The Great Irish Potato Famine*, p. 101.
98. Ibid., p. 92.
99. Trevelyan, *The Irish Crisis*, p. 1 & p. 201.
100. Donnelly, *The Great Irish Potato Famine*, p. 127.
101. Frank Neal, 'Black 47: Britain and the Famine Irish', in Breandán Ó Conaire (ed.), *The Famine Lectures* (*Roscommon Herald*, Boyle, 1997), pp. 334–335.
102. Smyth, 'The *Longue Dureé*', p. 57.
103. Ibid.
104. Cleary & O'Regan, *Dear Old Skibbereen*, p. 17.
105. Archibald G. Stark, *The South of Ireland in 1850: Being the Journal of a Tour in Leinster and Munster* (James Duffy, Dublin, 1850), pp. 178–179.
106. Donnelly, *The Land and the People of Nineteenth-Century Cork*, p. 121.
107. Ibid., p. 122.
108. Donnelly, *The Great Irish Potato Famine*, p. 102.
109. Kinealy, *This Great Calamity*, p. 219.
110. Donnelly, *The Land and the People of Nineteenth-Century Cork*, p. 124.
111. Cleary & O'Regan, *Dear Old Skibbereen*, p. 9.
112. Ibid., p. 9, and Jeremiah O'Callaghan, 'The Clearance System', *Cork Examiner*, 31 May 1847.
113. O'Callaghan, 'The Clearance System'.
114. Ibid
115. O'Callaghan, 'To the Editor of the Cork Examiner', *Cork Examiner*, 7 June 1847.
116. O'Callaghan, 'The Clearance System'.
117. Laurence M. Geary, 'Famine, Fever and the Bloody Flux', in Póirtéir, *The Great Irish Famine*, pp. 78–79.
118. Donnelly, *The Great Irish Potato Famine*, pp. 171–172.
119. Ibid., pp. 174–175.
120. Geary, 'Famine, Fever and the Bloody Flux', p. 83.
121. *Cork Constitution*, 14 May 1850.
122. Donnelly, *The Great Irish Potato Famine*, pp. 171–172.
123. Ibid., pp. 182–185.
124. Cleary & O'Regan, *Dear Old Skibbereen*, p. 43.
125. 'Wretched Condition of Emigrants', *Monmouthshire Merlin*, 6 February 1847.
126. Census of Ireland, 1851, Part VI, I, XIII, XIV.
127. Donnelly, *The Great Irish Potato Famine*, p. 178.
128. Foynes, *The Great Famine in Skibbereen*, p. 83.
129. Patrick Hickey, 'The Famine in the Skibbereen Union (1845–1851)', in Póirtéir, *The Great Irish Famine*, pp. 196–197. The parishes covered by the poll (census) were Kilcoe, Kilmoe, Schull, Caheragh, Drimoleague and Drinagh.
130. Foynes, *The Great Famine in Skibbereen*, p. 87.
131. Ibid., p. 89.
132. Kinealy, *This Great Calamity*, p. 219.
133. Stark, *The South of Ireland in 1850*, pp. 175–176.
134. 'Follow Up Report', Loans Funds Database, Baltimore Fund, May 1853, Skibbereen Heritage Centre Archive (uncatalogued).

5 - Marine Research

1. Terri Kearney, *Lough Hyne: The Marine Researchers – in Pictures* (Skibbereen Heritage Centre, Skibbereen, 2011), p. 1. The depth of the Western Trough was once estimated to be in the region of 53m, but the deepest current depth appears to be c. 48m. The base of the trough is an environment comprised of soft sediment and mud.
2. Christopher Moriarty, 'Marine Science' in Charles Mollen (ed.), *Science and Ireland – Value for Society* (Royal Dublin Society, Dublin, 2005), p. 149.
3. Jim MacLaughlin, *Troubled Waters* (Four Courts Press, Dublin, 2010), p. 288.
4. Moriarty, 'Marine Science', p. 149.
5. Ibid., p. 150.
6. T. Ó Raifeartaigh (ed.), *The Royal Irish Academy: A Bicentennial History, 1785–1985* (Royal Irish Academy, Dublin, 1985), p. 70.
7. Timothy Collins, 'The Clare Island Survey of 1909–1911: Participants, Papers and Progress', in Roisin Jones and Martin Steer (eds.), *Darwin, Praeger and the Clare Island Surveys* (RIA, Dublin, 2009), pp. 17–19.
8. Ibid., p. 19.
9. Ibid.
10. Ibid., p. 32. W.M. Tattersall, who later went on to work with Renouf, was part of the 1909–11 team.
11. Moriarty, 'Marine Science', p. 158.
12. Colm Ó hEocha, 'Biology', in Ó Raifeartaigh, *The Royal Irish Academy*, p. 308. Rowland Southern, Jean Stephens and George Farran continued to research fisheries, sponges and marine zoology respectively.
13. Moriarty, 'Marine Science', p. 159.
14. Louis P.W. Renouf, 'Preliminary Work of a New Biological Station (Lough Ine, Co Cork, I.F.S)', *Journal of Ecology*, Vol. 19, No. 2 (August 1931), p. 410.
15. Professor Haddon and Rev. W.S. Green, 'Second Report on the Marine Fauna of the South-West of Ireland', *Proceedings of the Royal Irish Academy*, Third Series, Vol. 1 (1891), pp. 33–34.
16. Robert Lloyd Praeger, *Some Irish Naturalists* (Dundaldan Press, Dundalk, 1949), pp. 88–89.

17. Haddon and Green, 'Second Report on the Marine Fauna of the South-West of Ireland', p. 31.
18. Ibid., p. 32.
19. Ibid., p. 33.
20. Ibid., p. 34.
21. Praeger, *Some Irish Naturalists*, Plate XVXX.
22. Haddon and Green, 'Second Report on the Marine Fauna of the South-West of Ireland', pp. 29–30. The 'Government Grant Committee' granted £100, while the RIA committed £40 towards the expedition costs.
23. Praeger, *Some Irish Naturalists,* pp. 186–187, lists cruise members for the 1885/6/8 trips.
24. Louis P.W. Renouf, 'Twenty Five Years at Lough Ine', in *Cork University Record*, 19 (Cork University Press, Cork, 1950), p. 19.
25. Ibid.
26. Renouf, 'Preliminary Work of a New Biological Station', p. 410.
27. Ó hEocha, 'Biology', p. 308.
28. Collins, 'The Clare Island Survey', p. 17.
29. Timothy Collins, 'The Helga/Muirchu: Her Contribution to Galway Maritime History', *Journal of the Galway Archaeological and Historical Society*, Vol. 54 (2002), p. 149.
30. Ibid., pp. 149–150.
31. Ibid., p. 151.
32. Ibid.
33. Renouf, 'Preliminary Work of a New Biological Station, p. 410.
34. Ibid.
35. Ibid.
36. Renouf, 'Twenty Five Years at Lough Ine', p. 19.
37. Renouf, 'Preliminary Work of a New Biological Station, p. 410.
38. Renouf, 'Twenty Five Years at Lough Ine, p. 19.
39. Renouf, 'Preliminary Work of a New Biological Station, p. 411.
40. Ibid.
41. Keith Wilson, 'A Bibliography of Literature Relating to Lough Hyne (Ine) Nature Reserve, 1687–1982', *Journal of Life Sciences of the Royal Dublin Society,* Vol. 5 (1984), p. 3.
42. Renouf, 'Preliminary Work of a New Biological Station, p. 410.
43. Fergus J. O'Rourke, 'Miss Marjorie Murphy, MSc., H.D.E. A Personal Tribute', *Cork University Record,* Vol. 37 (1962), p. 45. This was the second time that it had been washed into the lough by a tide.
44. Kearney, *Lough Hyne: The Marine Researchers – in Pictures',* p. 92.
45. Renouf, 'Preliminary Work of a New Biological Station, p. 411.
46. Renouf, 'Twenty Five Years at Lough Ine', p. 20.
47. Skibbereen Heritage Centre Archive, Visitors' Book, Lough Ine Biological Station, 'Easter 1929', entry by Prof. Tattersall.
48. Skibbereen Heritage Centre Archive, photo captioned 'the first visitors, Tattersall'. Date established from Visitors' Book entry.
49. Jones & Steer, *Darwin, Praeger and the Clare Island Surveys,* p. 32. His role was 'marine dredging'.
50. Skibbereen Heritage Centre Archive, Visitors' Book, W.M. Tattersall, Easter, 1931.
51. Ibid., 1930 entry by T. Kenneth Rees who records that Renouf lectured in Swansea in early 1930 and Violet M. Grubb records a visit by Renouf to Westfield College London in 1935.
52. Renouf, 'Preliminary Work of a New Biological Station, pp. 410–438.
53. Little, email, 6 April 2013.
54. Skibbereen Heritage Centre Archive, Visitors' Book, various entries.
55. Jean Hassett, 'My Father, the Naturalist', *Sherkin Comment,* Vol. 25 (2000), p. 24.
56. T. Kenneth Rees, 'Preliminary Observations on the Phaeophyceae of Lough Hyne, *Journal of Ecology,* Vol. 19 (1931), pp. 439–448; Rees, 'The Marine Algae of Lough Ine', *Journal of Ecology,* Vol. 23 (1935), pp. 69–133; L.P.W. Renouf and T.K. Rees, ' On Experiments Concerned with Biotic Factors of the Seashore', *Annals of Botany*, Vol. 4 (1932), pp. 1061–1062.
57. Information received from John Hassett, Renouf's grandson, on 2 February 2011.
58. Skibbereen Heritage Centre Archive, photo captioned 'The Bristol University Zoological Society 1937'.
59. Ebling's final visit date confirmed by his wife, Erica Ebling.
60. Skibbereen Heritage Centre Archive, 'The Lough Ine Rapids: Report of work carried out by the Bristol (1938) party at Lough Ine Biological Station', lists the participants' names. M.A. Sleigh, 'John Alwyne Kitching, OBE, 24 Oct 1908–1 April 1996', *Biographical Memoirs of Fellows of the Royal Society*, Vol. 43 (The Royal Society, November 1997), p. 284. Kitching began lecturing at Bristol in 1937.
61. Dr Colin Little, 'Memories of Lough Hyne', unpublished account of his memories of the lough, written for the author's referencing; 'Jack didn't come on expeditions to the lough after 1986'.
62. Sleigh, 'John Alwyne Kitching', p. 284.
63. John Ebling, 'The Exploration of the Rapids', in A.A. Myers, C. Little, M.J. Costello and J.C. Partridge (eds.), *The Ecology of Lough Hyne* (Royal Irish Academy, Dublin, 1991), p. 31.
64. Skibbereen Heritage Centre Archive, photo of 'Jerry Walton', established to have been taken mid-1960s by interview with Prof. Máire Mulcahy on 27 July 2012.
65. Sleigh, 'John Alwyne Kitching', pp. 284–285. Kitching awarded an OBE. Ebling, 'The Exploration of the Rapids', p. 31.
66. Prof. Tony Hawkins & Sue Hawkins, email, 21 April 2013.
67. Ibid.
68. Ebling, 'The Exploration of the Rapids', p. 31.
69. Interview with Dr Colin Little, 4 September 2011, who revised and subsequently approved this text.
70. Kearney, *Lough Hyne: The Marine Researchers,* p. 25.
71. Ebling, 'The Exploration of the Rapids', p. 32.
72. Ibid., p. 33.
73. Ibid.
74. Ibid., p. 31.
75. J.A. Kitching & F.J. Ebling, 'Ecological Studies at Lough Ine', *Advances in Ecological Research,* Vol. 4 (1967), p. 229; Little, email, 2 April 2013.
76. Kearney, *Lough Hyne: The Marine Researchers,* p. 49.
77. Cynthia Trowbridge, Oregon Institute of Marine Biology, email, 31 July 2012.
78. Kitching & Ebling, 'Ecological Studies at Lough Ine', p. 284; Little, email, 2 April 2013.
79. Trowbridge, email, 31 July 2012.
80. Ibid.
81. Sleigh, 'John Alwyne Kitching, p. 276.
82. D. Minchin, 'An Historical Summary of Scientific Activities', in Myers, Little, Costello and Partridge (eds.), *The Ecology of Lough Hyne*, p. 26.
83. Ebling, 'The Exploration of the Rapids', p. 39.
84. Correspondence between the author and Professor Michael Sleigh, Dr Colin Little, Professor Tony Hawkins, Dr Louise Muntz and Adrian Smith, as well as the diaries of the expeditions.
85. F.J. Ebling & J.A. Kitching, 'Exploration of the Lough Ine Rapids', *School Science Review,* No. 114 (1950), p. 229.
86. O'Rourke, 'Report on the Lough Ine Biological Station', pp. 6–15.
87. Interview with Prof. Máire Mulcahy, 27 July 2012.
88. Fergus J. O'Rourke, 'Marjorie Murphy, a Personal Tribute', p. 42.
89. Prof. Máire Mulcahy, 'Lough Hyne: Ireland's and Europe's First Marine Nature Reserve', Skibbereen Heritage Centre Archive, p. 2.
90. Information on UCC provided by Prof. Máire Mulcahy; Ebling, 'Exploration of the Rapids', p. 31, 'Students in 1939 ... Gerald Walton'.
91. Mulcahy, 27 July 12.
92. Dr Alan Myers interview, 30 July 2012. Student names at the time were Heidi Wilkins, Ruth O'Riordan and Simon Berrow.
93. Little, email, 2 April 2013.
94. Wilson, 'A Bibliography of Lough Hyne (Ine), pp. 1–22.
95. Ibid., p. 5.
96. Mulcahy, 27 July 2012.
97. Dr Conor Duggan, phone interview, 8 August 2012.
98. An Taisce, 'Lough Ine: Ireland's First National Marine Research Park?' (An Taisce, Cork, 1975), p. 1.
99. Professor Frank Hegarty, former Chairman of An Taisce, Cork, phone interview, 30 July 2012.
100. Duggan, 8 August 2012.
101. An Taisce, 'Lough Ine: Ireland's First National Marine Research Park?', pp. 1–19.
102. 'An Taisce Statement on Lough Ine', *Southern Star,* 8 November 1975.
103. Hegarty, 30 July 2012.
104. Mulcahy, 27 July 2012.
105. Dan Minchin, 'Dan Minchin, Lough Hyne', email, 28 July 2012.
106. 'Seminar and Survey Aid Lough Ine', *Southern Star,* 21 August 1976.
107. Minchin, 28 July 2012.
108. Statutory Instruments S.I. No. 206 of 1981, 'Nature Reserve (Lough Hyne) Establishment Order, 1981' (Stationery Office, Dublin, 1981), pp. 1–4.
109. Minchin, 28 July 2012, 'a management plan was then developed with the help of Martin Speight'. Brendan F. Keegan, WAC, 'Towards a Management Plan for the Lough Hyne Natural Reserve', 3 November 1982, Skibbereen Heritage Centre Archive.
110. Declan O'Donnell, interview 15 April 2013.
111. Little, 'Memories of Lough Hyne'.
112. Ibid.
113. Little, email, 2 April 2013.
114. Ibid.
115. Trowbridge, email, 31 July 2012.
116. Little, email, 31 January 2011.
117. Barnes to McAllen, email, 14 April 2013.
118. Little, email, 2 April 2013.
119. Prof. John Davenport, email, 14 April 2013.
120. Professor Mark Johnson, email, 17 April 2013.
121. Dr Mark Jessopp, email, 16 April 2013.
122. Rob McAllen, John Davenport, Karl Bredendieck, Declan Dunne, 'Seasonal Structuring of a Benthic Community Exposed to Regular Hypoxic Events', *Journal of Experimental Marine Biology and Ecology,* Vol. 368 (2009), pp. 67–74.
123. Julia Davenport & Rob McAllen, *Lough Hyne @ 30* (UCC, Cork, 2011), pp. 30–51.
124. Ibid., p. 30.
125. M.J. Costello & J.M.C. Holmes, 'A Bibliography of Lough Hyne to 1990', in Myers, Little, Costello & Partridge (eds.), *The Ecology of Lough Hyne,* pp. 171–174.
126. Lough Ine Visitors' Book, various entries.
127. J.A. Kitching, A.W.D. Larkum, T.A. Norton, J.C. Partridge & J. Shand, 'An Ecological Study of the Whirlpool Cliff, Lough Hyne (Ine)', *Progress in Underwater Science*, Vol. 15 (1990), pp. 101–132.
128. Johnson, email, 17 April 2013.
129. Little, email, 3 April 2013.
130. McAllen, email, 14 April 2013.
131. Little, email, 6 April 2013.
132. Hawkins, email, 22 February 2011.
133. Sue Hawkins, email, 21 April 2013.
134. Hawkins, email, 22 April 2013.

7 - Miscellany

1. Robert Lloyd Preager, *The Natural History of Ireland* (Reprinted EP Publishing, London, 1972), p. 129.
2. Mitchell & Ryan, *Reading the Irish Landscape,* p. 30.
3. Holland, 'The Origin of Lough Hyne', pp. 20-21.
4. Mitchell & Ryan, *Reading the Irish Landscape,* p. 30 & JB Whittow, *Geology and Scenery in Ireland (*Penguin Books, Great Britain, 1974), p. 225.
5. Mitchell & Ryan, *Reading the Irish Landscape,* p. 30.
6. Kitching, *Ecological Studies at Lough Ine,* p.201.
7. Holland, 'The Origin of Lough Hyne', p. 22.
8. Ibid, pp. 22–23.
9. Mitchell first presented his theory in 1976 in *Reading the Irish Landscape*, p. 30 and again reiterated his position in *The Way That I Followed* (Country House, Dublin, 1990) while Holland first offered his glacial erosion hypothesis in 1988 in 'On the Origin of Lough Hyne, Co Cork' in *Irish Naturalists Journal* 22, pp. 521-525 and again in 'The Origin of Lough Hyne', p. 22. Other scientists also disagree on this topic with Whittow supporting the tectonic subsidence suggestion in *Geology and Scenery in Ireland,* p. 225 while Coe and Selwood of the University of Exeter support the glacial erosion hypothesis in Kitching, *Ecological Studies at Lough Ine,* pp. 201-2.
10. Mitchell & Ryan, *Reading the Irish Landscape,* p. 30.
11. Buzer, 'Pollen Analyses from Lough Hyne and Ballyalla Lough, pp. 93-108.
12. Ibid.
13. Holland, 'The Origins of Lough Hyne', p. 23.
14. Breeda Cahalane, by email, 15 June 2013.
15. Holland, *History of West Cork*, p. 249: 'Carbery's ancestor, Sir Percy Freke, bought a large estate, which included the land to the east of Lough Hyne, in 1703, for £1,809'.
16. Deeds of Lough Hyne House/Lough Ine Cottage, Wolfe & Co. Solicitors, Skibbereen, consulted with the kind permission of the owners, the Beard family. 'Graceful-looking villa', see Donovan, *Sketches in Carbery*, pp. 121-2.
17. O'Regan, 'Two Catholic Gentlemen of the 1860s', pp. 28-29.
18. Obituary of Miss Mary Louise Bernadette McCarthy, *Southern Star,* June 15 1929.
19. George Pinchin was Sub-Inspector of the Constabulary in Skibbereen during the Great Famine and was a widower by this date; his first wife, Margaret died in 1852.
20. Deeds of Lough Hyne House.
21. Philip O'Regan, 'Macaura Family Maintains Links with "Home"', *Southern Star,* August 16 2003.
22. Ella Macaura, 'Gerald Macaura: A Biography', Skibbereen Heritage Centre Archive (unpublished), p. 5.
23. Macaura, 'Gerald Macaura', p. 6.
24. O'Regan, 'Macaura Family Maintains Links with "Home"'.
25. Interview with Neily and Annie Bohane, 7 June 2013, 'Donalín the piper was a cripple and came there by donkey you see'.
26. Ibid.
27. Interview with Neily and Annie Bohane, 7 June 2013.
28. Ibid.
29. Email Cathy Lynch, 16 June 2013.
30. Interview with Beatrice Hegarty, 12 April 2011 and Neily and Annie Bohane, 7 June 2013.
31. Interview with Andy O'Driscoll, 1 June 2011. Location of the stone later confirmed by Breeda Cahalane of Ballymacrown (née O'Sullivan of Coomavaridig).
32. Creagh Estate Records, Skibbereen Heritage Centre Archive [uncatalogued].
33. M. Cronin, 'Work and Workers in Cork City and County 1800-1900', in *Cork History and Society,* pp. 728-731 shows a daily wage rate of between 3 shilling and 3 shillings and 4 pence for a cabinet-maker in Cork city in the 1820s while McCarthy's daily wage rate worked out at 7.3 pence per day.
34. Properties with shoreline did not automatically have the rights to cut weed on their own land, such rights were dictated by the landlord. For example, the Bohanes of Dromadoon were not permitted to cut weed along their own shoreline, they were granted rights to cut a small strip of shoreline at Barlogue. Interview Neily Bohane, 15 June 2013.
35. Holland, *History of West Cork*, p. 252.

Select Bibliography

Hundreds of published and unpublished works were used in the research for this book. Information used from these sources is referenced in the footnotes for each chapter. The bibliography is confided to those sources of particular importance to Lough Hyne, or those repeatedly referenced within the book.

An Taisce, 'Lough Ine: Ireland's First National Marine Research Park?', AnTaisce, Cork, 1975.
An Taisce, 'Lough Ine: Ireland's First National Marine Research Park?' (Revised), An Taisce, Cork, 1979.
Archaeological Survey of Ireland, *Archaeological Inventory of County Cork,* Vol. 1, Office of Public Works, Dublin, 1992.
Archaeological Survey of Ireland, *Archaeological Inventory of County Cork*, Vol. 5, Government Stationary Office, Dublin, 2010.
Barry, Terence, *The Archaeology of Medieval Ireland*, Routledge, London, 1988.
Barry, Terry, *A History of Settlement in Ireland*, Routledge, London, 2000.
Bennett, George, *The History of Bandon*, Francis Guy, Cork, 1869.
Breen, Colin & Wes Forsythe, *Boats and Shipwrecks of Ireland*, Tempus Publishing, Gloucestershire, 2004.
Breen, Colin, *An Archaeology of Southwest Ireland 1570-1670*, Four Courts Press, Dublin, 2007.
Brindley, Anna, *Irish Pre-History: An Introduction*, Town and Country House, Dublin, 1994.
Burke, James M., 'Sir Fineen O'Driscoll', *Journal of the Cork Historical and Archaeological Society (JCHAS)*, Vol. 25 (1919), pp. 51-52.
Burrit, E., *A Journal of a Visit of Three Days to Skibbereen and Its Neighbourhood*, pp. 7-15, Available at: http://www.gutenberg.org/ebooks/25115, [accessed 25 October 2010].
Buzer, Jenny, 'Analyses of Sediments from Lough Ine, Co. Cork, Southwest Ireland', in *New Phytologist*, Vol. 86 (1980), pp. 93-108.
Chaster, George W., 'Proceedings of the Royal Irish Academy: Report Upon the Mollusca (excluding the cephalopoda and nudibranchiata)' obtained by the Royal Irish Acadamy Cruises of 1885, 1886 and 1888, *Proceedings of the Royal Irish Academy (1889-1901),* Third Series, Vol. 5 (1898-1900), pp. 1-33.
Clinton, Mark, *The Souterrains of Ireland*, Wordwell, Bray, 2001.
Cleary, Patrick and Philip O'Regan, *Dear Old Skibbereen*, Skibbereen Printers, Skibbereen, 1995.
Coleman, James, 'The Old Castles of South-West Cork', *JCHAS*, Vol. 30 (1925), pp. 29-35.
Coleman, James, 'The Old Castles of South-West Cork', *JCHAS*, Vol. 32 (1927), pp. 97-98.
Coleman, Samuel, 'A Tentative Chronology for Tower Houses in West Cork', *JCHAS*, Vol. 103 (1998), pp. 105-124.
Coombes, James, 'The Pilchard Fisheries of South-West Cork', *JCHAS*, Vol. 53 (1968), pp. 113-121.
Cooney, Gabriel, *Landscapes of Neolithic Ireland,* Routledge, Oxon, 2000.
Copinger, Walter Arthur, *History of the Family of Copingers or Coppingers of the County of Cork, Ireland and the Counties of Suffolk and Kent, England*, Southern, Manchester, 1884.
Crowley, John, and John Sheehan (eds.), *The Iveragh Peninsula: A Cultural Atlas of the Ring of Kerry,* Cork University Press, Cork, 2009.
Crowley, John, William J. Smyth and Mike Murphy (eds.), *The Atlas of the Great Famine*, Cork University Press, Cork, 2012.
Davenport, Julia & Rob McAllen (eds.), *Lough Hyne Marine Reserve @ 30,* University College Cork, Cork, 2011.
Day, Robert, 'St Bridget's Church, Lough Hyne', *JCHAS*, Vol. 10 (1904), pp. 18-22.
Donnelly, James S. Jr, *The Land and the People of Nineteenth-Century Cork: The Rural Economy and the Land Question,* Routledge & Kegan Paul, London, 1987.
Donnelly, James S. Jr, *The Great Irish Potato Famine*, Sutton Publishing, Gloucestershire, 2002.
Donovan, Daniel, *Sketches in Carbery*, McGlashan and Gill, Dublin, 1876.
Dúchas The Heritage Service, *Lough Hyne Marine Nature Reserve*, Heritage Service, Dublin, 2000.
Dufferin & Ava, Marquis of, & G.F. Boyle, *Narrative of a Journey From Oxford to Skibbereen During the Irish Famine,* London, 1847.
Duffy, Seán, *Ireland in the Middle Ages*, Gill and Macmillan, Dublin, 1997. Edwards, Nancy, *The Archaeology of Early Medieval Ireland*, Batsford, London, 1990.
Flanagan, Patrick and Cornelius Buttimer (eds.), *Cork History and Society*, Geography Publications, Dublin, 1993.
Foynes, Peter, *The Great Famine in Skibbereen*, Irish Famine Commemoration Ltd, Skibbereen, 2004.
Gillespie, Raymond, *Seventeenth-Century Ireland*, Gill and Macmillan, Dublin, 2006.
Hadden, Prof. A.C. and Rev. W.S. Green, 'Second Report on the Marine Fauna of the South-West of Ireland', *Proceedings of the Royal Irish Academy, Third Series*, Vol. 1 (1898), pp. 29-56.
Hall, S. C., *Hall's Ireland: Mr & Mrs Hall's tour of 1840,* Hall Virtue and Co., London, 1984: first published 1841.
Hickey, Patrick, *Famine in West Cork: The Mizen Peninsula, Land and People, 1800-1852*, Mercier Press, Cork, 2002.
Holland, Rev. W., *History of West Cork and the Diocese of Ross*, Southern Star, Skibbereen, 1949.
Irish University Press, *The Irish University Press Series of the British Parliamentary Papers: Subject Set on Famine (Ireland)*: Volumes 5-8, Irish University Press, Shannon, 1970.
Jeffries, Henry A. 'The History and Topography of Viking Cork', *JCHAS*, Vol. 90 (1985), pp. 10-25.
Jones, Roisin and Martin Steer (eds.), *Darwin, Praeger and the Clare Island Surveys,* Royal Irish Academy, Dublin, 2009.
Kearney, Terri, 'Bronze Age Copper Mine at Lick Hill/Coombe', DLRS essay, University College Cork, 2009.
Kearney, Terri, 'Lough Hyne's Archaeology and its Associated Folklore', DLRS dissertation, University College Cork, 2009.
Kearney, Terri, *Lough Hyne: The Marine Researchers – In Pictures*, Skibbereen Heritage Centre, Cork, 2011.
Kearney, Terri, 'The Lough Hyne Area Through History', MA Thesis, University College Cork, 2013.
Kelleher, Connie, 'The Gaelic O'Driscoll Lords of County Cork', in Linda Doran and James Littleton (eds.), *Lordship in Medieval Ireland: Image and Reality*, Four Courts Press, Dublin, 2007, pp. 130-159.
Kingston, William, *The Story of West Carbery*, The Friendly Press, Waterford, 1985.
Kinealy, Christine, *This Great Calamity: The Irish Famine 1845-52*, Gill and Macmillan, Dublin, 2006.
Kitching, J.A., and F.J. Ebeling, 'Exploration of the Lough Hyne Rapids', in *The School Science Review*, Butler & Tanner, Frome and London, 1955, pp. 222-29.
Kitching, J.A., and F.J. Ebeling, 'Ecological Studies at Lough Ine', *Advances in Ecological Research*, Vol. 4 (1967), pp. 177-291.
Lankford, Éamon, *O Driscolls Past and Present,* Cape Clear Museum, Co Cork, 2005.
Lennon, Colm, *Sixteenth-Century Ireland: The Incomplete Conquest*, Gill and Macmillan, Dublin, 1994.
Marten, Brian, 'Previously Unrecorded Bronze Age (?) Copper Working, West Cork, Ireland' [unpublished], 1998.
McCarthy, Bernie, *Dún na Séad Castle*, Bernie McCarthy, Baltimore, 2006.
McCarthy, Bernie, *Baltimore Castle: An 800-Year History,* Baltimore Castle Publications, Baltimore, 2012.
McCarthy-Morrogh, Michael, *The Munster Plantation: English Migration to Southern Ireland 1583-1641*, Clarendon Press, Oxford, 1986.
Mackey, Mary, (ed.), *Mizen Journal: Selection from Mizen Journals 1993-2004*, Part 2, Mizen Archaeological Society, Cork, 2010.
McVeigh, John (ed.), *Richard Pococke's Irish Tours*, Irish Academic Press, Dublin, 1995.
Mitchell, Frank, *The Way That I Followed,* Country House, Dublin, 1990.
Mitchell, Frank and Michael Ryan, *Reading the Irish Landscape*, Town and Country House, Dublin, 1998.
Monk, Michael A. and John Sheehan (eds.), *Early Medieval Munster: Archaeology, History and Society,* Cork University Press, Cork, 1998.
Myers, A.A., Colin Little, J.J. Costello, J.C. Partridge (eds),*The Ecology of Lough Hyne,* Royal Irish Academy, Dublin, 1991.
Nichols, Kenneth, W., *Gaelic and Gaelicised Ireland in the Middle Ages*, Gill and Macmillan, Dublin, 1972.
Norton, Trevor, *Reflections on a Summer Sea*, Century, London, 2001.
O'Brien, William, *Mount Gabriel: Bronze Age Mining in Ireland*, Galway University Press, Galway, 1994.
O'Brien, William, *Sacred Ground: Megalithic Tombs in Coastal South West Ireland*, National University of Ireland, Galway, 1999.
O'Brien, William, *Local Worlds: Early Settlement Landscapes and Upland Farming in South-West Ireland,* The Collins Press, Cork, 2009.
O'Brien, William, *Iverni: A Prehistory of Cork*, The Collins Press, Cork, 2012.
Ó Conaire, Breandán, *The Famine Lectures*, Roscommon Herald, Boyle, 1997.
Ó Corráin, Donncha, *Ireland Before the Normans,* Gill and MacMillan, Dublin, 1973.
Ó Cróinín, Dáibhí, *Early Medieval Ireland: 400-1200*, Longman, London and New York, 1995.
Ó Cuileanáin, Conchubhar, 'Excavation of a Circular Stone House at Glannafeen (Lough Ine) Co. Cork (1955)', *Journal of the Royal Society of Antiquaries*, Vol. 85 (1955), pp. 94-99.
O'Donovan, John, *Miscellany of the Celtic Society*, The Celtic Society, Dublin, 1849.
O'Flanagan, Patrick & Cornelius G. Buttimer (eds.), *Cork History and Society,* Geography Publications, Dublin, 1993.
Ó' Gráda, Cormac, *Famine 150: Commemorative Lecture Series,* Teagasc, Dublin, 1997.
O'Kelly, Michael, *Early Ireland: An Introduction to Irish Prehistory*, Cambridge University Press, 1997.
O'Mahony, Edward, 'Baltimore, the O'Driscolls and the End of Gaelic Civilisation, 1538-1615', *Mizen Journal*, Vol. 8 (2000), pp. 108-112.
O'Mahony, Edward, 'The O'Driscolls and Their Revenue from Fishing - The 1609 Inquisition', *Mizen Journal*, Vol. 8 (2000), pp. 128-130.
Ó Maidín, Pádraig, 'Pococke's Tour of South and South West Ireland in 1758', *JCHAS*, Vol. 65 (1960), pp. 130-141.
O'Regan, Liam, 'Two Catholic Gentlemen of the 1860s and Whatever Happened to the Skibbereen Show', *Mizen Journal*, Vol. 4 (1996), pp. 27-42.
O'Rourke, Canon John, *The Great Irish Famine*, Veritas Publications, Dublin, 1989.
Ó Siochrú, Micheál, *God's Executioner: Oliver Cromwell and the Conquest of Ireland,* Faber & Faber, London, 1988.
O'Sullivan, A., John Sheehan, The *Iveragh Peninsula: An Archaeological Survey of South Kerry,* Cork University Press, Cork, 1996.
Póirtéir, Cathal (ed.), *The Great Irish Famine: The Thomas Davis Lecture Series,* Mercier Press, Cork, 1995.
Praeger, Robert Lloyd, *Some Irish Naturalists*, Dundalgan Press, Dundalk, 1949.
Praeger, Robert Lloyd, *Natural History of Ireland*, E.P. Publishing, Yorkshire, 1972.
Praeger, Robert Lloyd, *The Way That I Went*, The Collins Press, Cork, 1997.
Raftery, Barry, *Pagan Ireland*, Thames and Hudson, London, 1997.
Raftery, Joseph, *Prehistoric Ireland*, Batsford, London, 1951.
Renouf, Louis P.W., 'Preliminary Work of a New Biological Station (Lough Ine, Co. Cork)', *Journal of Ecology*, Vol. 19 (1931), pp. 410-438.
Renouf, Louis P.W., 'Twenty Five Years at Lough Ine', *Cork University Record*, Vol. 19 (1950), pp. 18-22.
Ryan, Michael, *Irish Archaeology: Illustrated*, Country House, Dublin, 1994.
Samuel, Mark, 'A Tentative Chronology for Tower Houses in West Cork', *JCHAS*, Vol. 103 (1998), pp. 103-9.
Sheehan, John, 'The Viking Age Hoard at Castlefreke', *Ardfield Rathbarry Journal,* Vol. 5 (2006), pp. 42-56.
Shee Twhoig, E. and M. Roynayne (eds.), *Past Perceptions: The Prehistoric Archaeology of South-West Cork*, Cork University Press, Cork, 1993.
Sleigh, MA., 'John Alwyne Kitching, O.B.E. 24 Oct 1908-1 April 1996', *Biographical Memoirs of Fellows of the Royal Society,* Vol. 43 (1997), pp. 269-284.
Smith, Charles, *The Ancient and Present State of the City and County of Cork*, Vol. 1, Connor, Cork, 1815.
Smyth, William J., *Map Making, Landscapes and Memory*, Cork University Press, Cork, 2006.
Stafford, Thomas, Sir, *Pacata Hibernia*, Downey and Co., London, 1886.
Stark, Archibald G., *The South of Ireland in 1850: Being the Journal of a Tour in Leinster and Munster,* James Duffy, Dublin, 1850.
Stewart, A.T.Q., *The Shape of Irish History*, Blackstaff Press, Belfast, 2001.
Stout, Matthew, *The Irish Ringfort*, Four Courts Press, Dublin, 1997.
Sweetnam, David, *Medieval Castles of Ireland*, The Collins Press, Cork, 1999.
Townsend, H., *Statistical Study of the County of Cork*, Graisberry and Campbell, Dublin, 1810.
Trevelyan, Charles Edward, *The Irish Crisis*, Longman, Brown, Green & Longmans, London, 1848.
Waddell, John, *The Prehistoric Archaeology of Ireland*, Galway University Press, Galway, 2006.
Webster, Charles, *The Diocese of Ross and Its Ancient Churches*, Hodges, Figges and Co., Dublin, 1932.
Weld, Isaac, *Illustrations of the Scenery of Killarney and the Surrounding Country*, Longman, Hurst, Rees & Orme [etc.], London, 1807.
Went, Author E.J., 'Pilchard in the South of Ireland', *JCHAS*, Vol. 51 (1946), pp. 137-156.
Whitlow, J.B., *Geology and Scenery in Ireland*, Penguin Books, Middlesex, 1974.
Wilson, Keith, 'A Bibliography of Literature Relating to Lough Hyne (Ine) Nature Reserve 1687-1982', *Journal of Life Sciences of the Royal Dublin Society*, Vol. 113 (1984), pp. 1-11.
Woodham-Smith, Cecil, *The Great Hunger: Ireland 1845-1849*, Penguin Books, London, 1962.

About the Contributors

Author:

Terri Kearney is a native of Skibbereen and spent much of her childhood in Lough Hyne and nearby Tralispean. As a regular walker in the area, she got to know those who live around the lough. These people generously shared their properties and knowledge with her when she carried out a survey of the archaeology of the area in 2009-10 as part of a UCC Diploma in Local and Regional Studies. She went on to investigate other aspects of Lough Hyne's heritage as part of an MA in Local History at UCC. She published a pictorial history of the marine research at Lough Hyne in 2011, *Lough Hyne: The Marine Researchers – in Pictures*. She works at Skibbereen Heritage Centre, which hosts an exhibition on Lough Hyne.

Illustrator:

A self-taught artist with an interest in Irish archaeology, Peter Murray specialises in watercolours of landscapes and cities. Originally from Dublin, he now lives near Lough Hyne.

Contributors of Chapter 6:

Colin Little, a retired Senior Lecturer from Bristol University, has worked at Lough Hyne annually since 1979 (see pages 151-153). Working with Penny Stirling, and others, he has monitored the shores of the lough since 1990.

Cynthia D. Trowbridge is a Senior Research Associate at the Oregon Institute of Marine Biology (USA). She has worked at Lough Hyne since 2002, investigating herbivorous sea slugs and invasive seaweeds (see page 160).

Foreword:

Eoghan Harris is a political columnist and playwright. His play Souper Sullivan, set in West Cork during the famine, was staged at the Abbey Theatre for the Dublin Theatre Festival 1985. He has swum in Lough Hyne, in all seasons, over the past 33 years.

Photographic contributor:

Redmond O'Regan is from the Skibbereen area and, having qualified as a solicitor, he spent over 30 years in the midlands. He has returned to live in Tragumna and explore his love of art and photography and Lough Hyne plays a significant role in this, as it did in his childhood and teenage years.

This publication has been financially supported by the Gwendoline Harold Barry Trust and WCDP.